Climate Action Upsurge

In the late 2000s climate action became a defining feature of the international political agenda. Evidence of global warming and accelerating greenhouse gas emissions created a new sense of urgency and, despite consensus on the need for action, the growing failure of international climate policy engendered new political space for social movements. By 2007 a 'climate justice' movement was surfacing and developing a strong critique of existing official climate policies and engaging in new forms of direct action to assert the need for reduced extraction and burning of fossil fuels.

Climate Action Upsurge offers an insight into this important period in climate movement politics, drawing on the perspectives of activists who were directly engaged in the mobilisation process. Through the interpretation of these perspectives the book illustrates important lessons for the climate movement today. In developing its examination of the climate action upsurge, the book focuses on individual activists involved in direct-action 'Climate Camps' in Australia, while drawing comparisons and highlighting links with climate campaigns in other locales.

The book should be of interest to scholars and researchers in climate change, environmental sociology, politics, policy and activism.

Stuart Rosewarne is Senior Lecturer in the Department of Political Economy at the University of Sydney, Australia.

James Goodman is Associate Professor in the Social and Political Change Group at the University of Technology Sydney, Australia.

Rebecca Pearse is a Doctoral Candidate at the School of Social Sciences, University of New South Wales, and Research Associate at the Cosmopolitan Civil Societies Research Centre, University of Technology Sydney, Australia.

Climate Action Upsurge
The ethnography of climate
movement politics

**Stuart Rosewarne, James Goodman
and Rebecca Pearse**

Routledge
Taylor & Francis Group

LONDON AND NEW YORK

First published 2014
by Routledge
2 Park Square, Milton Park, Abingdon, Oxfordshire OX14 4RN

and by Routledge
711 Third Avenue, New York, NY 10017

First issued in paperback 2015

Routledge is an imprint of the Taylor & Francis Group, an informa business

British Library Cataloguing in Publication Data
A catalogue record for this book is available from the British Library

Library of Congress Cataloging in Publication Data
A catalog record has been requested for this book

ISBN13: 978-0-415-81616-8 (hbk)
ISBN13: 978-1-138-94159-5 (pbk)

Typeset in Times
by Taylor & Francis Books

Contents

Preface to Climate Action Politics

The world is confronted by extraordinary business-as-usual myopia in our continuing reliance on fossil fuels to meet our energy needs. Indeed there has been an upsurge in energy consumption, with the burning of coal its chief source. Adding to the mix has been the turn to gas, produced from a range of sources – natural gas, coal seam gas and shale gas – and represented as a bridge between the highly polluting coal and renewable sources of energy. Worse has been the intensification in the exploitation of the intensely polluting tar oil sands. Yet, despite all the modelling and the signs that justify the warnings, such as those by the International Energy Agency's 2012 that the world is on track for a 6C° warming, governments and key multilateral financial institutions, such as the European Bank for Reconstruction and Development, can't seem to shake the commitment to a fossil fuel sourced energy future. Australia is no exception to this.

For a brief period of time, it seemed that this commitment to fossil fuels would be successfully contested. The preoccupation with addressing the imminent threat of climate change had galvanised climate as the most potent political cause at the turn of the century. Non-government environment organisations focused all of their energies on this cause; climate politics captured the imagination of civil society. Climate became the *cause célèbre* making a mockery of Anthony Giddens' claim that the world was in desperate need of a climate politics. Indeed, an emergent climate politics heralded a renewal of a deep engagement in political activism. This turn captured the measure of what James O'Connor has contended is the politicisation of the environment, resulting in the call for states to regulate and contain the destructive force of the fossil-fuel intensive systems of production and consumption. Governments came under considerable pressure and wrestled with various policy options designed to mitigate the issue of greenhouse gas emissions. Calls for more radical transformations, based on more social forms of production and engagement with the environment, gave further meaning to O'Connor's thesis, and these calls marked a critical shift in the environment movement as it engaged with climate politics, supported and injected with a new momentum by a veritable army of community-based climate action groups and climate activists. The vitality and determination of this new political force was evident in the thousands of activists who journeyed to the United Nations Climate Change Conference held in Copenhagen in December 2009 amassed under the banner of the climate justice movement.

The momentum of this movement did not survive Copenhagen. State resistance to any agreements for meaningful action that would generate a tangible pathway forward was the immediate obstacle. But the failure of this political moment to break through the logjam, and the political ambivalence that seems to have defined climate politics over the successive years, has paradoxically prompted comparatively little critical reflection. There have been some critics, such as Tim Doyle, Erik Swyngedouw and Raphael Schlembach, who have represented the failure of this moment as not so much the consequence of state resistance, but rather the product of an ill-considered politics. They argue that climate politics tended to be captured by an uncritical echoing of climate science and the appeal for urgent action. However rich and inclusive the climate movement and action forums were in igniting climate politics, it is argued that a lack of political vision tended to be compounded by the endeavours to hold together the disparate array of activists coming from diverse political backgrounds and experiences. There was a determination to avoid any contentious debate on political strategies for fear that this would fracture the movement, and this resulted in retreat to conventional options, to ecological modernisation and the technological solutions it promises, the neoliberal panacea of market-based mechanisms and a focus on managing carbon rather than the foundations of the fossil-fuel energy-intensive system that calls forth the carbon economy.

This critique, we argue, is overstated. It portends the failure of climate politics more or less at its birth. Our engagement in this emergent politics suggests otherwise, that the movement held out the hope of building a different future. The radical climate politics that took off in the first decade of the new millennium was very much an exploration of a political panorama, a laboratory for climate politics beyond pragmatism of mainstream environment organisations. In all its complexity it canvassed an array of political positions, contesting the legitimacy of carbon-intensive activities, challenging the authority of the state and the legitimisation of the fossil-fuel energy-intensive economy. It sought to demonstrate by example the capacity to build a low-carbon community, forming deeply democratic structures that afforded a voice for all participants, and offered the means for consensus-based decision making. Climate politics brought together people from diverse backgrounds and interests to lay the foundations for moulding a new political force. This was not without its challenges, but it was the start of something new.

The movement did not disavow climate politics, but on the contrary sought to provoke it. The key questions faced by the climate movement in this moment of upsurge, we argue, centred on how to translate climate science into climate politics. Considerations of how to develop political vision and strategic direction, how to strengthen capacity to mobilise directly in order to achieve this, and how to create personal political agency as part of the movement, became central. These questions shape this study, and are addressed together as instances of the much broader challenge of how to socialise the climate crisis. In this respect we draw from James O'Connor's work on the second contradiction of capitalism, as a contradiction between capital and nature (distinct from the labour-capital contradiction). For O'Connor, internal social contradictions create crises that cannot be repressed, producing the necessity for public intervention whether through the state or other social agencies. This process of socialisation may be aimed at saving capitalism – but it also points to the process of superseding it. This book serves in large part as exploration of how the capital-nature contradiction, as played out in climate change, forces governments and social movements into action. Whether this climate socialisation serves the vast bulk of the population or is simply a bail-out for corporates became a central concern for the climate movement.

In mobilising to target the false solutions and prevarications and the deliberate and malign neglect that passes for much of climate policy, the climate movement put the question of socialisation at the heart of climate politics. In this study we recount how activists wrestled with the resulting problems and dilemmas. In the process we show how the challenge of socialisation is confronted, and gain key insights into the conditions under which it may be realised in the future. Self-evidently, climate change is intensifying, and climate politics is likely to rise up the political agenda, especially in anticipation of a new attempt at global agreement through the United Nations in 2015. As such, since 2010 the climate movement has been in relative abeyance, but it is not superseded. Key ideas of the movement are being deepened, with something of the potential vision embodied in the program for 'bio-civilisation' and 'living well' advanced by the World Social Forum in its counter-manifesto, 'Another Future is Possible' at the 2012 Rio+20 United Nations Conference on Sustainable Development. As the institutionalisation of elite power is renewed, in the lead-up to 2015, through new agreement-making on climate, we can anticipate a renewed upsurge. We anticipate that this return to climate movement will be inscribed with many of the potentials and struggles outlined in this book. We believe that only by documenting and reflecting on these experiences will climate movements begin to realise the urgently-required historical agency to address climate crisis. Our intent here is assist in that process. The story that unfolds in the pages that follow explores this journey and takes us beyond the dismissive accounts of climate politics, mapping instead some of the priorities in making 'Another Future'.

Stuart Rosewarne, James Goodman and Rebecca Pearse
June 2013

Acronyms

ACF	Australian Conservation Foundation
ACOSS	Australian Council of Social Service
ACTU	Australian Council of Trade Unions
ASEN	Australian Student Environment Network
AYCC	Australian Youth Climate Coalition
BZE	Beyond Zero Emissions
CAG	Climate Action Group
CANI	Climate Action Network International
CANA	Climate Action Network Australia
CCS	Carbon Capture and Storage
CDM	Clean Development Mechanism
CEF	Clean Energy Future (legislative package announced in 2011)
CJN!	Climate Justice Now!
CPRS	Carbon Pollution Reduction Scheme (legislative package announced in 2008)
CTW	Carbon Trade Watch
ESD	Ecologically Sustainable Development
ETS	Emissions trading scheme
EITE	Emissions Intensive Trade Exposed industries
EU ETS	European Union emissions trading scheme
FoEA	Friends of the Earth Australia
FoEI	Friends of the Earth International
GCC	Global Climate Coalition
IPCC	Intergovernmental Panel on Climate Change
NSW	New South Wales
PWCCC	World People's Conference on Climate Change and the Rights of Mother Earth
REDD+	Reducing Emissions from Deforestation and forest Degradation
SCCC	Southern Cross Climate Coalition
TEC	Total Environment Centre
UNFCCC	United Nations Framework Convention on Climate Change
WALHI	Wahana Lingkungan Hidup Indonesia (FoE Indonesia)
WWF	World Wide Fund for Nature
YPD	Yayasan Petak Danum

1 Climate Change and Political Agency

Climate change marks as an unprecedented moment, where humankind becomes capable of manipulating global geology. What Paul Crutzen and others have labeled the Anthropocene marks a new chapter in human history (Chakrabarty, 2009; Crutzen & Stoermer, 2000). The advent of climate crisis, and the existential threat it now poses, directly raises the question of political agency. The horizon of politics is suddenly extended into millennia, the significance of 'what is to be done' magnified into universal planetary scope. In the process, the dialectic of history is radically transformed; the structures on which we have to gain political purchase exist in an entirely different register. People are only beginning to imagine the implications for political community, and for the very practice of politics, as we start to directly experience humanity's collective force in the new climate era. As the sociologist Mike Hulme puts it, 'we have only tentative understanding of the implications of such a new role and only limited means at our disposal to exercise purposeful, as opposed to inadvertent, agency' (Hulme, 2010: 1). This book is centred on the question of gaining 'purposeful agency' in an era of human-induced climate change.

Climate agency is a directly political matter. Politics encompasses domination and contestation in society and is at the centre of any possibility for 'purposeful' agency. The key parameters for climate politics, both as domination and contestation, are set by the logic of global capitalism. Self-evidently we live in a capitalist society and capitalist development is the key contemporary driver of climate crisis. Indeed, the asymmetries of climate change directly reflect capitalism's uneven development – from early industrialisers to today's 'emerging economies' – and hierarchies of wealth and accumulation are central to addressing global climate change. The seventy million 'one per cent', who according to the World Economic Forum now own half the planet, have no immediate interest in addressing the causes of climate change (WEF, 2012: 18). Meanwhile, the seven billion others bear the brunt of climate change, most of them far from the levers of power in the already underdeveloped world, with next to zero responsibility for greenhouse gas emissions and no capacity to adapt (Goodman, 2009; Redclift & Sage, 1998; Roberts & Parks, 2007). In the long run we are certainly 'all in this together', but, as Keynes famously reminded us, in the long run we are all dead. In any case the 'one per cent' will always find a new bunker, although as demonstrated by the closure of Wall Street in the face of Hurricane Sandy in November 2012, there may be inconveniences.

More fundamentally, as demonstrated by these asymmetries, the political question of climate change is clearly a question of power and justice. Climate change as such makes visible climate injustice, forcing it onto the political agenda. The question of who is to be the arbiter of our collective climate agency is the key political question of our times. Will humanity's collective force to transform the climate be appropriated by the powerful, against our collective future?

Climate change itself expresses the reflexive logic of ecological domination. It demonstrates what Neil Smith has called 'the production of nature on a global scale', expressing the dream of centuries of capitalist domination over nature, the 'idea of control over nature ... dreamt each night by capital and its class, in preparation for the next day's labour' (Smith, 1984: 31). But control comes at a systemic price. The accumulation of capital directly produces the accumulation of greenhouse gases, and drives climate change. Indeed, the capitalist social system produced the steam engine that announced the Anthropocene. The production of climate change, through accumulation, signals the production of nature by the domination of the capitalist world system.

Domination of nature produces a sharp contradiction or 'metabolic rift' between society and nonhuman nature and is ultimately self-destructive (Foster, Clark and York, 2010). Climate change signals the 'revenge' of nature, as Engels coined it, demonstrating on a world scale 'that we by no means rule over nature like a conqueror over a foreign people, like someone standing outside nature – but we, with flesh, blood and brain, belong to nature and exist in its midst ... ' (Engels, 1953[1876]: 10). Healing the metabolic rift requires a transformative move, for a mutual immersion of society and ecology, where neither dominates the other (see Harvey, 1996). The move can be conceptualised as a process of recognising ecological 'embeddedness' (as per Polanyi, 2001[1944]), perhaps to recognise the 'naturalization of man and the humanism of nature', as Marx put it (Marx, 1964: 104).

The production of climate change is a systemic outcome, but certainly not planned, or at least not before 1988, when it became widely recognised that greenhouse gas emissions were warming the planet. But it is also not an accidental agency, of simple carelessness, but rather a product of social-systemic agency. Climate change is not an externally imposed catastrophe, an accident of natural history, but rather a product of the internal contradictions of society. Attempts to mitigate greenhouse gas emissions and to prevent dangerous climate change involve purposive action that, if it is to have any real purchase, must be anti-systemic. 'Inadvertent' systemic agency can only be countered by purposive anti-systemic agency.

Current climate policy, in so far as it seeks to rescue 'business as usual', is by definition pro-systemic and subject to failure. This applies, for instance, to efficiency-focused efforts that seek to reduce the carbon intensity of growth while maximising growth. The contradiction is sharper still with the various 'end of pipe' solutions that facilitate increased emissions by creating mechanisms to absorb them or to deflect their effects. Pro-systemic climate policy is by definition a moral hazard that hoists itself on its own petard. The drive to accumulate will always see the hazard realised. As amply demonstrated by the global rush to oil shale and coal seam gas, capitalism is not a moral force, even when it comes to its own long-term survival.

Climate change creates the necessity for purposeful anti-systemic agency. In doing so, it opens the door to a new form of global transformative agency. The climate movement, by definition, is (or must be) an 'anti-systemic movement', to borrow the terminology used by Immanuel Wallerstein and others to describe socialist and anti-colonial movements, and, latterly, global justice movements (Arrighi et al., 1989; Wallerstein, 2002). As climate change proceeds, the anti-systemic imperative can only be deepened. One can anticipate a simple choice as the various pro-systemic climate policies fail to reduce aggregate greenhouse gas emissions – between more-of-the-same, with heightened climate disruption and the displacement of many millions of people worldwide, and the alternative of anti-systemic post-capitalist society. As such, a sharp polarisation is likely to emerge between the barbarism of dangerous climate change and the anti-systemic imperatives of climate justice.

Writing about the industrial revolution, Rosa Luxemburg posed a similar polarity between 'transition to Socialism or regression into Barbarism' (Luxemburg, 1916). In the event, the state reformed capitalism, modifying its contradictions through welfarism. But can capitalism outlive ecologism? As O'Connor identifies, the state enabled the labour-capital contradiction to be socialised in a way that gave rise to and complemented a new phase of capitalist accumulation (O'Connor, 1998). He predicts a new process of ecological socialisation to address the capital-nature contradiction, albeit one that only ever provides a temporary resolution of the contradictions within capitalism. But how far can ecologism be achieved within capitalism? There is a radical incommensurability between commodity production for profit and ecological sustainability, and despite the modelling it is hard to imagine how capital accumulation can be maintained in a steady-state or post-growth society (see Jackson, 2009). Those who argue it is possible do so on the basis of extensive state regulation of production, to the extent of rendering capitalism unrecognisable. In this context, ecologism begins to look like a transitional programme for post-capitalism.

The question of how to define an anti-systemic climate movement, and how to produce its praxis in terms of mobilisation, vision and programme, is at the core of this book. We may anticipate anti-systemic climate movements as the necessary outcome of the current situation but how can such a movement come into being? This is at the nub of O'Connor's socialisation process. We argue in this book that experimentations for an anti-systemic climate movement have begun, and that we should be alert to the problems and possibilities this raises. Clearly O'Connor's agenda for ecological socialisation will not arrive fully formed from some supreme strategist. If it is to emerge at all, it will do so from the exercise of movement agency, and in the process of contestation and reflection amongst movement participants that this agency produces.

This book aims to contribute to this process of developing anti-systemic climate agency as a sustained reflection with climate activists on the process of realising agency. Here we investigate whether climate politics is breaking the political mould. To what extent does climate change define a new political era, as well as a new geological era? As humans gain geological agency, what are the implications for politics? We investigate the spectrum of climate mobilisation, finding that the dominant tendency to pragmatic environmentalism is increasingly supplemented, if not displaced, by an emergent climate 'radicalism'. In the process, climate agency breaks the official straitjacket, and new social forces enter the political arena.

To explore these emergent horizons of climate politics we focus on a brief upsurge of climate 'radicalism' in the late 2000s. We directly engage with the upsurge in Australia, a strategic vantage point as a rich country reaping the benefits of the coal and gas boom. We chart both possibilities and pitfalls revealed by the upsurge, both internationally and in Australia, interpreting it as a prefigurative moment for an anti-systemic climate agency.

We ask what social forms are created by climate movements and in what ways familiar collective-action problems, such as the ethics and politics of resistance, are changed in the age of climate crisis. We find movements constructing agendas to produce mobilisation, but also, on the flipside, a tendency to despair and demobilisation, raising the spectre of securitised responses and unilateral experiments with geoengineering. In this context it is noteworthy that, in the face of demobilisation, some key movement intellectuals such as George Monbiot in the UK and Tim Flannery in Australia joined the US-based James Hansen and James Lovelock in arguing that nuclear energy may offer the only viable means of buying time for reductions in greenhouse gas emissions (see Flannery, 2006a; Hansen, 2009; Lovelock, 2004; Monbiot, 2011). Setting aside the option of pro-systemic action, we treat this period as a laboratory where many approaches and demands for anti-systemic climate agency were created and trialed. In the period of mobilisation we account for, we document how activists developed anti-systemic or 'radical' approaches against the pragmatism of NGOs and governments, sustaining activism against elite capture of the climate debate.

Inverting pragmatism and radicalism?

The identified relationship between climate radicals and climate pragmatists replicates a broadly identified divide in modern politics between the 'mainstream' and the 'fringe'. That divide has its origins in the emergence of nation states, which for the first time enabled mass social movements to make demands in the name of society as a whole. Articulated in relation to state power, social movements were defined in a spectrum from reform to revolution (Tarrow, 1998). The reform-revolution dichotomy became a key political tension, beginning with the diagnosis of social problems – as either contingent, and hence subject to reform, or systemic and entrenched in structural power. The same bifurcation informs much theoretical investigation of social movements in the political process. For Manuel Castells, for instance, social movements can make appeals to the authorities that promote 'legitimation' identities; alternatively they can promote 'resistance' or 'project' identities that challenge legitimacy structures (Castells, 2004). The idea of a 'project' identity is particularly rich as it suggests an agenda and capacity to not simply oppose the existing order, but to 'project' an alternative. The distinction also surfaces in Fraser's distinction between social movements that seek 'affirmation' of their status from power-holders, and those that pursue transformative agendas designed to overturn the power structure (Fraser, 1995). The distinction is between movements that seek reform in relation to a given set of constraints and those that seek to break those constraints.

In climate politics we find a similar bifurcation, and we ask if it has been realigned and reordered by the Anthropocene. Our proposition, or rather provocation, is that the Anthropocene inverts the pragmatism-radicalism bifurcation. Under climate change, 'realism' becomes utopian, and the 'utopian' fringe becomes the new realism. Pragmatism becomes an impossible demand, upending Bismark's definition of politics as the 'art of the possible'.

Climate radicals, as we shall see, seek to apprehend climate change in its full implications. They are aware that dangerous climate change is already upon us, and that catastrophic climate change is already built into even the more optimistic scenarios for greenhouse gas emissions. They take the warnings of climate scientists seriously and seek responses that address its root causes – for instance, through programmes for sufficiency. In this respect, we suggest, climate 'radicals' aim for a realistic reflexivity. They pragmatically apprehend the challenge and seek to produce responses that have a realistic chance of delivering climate stability. Climate pragmatists also accept the climate science, but fail to calibrate their response to the challenge this poses. Less pessimistic scientific assessments are referenced to demonstrate the effectiveness of policy confined to existing parameters. The utopian visions of global carbon markets, carbon capture and storage, or clean coal, for instance, gain traction as they promise 'end-of-pipe' decarbonisation within the existing status quo. These unrealistic models are promoted, and grossly overstate the capacity to 'delink' economic growth from greenhouse gas emissions. The fantasies gain a hold on the elite imagination, including through the United Nations.

The inversion of pragmatism and radicalism reflects the transformative impact of climate change on political agency. Climate politics changes the definition of political agency, situating it in the long view of what Chakrabarty calls 'species history'. He captures the phenomenological and political challenge climate change poses by eliciting what he argues is our dual ontology as geological force and political agents. Human agency producing climate disruption operates at the level of species. Collectively we have become a geological force. Chakrabarty argues that this side of our ontic being is 'justice-blind', and a limit to social action (Chakrabarty, 2012: 14). He argues that whilst we will always be concerned with questions of justice, our new-found geological agency is a new register through which societies must simultaneously come to know themselves.

With regard to politics, the challenge for social movements is to materialise the climate problem beyond apolitical abstractions. The universal urgency of climate crisis, and the necessity to act on the causes of climate change, has the effect of enveloping and subsuming all political antagonisms. Some have characterised the result as a form of 'post-politics', where the meta-imperative cancels out political identification and the political process (Catney & Doyle, 2011; Swyngedouw, 2010). Erik Swyngedouw argues that climate politics is a frontier of post-politicisation, constituted through populist apocalyptic rhetoric, and the invention of an asocial universal enemy in CO_2. The political outcome is the advent of techno-managerialism and marketised climate policy effecting the commodification of the atmosphere. Mainstream 'climate governance' has cemented scientific and economic authority in a new class of carbon managers convening complex and opaque carbon markets. Whilst this narration of climate politics holds all too often, we argue that Swyngedouw offers an overdetermined account of the social dynamics of climate politics. Others have pointed out that recourse to a former 'properly political' time is unsubstantiated, and a grounded analysis of the social-movement response to climate change is missing in this thesis. Swyngedouw seems unaware of the array of climate subjects emerging in activism of various stripes, particularly the politics of 'climate justice' (see Chatterton et al., 2012; Urry, 2011).

As a counterpoint, we argue for a engaged investigation into the sites of resistance. Certainly, the meta-political logic visible in climate politics reflects the scope of the challenge. The resort to the post-political, though, is not a foregone conclusion. Rather, it is a predictable response to what is an overwhelming challenge, reflecting the difficulty expressed by Chakrabarty, of translating the 'long view' into the immediate contexts of political claim-making. The problem this poses is profound. How can a demand for 'system change not climate change' be translated into a coherent political programme that can be brought into effect against the prevailing order? The task, one may say, is a uniquely challenging one, although it may be compared with other world-historical transformations, such as from autocracy to social democracy or from imperialism to post-colonialism.

In this book we find 'radical' climate activists directly engaged in the struggle to produce a realistic politics of climate change, one that meets the challenge of climate science in ways that cannot be dismissed. We find this challenge can be overwhelming, and that activists tend to lapse into the meta-political realm and into individual or 'community' actions, avoiding the question of society-wide transformation. The result can be a default into pragmatism, of accepting what is presented as the official solution as 'better than nothing', whilst being aware that it is inadequate and in fact counter-productive. Here the temporal gauntlet can breed despair and demobilisation. The narratives in this book track these efforts at constructing an adequate climate politics, one that could be adequate to climate science, and the difficulties activists encounter along the way. Indeed the precipitous rise and fall of the 'radical' climate upsurge bears out this political difficulty. At one level it reflects a wilfull reluctance to engage the state; at another level, and much more funda-mentally, it reflects the underlying difficulty of constructing a state response that is capable of addressing the deep social contradictions that drive climate change.

We do not want to suggest, though, that this is an impossible task. Anthropogenic climate change is a product of capitalist society and, as something created by human society, in principle it can be reversed. What humans are responsible for, they can correct, provided there is sufficient political will and capacity. O'Connor understands this as a 'socialisation process' which sees a regrounding of the logic of accumulation, especially through state action, to recreate a stable climate. The difficult question is one of capacity, as arguably accumulation by definition produces ecological degradation (Foster, 2002). Even efficiency gains only offer limited respite as the drive for profit growth draws on any available extra capacity made avail-able through delinking efforts (the so-called 'Jevons Paradox'). Efficiency efforts in this respect can tend to backfire, or even become counterproductive, as they enable further throughput. In a system driven by the profit margin, rising efficiency and falling emissions intensity of growth enables more growth and more emissions, not less.

Here we arrive at the central dilemma of climate politics. Developing cli-mate policy that can have a reasonable chance of gaining the support of state elites must not significantly hamper growth prospects. Under Article 2 the UNFCCC objective is to achieve stabilisation of greenhouse gases to prevent 'dangerous' climate change, while at the same time to 'enable economic development to proceed in a sustainable manner' (Article 1, UNFCCC, 1992). To achieve this, the definition of 'stabilisation' has been massaged to enable high-risk rates of emissions, while the notion of 'sustainable' economic development has been reduced to the growth imperative.

The issue is demonstrated by the IPCC report of 2007 which reasserted the 2°C target and the claim that atmospheric greenhouse gases could rise to at least 450 parts per million. Unfortunately, as the IPCC stated, the 450 limit had a 30–70 per cent likelihood of breaching the 2°C target, and as such was only likely, 'on balance', to achieve the necessary 'stabilisation' (Fig 19.1, IPCC, 2007). Any less risky target below 450 was 'already outside the range of scenarios' (IPCC, 2007: 2). Even the 450 option was deemed likely to be unrealistic as it required emissions to peak at 2015 and halve by 2050. The IPCC scenarios began at the 450 limit, rising above it, posing the possibility of a rise by to 6°gC or more. The report thereby directly violated the 'stabilisation' objective of the UNFCCC (Simonis, 2009).

As greenhouse gas concentrations rise, the cost of achieving a stabilised climate increases beyond what is considered achievable within the current economic system. The Stern Report on climate change, commissioned by the UK Government, endorsed a highly risky target of 500–530ppm to limit the impact in terms of lost economic growth to 1 per cent a year. At the same time it acknowledged that even a 500ppm target carried a 48–96% probability of forcing temperatures rises above the 2°C target (Stern, 2007: 8.1). For Stern, the rate of growth was sacrosanct.

In 2006 the 2°C target was already being counted as unlikely, and, for some, as next to impossible. In 2012, with global greenhouse gas concentrations rising to 400ppm, the 2°C target set by the IPCC in 2007 is being superseded as expectations of a 4°C or 6°C scenario start to emerge, for instance from the World Bank and the International Energy Agency (Bank, 2012; IEA, 2012). The management consultancy Price Waterhouse Coopers (which may have a conflict of interest on this issue), declared in November 2012 that 'one thing is clear: businesses, governments and communities across the world need to plan for a warming world – not just 2°C, but 4°C, or even 6°C' (PWC, 2012: 3). There is a palpable panic at work within these agencies as they come to the realisation that global growth is not decarbonising at the rate needed to prevent a climate catastrophe. Horror at the likely impacts is expressed in the title of the World Bank report – *Turn Down the Heat: Why a 4°C World Must Be Avoided* – a title that could have been borrowed from a climate-action campaign from the mid-1990s. The PWC Report is no less frank, stating that decoupling has so far been a dismal failure. Despite the looming threat, all three agencies declared their faith in (green) growth and faster decarbonisation.

The growing dissonance reflects the diffused 'growth imperative', or more accurately, 'profit imperative'. As UN emissions data reveals, there is a direct relationship between emissions reduction and economic growth: during recession, emissions fall; during a boom, emissions rise (UNFCCC, 2011). The PWC Report went further, stating that 'emissions tend to grow proportionally with economic growth, but fall by less than the rate of economic decline' (PWC, 2012: 16). Ultimately the ecological costs of growth must become too high, but when that point is reached is unclear. The International Energy Agency now states that two thirds of existing known fossil fuel reserves must remain in the ground if the world is to keep global warming below 2°C (IEA, 2012). Yet the exploration for new resources continues apace as the world embarks on a new fossil-fuel bonanza. The problem, as pointed out by climate scientists, and by many of the climate activists we interviewed, is that growth cannot proceed under catastrophic climate change.

We may say, then, that climate change transforms agency because it presents a material zero-sum imperative that cannot be displaced: more emissions, less climate stability. There is no negotiating with the inexorable logic of global warming. In 2008 the Australian Prime Minister spoke of seeking to 'steer a balanced course' between the demands of industry and climate science (Rudd in O'Brien, 2008). The comment was highly revealing of the failure to appreciate the transformed context for political agency. As some pointed out at the time: 'Climate targets must be set according to the scientific imperatives, and putting them through a political filter can only imperil the planet' (Spratt & Lawson, 2008; see also Flannery & Rowley, 2009). Seeking to compromise with global warming was clearly nonsensical, yet it accorded with prevailing anthropocentric and historical assumptions about political agency, that there is always room for compromise in what is always assumed to be a social process.

Climate change finally makes it impossible to avoid the reality that human agency is embedded in the ecosystem. From the first days of profit-based commodity production a conflict opened up between the push for profit and ecological viability. While exhausted environments could be abandoned for 'greenfield' sites, the profit motive would triumph. A sharp divide opened up – a metabolic rift – between the success of capitalism, measured in terms of rising financial accumulation, and the degradation of ecologies.

With climate change the financial success of capitalism is now in direct collision with the material logic of degradation, directly measured in greenhouse gas accounting. The more successful capitalism is in financial terms, the more destructive it is in terms of climate change. The financial collapse of 2008 slowed emissions growth; the financial recovery since the bank bailouts has accelerated emissions. The inverse relationship between growth and climate stability is now a defining one for climate politics. Climate pragmatists attempt to restore the dominance of the cash nexus by trading off growth and climate stability through commodified emissions. Climate radicals insist on the intrinsic, unique value of climate stability, and its infinite value to humankind. Abstracted and disembedded models designed to enable continued growth on the basis of 'fungible units' of carbon, traded and brought into arbitrage, are confronted by 'radical' campaigns that focus on actual emissions in material places as concrete manifestations of the climate crisis, and of the failure of pragmatic utopia.

We can say very immediately, in the first instance (rather than ultimately in the last instance), that agency is now ecologically embedded. What this means for our capacity to act is profound. Human history is replete with examples of where innovation has overcome local ecological limitations, only to then encounter new larger-scale impacts. Coal is a very apposite case as it enabled urbanising societies to overcome their dependence on limited supplies of timber (Freese, 2006). Urban conglomerations were close to exhausting wood supplies in Western Europe when the steam engine was invented, enabling the large-scale mining of coal. The burning of coal made cities a health hazard until coal-fired electrification, which in turn has become the most important source of greenhouse gas emissions and of climate change on a planetary scale.

The temporal closure of what could always in the past be projected into the future is what, in our view, explains the transformative logic of climate change. Human society is by definition part of the biosphere, but until now the truism has always been avoided. As Foster et al. outline, capitalist development has proceeded through a succession of local, then national and regional exhaustions, and has finally reached the planetary level with climate change (Foster et al., 2010). The temporal horizon has arrived, creating a new 'climate sensibility', where corporates and governments act in the knowledge of their impacts on climate change (albeit in spite of this knowledge). The question, which 'radical' activists grapple with, is how to translate this meta-imperative into a climate politics, or, in O'Connor's terms, a 'socialisation agenda' that is truly transformative, against the failures of 'pragmatic' utopia.

A new political conjuncture?

What we identify in this book as the 'climate upsurge' emerged principally from the conjuncture between intensifying evidence of climate risk and the continuing failure of global climate governance. In the closing years of the Twentieth Century the question of climate change quickly emerged as a pivotal political issue. There was mounting scientific data and modelling that confirmed the build-up of greenhouse gases in the global atmosphere, that in all likelihood human activity was the paramount cause, and that this was driving increases in temperatures and changes in climate patterns across the world. Climate change had become an explosive political issue.

While governments generally recognised the scale of the threat and the need to act, negotiations under the umbrella of the United Nations Framework Convention on Climate Change (UNFCCC) were fraught. Resistance from some parties to agreeing any targets that would impede industrial expansion and economic growth blocked a comprehensive and effective agreement. Environmental non-governmental organisations were mostly unsuccessful in their lobbying efforts to secure any meaningful progress. The culmination of international negotiations in the signing of the Kyoto Protocol in 1997, and subsequent efforts to specify and expand some of its provisions, did nothing to assuage the politically charged nature of climate change. The well-financed efforts by climate sceptics and the fossil-fuel industry to oppose any restrictions on emissions – beginning with their Global Climate Coalition of 1988 – made sure of this (Gelbspan, 1998, 2005; McGregor, 2009).

Paradoxically, international negotiations had provided a focus for mobilisation by environmental NGOs. The elaboration of international climate policy enabled them to mobilise, providing a heightened sense of purpose and lifting their profile in domestic domains (Bullard & Müller, 2012). With international environmental NGOs forming the 'Climate Action Network' in 1989, and the creation of national branches through the 1990s, the issue of climate change began to encompass and eclipse other environmental concerns. Environmental politics had metamorphosed into climate politics.

Yet involvement in policy negotiation entailed compromises even when there was little progress, especially in national policy design, and exposed the political ineffectiveness of environmental NGOs. By the early 2000s the political limits of NGO lobbying on climate change were self-evident. The Climate

Action Network (CAN) had channeled NGO opinion, yet had achieved little. As it calibrated its own demands to the limits of the negotiation process it became, itself, an extension of that process. Quickly, CAN began acting as a disciplinary constraint on public concerns, diminishing aspiration to the limits of what was considered pragmatically possible. This capture of international environmental NGOs by the UNFCCC process begged the question of an alternative counterpoint 'from below'. Hopes were quickly vested in aspirations for a more radical climate movement.

By 2008 even the UK's Energy Secretary Ed Miliband was calling for a more effective movement-based counterpoint, commenting that: 'When you think about all the big historic movements, from the suffragettes, to anti-apartheid, to sexual equality in the 1960s, all the big political movements had popular mobilisation. Maybe it's an odd thing for someone in government to say, but I just think there's a real opportunity and a need here' (Miliband in Adam & Jowitt, 2008).

Following a series of environmental disasters in 2005, the popular con-sensus for global climate action was fortified by *An Inconvenient Truth*. Al Gore's movie sought to establish a new 'planetary ethics' (Luke, 2005, 2008) and was neatly dovetailed with Nicholas Stern's (2007) call to action with an economic blueprint for managing the climate commons. Meanwhile popular books written by politically engaged scientists and environmental authors were telling stories of the coming catastrophe (Flannery, 2006b; Lowe, 2005; Lynas, 2007; Monbiot, 2006). The increased political and public engagement was framed by the momentous Fourth Report of the Intergovernmental Panel on Climate Change (IPCC) and by the wider imperative to frame a climate agreement to supersede the Kyoto Protocol of the UNFCCC, which was due to pass into history in 2012.

The apparent magnification of elite commitment to climate action was paralleled by a promising flurry of social movement activity seeking trans-formative change. New groups, primarily in the global North, were germi-nated from the networks of the global justice movement and various environmental movements, including the anti-roads campaigns in the UK and anti-nuclear and forest-activist campaigns in Australia. They addressed the striking contradictions behind the rhetoric of climate action on display in high-level politics. Climate action in the 2000s took on an entirely different meaning as a new climate activism emerged to contest and seek to reframe the debate around climate change. Local community groups began to be formed, providing forums to discuss the challenge of climate change and for concerned individuals to engage others in exploring ways they might bring pressure to bear on governments, to encourage them to act. These groups engaged people in a way that the environmental NGOs had not. While the groups were principally occupied with arousing interest within the local community, such as through setting up information stalls in shop-ping precincts, conducting discussion events or holding local protest actions, they also engaged in collaborative endeavours with other groups and in developing networks. They were also crucial in underwriting the momentum of more ambitious actions calling for decisive policy initiatives from government.

The creation of new grassroots groups and networks offered the possibility of mass climate mobilisation, giving voice to human agency beyond the constraints of environmental NGOs. Climate-focused member-based organisations had not existed prior to the emergence of these local groups, and the turn in climate politics that they announced was associated with a more antagonistic and radical approach to doing politics. Against expert-based NGO lobbying there was a conscious effort to establish organisational forms that honoured a commitment to the democratic processes, and to an open process founded on principles of grass-roots activism. Insights drew variously from community organising traditions grounded in liberal pluralism, from relatively 'flat' network models of political organisation, and from both socialist and anarchist practice. Aspects of these approaches then became firmly embedded in the larger initiatives that were organised, presented as loose collaborative ventures, lacking hierarchical organisational form, and held to be integral to invigorating mass involvement in climate activism.

Another distinctive feature of the upsurge in the number of alternative grass-roots climate groups was the declared intention to pursue a more vigorous and provocative approach to challenging the root causes of climate change, and to contesting the legitimacy of the 'business-as-usual' agendas of government. The grass-roots movements diagnosed the weakness of climate policy in terms of systemic problems of carbon-intensive economies, especially in the industrially developed global North, which were now framing the dramatic economic expansion of developing countries. Rather than defining climate change as a managerial or technical challenge for governance, these groups positioned climate at the centre of global uneven development and growing disparities in human well-being, issues that had been put on the agenda by global justice movements from the mid-1990s (Della Porta, 2007). Much of this shift in appraising the climate challenge was based on an engagement with critical readings of global capitalism, and critiques of corporate globalism and neo-liberalism more particularly, some drawn from Marxist critics and insights from anarchist-influenced critiques, that emphasised the vital role of the state in supporting fossil-fuel based accumulation regimes.

Instead of the environmental lobbying and efforts at influencing policy solutions with government or business, measures that invariably ended in compromised outcomes or nothing constructive at all, the new climate politics confronted the status quo. The grass-roots movements sought to challenge the inaction and question the legitimacy of government and the authority of big polluters through a range of campaigns and actions. Foremost among these was the appeal to direct action, defined as non-violent civil disobedience. This necessitated a more critical acquaintance with the issues, challenges and political strategies that could be deployed in place of the passive role that was generally associated with supporting an environmental NGO campaign.

Climate activists thereby became active agents, personally and actively engaged in constructing this new climate politics.

The upsurge in climate politics was multiscalar in its organisational form. The local grass-roots groups had provided the foundation for the invigoration of climate politics. The interaction, the establishment of networks and collaborations, from the national day-of-action rallies through to the longer-duration campaigns launched against particular carbon-intensive activities, such as actions to block the operation of coal mines and coal loaders or coal-fired power stations, highlighted the purchase of antagonistic politics in reinvigorating climate politics. These actions were networked internationally, with much co-inspiration across local and national contexts. Informal and mediated interactions across the spatial plane have been crucial in constructing an imagined network of correlated actions, a trans-local 'movement of movements'. Local movements drew upon the experience of actions and campaigns in other localities, developed cross-border links and formed networks to foster movement ideas, practices and strategies to reframe the climate-change debate.

While a far from exhaustive list, among the more prominent of those climate movements that have captured attention we can note the Camp for Climate Action in Britain, and similar camps in a number of other countries, including Australia, the US-based Indigenous Environment Network, La Via Campesina, Climate Justice Action and Rising Tide networks (discussed in detail in Chapter 3). A loose transnational front was formed across these groups that saw the coordination of some iconic actions linked with the objective of promoting a transformative political agenda of social change and climate justice. This critical and unique moment is the subject of this study. Many of these were mobilised for the UNFCCC conferences, reaching a peak involving some 100,000 activists who descended on Copenhagen to demand effective climate action at the Conference of the Parties in December 2009.

Collective mobilisations in Northern countries targeted sites of pollution that continued to expand (coal power plants, mines, airports), as well as institutional sites of policy obfuscation, emissions displacement and marketisation (the UN climate meetings, the Australian parliament, the EU carbon trading hub). As noted, the movement that emerged in this short period of time stood in contrast with the pragmatic approach to negotiating climate action with nation states and business taken by professionalised NGOs from the 1990s (Bond, 2012; Rootes, 2011). And in a more routine set of practices, the groundswell of grass-roots movement involved an ongoing process of energetic debate and strategising about how to build movement power, and how to articulate a new climate politics at the turn of the twenty-first century.

From Canberra to Copenhagen, the pragmatism of the 1990s reasserted itself in 2009. The upsurge was disrupted by the global financial crisis in late 2008, and outside of Australia was cut short by the ensuing recession. By 2010, movements against austerity were gaining a new urgency; by 2011, with the 'occupy' movement, climate issues had become subsumed into a wider push against corporate power. In Australia, relatively insulated from recession by the minerals boom, climate activists watched as their government constructed a signally inadequate response to climate change. In December 2009 they witnessed the collapse of what was presented at the time as a last chance for a new multilateral deal on climate action.

The network of commentators and activists in Australia that formed to oppose coal expansion had been highly visible at times, with some gains against planned coal power plant extensions, but they had little impact on the minerals boom. Coal and the climate policy became a benign abstraction on the periphery of everyday life for Australia's largely urban affluent population. While the mining boom extended colonial settlement into the interior, the longstanding imaginary of the mining industry as the engine room of the national economy was reasserted. Reflecting this, mining industries, including the coal-mining sector, were able to maintain their legitimacy in the context of climate-policy debate. Activists' calls for dramatic reductions in emissions came into direct conflict with narratives of the inexorable link between resource extraction and prosperity. In the rush of soundbites that came in response to movement mobilisations, threats of capital flight and economic downturn from industry, as well as accusations of green extremism, were commonplace.

Australia – a strategic site

In this book we interpret the climate upsurge from an Australian perspective. At one level this is an epistemological stance, that knowledge production for climate agency must be embedded in material lived contexts. At another level it reflects a desire to analyse climate action in what is one of the world's most fossil-fuel dependent societies.

Australia offers an important vantage point from a number of perspectives. A high-income settler country, it has one of the highest per capita CO_2 emission rates in the world, at 24.4 tonnes per person in 2012 (DCCEE, 2012: 16). Australia acts as a crucial node in the booming carbon economy, and, increasingly, in the global networks of the new climate movement. Australia is a recalcitrant figure in global climate politics, known for special pleading within the United Nations climate regime on the basis of being uniquely fossil-fuel reliant compared to other affluent nations. The national economy has developed with massively increased energy production since the 1990s, notably through coal mining. Coal generates 75 per cent of Australia's electricity, and while the 2011 Clean Energy Act introduced a range of measures to reduce Australian emissions, coal will still generate more than a third of Australia's electricity in 2035 (DRET 2012: 88). The Government's 'unconditional' target for reducing emissions by 5 per cent below 2000 levels by 2020 is below the international minimum requirement of 25 per cent for industrialised countries set out by the IPCC (IPCC, 2007: 776). The Australian

Government has pledged to increase this target to 15 or 25 per cent only in the context of major developing countries reducing their emissions. Further, the majority of emissions reductions are projected by the Treasury to be achieved by buying carbon offset credits internationally (Commonwealth of Australia, 2011: 77, 96; Pearse, 2013).

More significant, though, Australia is swiftly becoming a fossil-fuel export platform, predicted to rival Saudi Arabia in terms of exported climate change (BREE, 2012a; Pearse, 2010a). Already Australia is the world's largest coal exporter. Coal exports have driven a coal boom, production rising from 304mt to 420mt annually between 2005 and 2010, with 75 per cent exported. A further increase is now expected, to 689mt by 2025 (DRET, 2012: 67). Coal exports are bolstered by exports of gas, and most controversially coal seam gas, which is set to dramatically expand Australia's climate-change exports.

Australia has been described as a quarry economy, reflecting the booming coal industry, and also other mining sectors; mining accounted for a third of company profits and two thirds of exports in 2011 (BREE, 2012b: 80). With the growing power of mining companies, and the expanding reach of their operations, mining has become increasingly politicized. In 2010, mining executives successfully mounted an advertising campaign against a Federal Government proposal to tax 'super-profits' from mining, and in 2012 political controversy erupted in New South Wales, with allegations of corruption in the allocation of coal concessions. Coal mining and coal seam gas extraction, along with associated transport corridors, power stations and port terminals, have become sites of political controversy and are now increasingly contested by affected communities, civil society and campaign organisations (Burgmann & Baer, 2012; Connor et al., 2009; Connor, 2012).

Indeed, if there is a global 'front line' to keep fossil fuels in the ground then it is in Australia. Australia has sufficient known fossil-fuel reserves to substantially alter the global climate. The stakes are high, and getting higher. In 2012 Greenpeace calculated that the emissions resulting from the burning of coal from nine mines proposed for Queensland's Galilee Basin would release more than 700mt of CO_2 annually, more than the UK's entire annual emissions of 550mt (Milman, 2012). Across the country's eastern states, 76bt of black coal and 110 trillion cubic feet of natural gas sit at a commercially viable distance from the surface. These carbon commodities 'in-waiting' are ancient vegetation formed over millennia through microbial action, heat and pressure. Above ground, the churn of earth movers, trucks and cranes building the industrial complex necessary for expanded coal and gas extraction has been moving at great pace. Private and state-owned corporations investing in the boom have rapidly expanded, eager to meet demand in the emerging economies of the Asia-Pacific.

From an international perspective, halting the Australian coal boom is critical. In 2012 the International Energy Agency stated that two thirds of the world's known fossil-fuel reserves must be left in the ground if the world is to prevent global warming above 2°C. Its *World Energy Report* stated unequivocally that no more than a third of proven reserves of fossil fuels should be burnt: coal consumption would have to fall to 3.3bt by 2035, 4.5bt below the 'business as usual' scenario of 7.8 bt (IEA, 2012: 3, 157). Australia, as a high-income country with 6 per cent of the world's known black coal reserves, may be expected to take the lead and leave its reserves in the ground. Indeed, if a country like Australia cannot achieve this then how can other countries such as China and India, with between them a third of the world's known coal reserves, be expected to act? (IEA, 2012: 164). Accordingly, Australia's movements for climate justice sit at a key pivot in climate policy: advances in Australia to halt the fossil-fuel economy are of critical political importance for addressing global climate change.

Analysing climate agency

Any kind of social agency is by necessity caught between involvement in the daily troubles of society and the need to gain an external perspective, in order to act on it. Involvement is necessary for the insights it allows into social experiences; detachment is necessary to acquire a perspective on these experiences, to enable social agency (Elias, 1956, 2007). The responsibility of the sociologist – indeed of anyone involved in social action – is to bridge these worlds, to create the imagination needed for transformative agendas and visions, enabling us to become subjects of history, rather than its objects (Mills 1959/2000). The challenge is to produce grounded explanations in dialogue with subjective or affective knowledge (Juris, 2008). Indeed, using embedded explanations to produce normative claims is central to any possibility of a collective social movement 'subjectivication' (Touraine, 1995). The resulting practice-theory exchange, or praxis, is an important site in the production of emancipatory knowledge, to transform social relations (Johnston & Goodman, 2006).

Global warming poses very directly the question of human agency in the face of crisis, writ large on a global scale. In his writings on 'Involvement and Detachment', Norbert Elias (2007) addresses exactly this nexus, retelling Edgar Allan Poe's story of two mariners caught in a whirlpool created by their sinking ship. One mariner is so involved in the crisis that he panics and flails around despairingly. The other mariner is able to reflect critically on their situation, and realises that a wooden barrel appears to be falling more slowly into the vortex. The second mariner grabs the barrel and floats free; the first mariner is drowned. The metaphor nicely encapsulates the global-warming crisis, where engagement with the intensity of the crisis can produce a politics of avoidance, a form of 'apocalypse blindness' (Beck, 1992) or 'collective avoidance' (Norgaard, 2006). Alternatively, climate change accentuates the tendency to self-exhaustion, or 'burnout', typical of activism (Chapter 10, Maddison & Scalmer, 2006). Here, the involvement/detachment dilemma is thrown into sharp relief.

We argue that the potential for climate agency comes from precisely this combined engagement with the intensity of the crisis and an ability to reflect on how to act on society to address the crisis (Melucci, 1996). Climate crisis and climate agency are, in this way, locked into a dialectical struggle – the one enables the other and vice versa. Drawing on Paolo Friere, we can conceptualise the process as a praxis between 'activism' at the coalface, where strategic possibilities may not be apparent, and 'verbalism', where there is no engagement with the political process (Freire, 1970). Praxis signifies an active dialogue between these positions to produce forms of knowledge that enable political agency: these are 'emancipatory knowledges' that take us beyond the current limits of the politically 'possible' (Johnston & Goodman, 2006).

Our analytical framework posits a particular challenge for climate movements, of bridging the abstract universal claims of climate science with the concrete lived experience that makes human history. The news of global warming came in the form of 'an impersonal, apolitical and universal imaginary', cutting against the grain of human experience (Jasanoff, 2010: 233, 237). As with Elias' mariners, the intense immersion in the science of climate crisis can overwhelm movement participants, bringing them to a point where they suspend reflection and self-critique. Translating the abstract knowledge of climate science into concrete political agendas and programmes requires a degree of strategic detachment in order to reflect on how best to act on the problem of climate change, given the political context. We can think of this bridging as a form of movement praxis, in the Freirean sense of bridging verbalism and activism.

Our conundrum, we believe, is general to all movements, but is particularly sharply posed for climate movements. As noted, theory of climate change relies for its claims on scientific discourse rather than direct experience (although that may be changing), and is especially abstracted. The claims, furthermore, relate to a timeframe of species history, and assert an absolute universality, far beyond the particular material logic of present-day existence. Translating these meta-political claims into the mundane politics of everyday life, into a directly embodied political process of movement mobilisation for a genuine strategy for transformation, presents a profound challenge. Our analysis centres on how this is achieved – or not – by the would-be climate movement.

In taking this analytical stance, we position ourselves in relation to the field, applying a particular lens of inquiry to the ethnographic data we have gathered. We are indeed positioned – in the sense that all analysis is positioned, explicitly or otherwise – but our analysis is not predetermined. We point to what we believe to be the key conundrum for the movement, and seek to document how participants negotiate it. As outlined below, we focus on how participants negotiate the dialectic between involvement and detachment across four dimensions of their engagement: in terms of their personal trajectory, their hopes and fears, their commitment to direct action, and their views on policies and alternatives.

Ethnography of climate agency

Climate Action Upsurge is an ethnography of the Australian arm of the climate-action movement that emerged in 2006. The movement was transnational in scope, centred on affluent emissions-intensive countries, but also to a degree interlinked with counterpart organisations in low-income developing countries. With mobilisations for climate action at critical sites of carbon pollution in Australia's coal industry, the movement sought to materialise the problem of climate change. It aimed to produce a more grounded climate politics than previously created by policymakers, scientists and lobbyists. Through these actions activists sought to redraw the stakes of climate politics.

Our ethnographic method captures their experimentation in climate action, the personal and collective challenge of coming to terms with the climate problem, of sustaining collective energy for mobilisation, and the play of hope and despair in the lives of climate activists. We witnessed, and in fact were part of, a decline in movement activity precipitated by the underwhelming pragmatism that engulfed both the Australian Government and the Copenhagen talks in late 2009. By decline we mean diminishing energy across the network of movement groups, marked by waning numbers at protests across 2010, but more generally, ambivalence about the direction of debate over climate policy. We draw on discussions with climate activists and our participation in movement events and organising work, primarily in Australia, and brief visits to the UK. The visions for change held by activists and difficulties in building collective power in this period are presented not as definitive, but as an account of sustained engagement with the movement.

Through sustained engagement with the movement we sought to track the process of constructing climate agency. To do so we deployed a range of ethnographic methods: participant observation at movement events, in-depth and longitudinal sets of interviews with movement activists over three years, as well as collection and analysis of movement and mainstream media.

Data from participant observation was gathered from our existing commitments to the climate movement in Australia, and briefly in the UK. We have joined climate protests, including Climate Camps in Newcastle, the La Trobe Valley, Helensburgh, Muswellbrook, Yorkshire and London, and other climate events such as the annual People's Blockades of Newcastle coal port, sit-ins at the Sydney Labor Party office and Parliament House, protests against electricity privatisation in New South Wales, the annual Walks Against Warming in Adelaide and Sydney, and the annual Climate Summits where groups from across Australia come together to discuss movement strategy. We are all members of the Friends of the Earth Sydney collective, which agreed as a constituent member of the climate camp organising group to participate in the research programme and to assist in sourcing interviewees.

In terms of interviews, between 2008 and 2010, 25 participants in climate activism in Australia were interviewed at least twice, some up to five times.

This allowed us to longitudinally track the personal and political shifts for participants in the movement. The interactions with activists in the research-participant dialogue began as relatively formal encounters, but over time became more fluid and reflexive. The group of 25 was largely representative of the climate movement that organised and attended Australian Climate Camps. All participants identified as being involved in grass-roots activism, and, as outlined in the Appendix, several interviewees were directly linked to campaign groups. There was a political-geographic bias toward Sydney-based activism, with 11 of the participants coming from Sydney, the rest from Newcastle, the Hunter Valley, Brisbane or Melbourne. Six participants were linked to environmental non-governmental organisations, as campaigners or members of action collectives, including three from Friends of the Earth (FoE). Of the remaining participants, two were from a socialist organisation, six from student organisations, two from community radio collectives, and one participant each from a Climate Action Group, a local residents group and a solar energy cooperative; one indigenous activist from the Gunai/Kurnai Nation in Victoria was also interviewed. Finally, a Green Party Member of Parliament was included in the mix.

In terms of interview themes, there were four main aspects: personal biography; motivation; mobilisation; political strategy. Participants were first questioned about why they were attending the camps and how they came to identify as climate activists. They were prompted to tell the 'longer story' behind their participation in the movement. Second, participants were asked about their motivations and how they sustained their activism. They were questioned about their understanding of social change, and their hopes and fears for the future. Third, the interviews posed questions of political strategy, including the role of collective mobilisation, the politics of 'direct action' (civil disobedience), and more generally the process of social and political change. Fourth, they were asked about the causes of climate change, its impacts and solutions. All interviews and focus groups were taped and transcribed, and analysed according to these four themes, which then formed the basis for Chapters 4, 5, 6 and 7.

As researchers and participants in the movement, we begin from the assumption that only a reflexive method of inquiry, of this sort, can embed the needed dynamics of involvement and detachment (Steier, 1991). Our close engagement with the climate movement raised a series of questions about our place as researcher-participants. Such questions are commonplace for ethnographers, especially those who have stake in their field of study. How should academics conduct themselves when intellectual and political interests align? What relationships and responsibilities does one have to the movement? How far is it possible to produce productive critiques, at a distance from 'the field', when the researcher is already embedded in the field of study? This common dilemma for researchers can be presented as a methodological polarity between complete submersion in movement activity and the pursuit of detachment (Johnston & Goodman, 2006). On the one hand, involvement in the movement can compromise analytic rigor, and undermine effective analysis. On the other hand, the detached study of movements falsely positions the movement as a discrete object, and dis-embeds the researchers from an ethical relationship with those studied. The sharp division between these choices is unsatisfactory in analytic and ethical and practical terms. We argue that a critically engaged ethnography charts a way between these poles, in terms of providing a method with which to grasp the climate problem and our role as researchers in the movement.

We are particularly concerned, as academics employed in the university system, to refuse the stance of self-distancing, not least because no-one is ever 'outside' the society they are engaging with. As researchers and participants in the movement, we have consciously sought to overcome what Bourdieu and Wacquant (1992: 39) call an 'intellectual bias' where the researcher as outsider is tempted to 'construe the world as a spectacle, as a set of significations, to be interpreted rather than as concrete problems to be solved practically'. The problems we address in this book are practical problems, and we are motivated as researchers to address them substantively rather than simply to describe them. In this respect we are engaged with the very same concerns that climate activists are grappling with, and certainly identify strongly with the sets of issues that they are raising. We come to this issue from a normative standpoint, and have sought to make this self-evident, as reflected for instance in our opening provocation on the 'realism' of anti-systemic climate agency.

Normative proximity enables engagement with issues and insights that would otherwise be unavailable to us. Simultaneously we have our own intellectual trajectories and agendas that influence what we have sought to find out, and how we attempt to make sense of the material we have collected. We have, for instance, as co-authors, had extensive discussions about the extent to which we should faithfully report on the interview data, and how far that should delimit active interpretation, analysis and critique. We certainly have our own views on climate change and how it should be addressed, and also face our own difficulties in translating these views into a viable 'climate politics'. We are conscious that our positions shape what we are writing, and seek as far as possible to foreground what assumptions are at play.

In order to anticipate the readers' interest in these underlying assumptions, we take up three areas of concern: our social background, our relationship to the movement, and to the academic field (Bourdieu & Wacquant, 1992). We proceed with care here, aware that an overemphasis on the process of inquiry can call into question our very capacity to arrive at a satisfactory account of events. The *tu quoque* arguments about reflexivity turn the weapon of reflexivity upon itself, leaving us without a resolution to the problem of ethical knowledge production (Lynch, 2000: 46). Rather, we introduce our involvement with the movement as an exercise in 'ordinary reflexivity', a position that refuses a choice between ceaseless self-inquiry and claims to detached objectivist knowledge. Accordingly, we seek to avoid academic 'self-fascination', and instead explore reflexivity as everyday activist practice, or indeed everyday life, as much as research method (Bourdieu & Wacquant, 1992: 72; Riach, 2009).

Rebecca Pearse has been engaged with questions of climate change – as an activist since 2005 – and from 2008 developed an academic interest in the field through research undertaken for this book. Through this process the academic pursuit has sat uncomfortably at times with engagement with climate movements. In the process of undertaking interviews, she felt a tension between a sense of obligation to participate in processes of movement organising, and the need to fulfil the tasks for the research project. The sense of detachment resulting from the time spent on research tasks produced in her a more intense sense of involvement in the question of climate-movement agency. Over time, the research process politicised and immersed Pearse in the climate movement to a degree that is likely to have not occurred otherwise.

James Goodman works mainly as a political sociologist, drawing on a disciplinary background in political geography, political economy and international relations. Over the last twenty years he has allowed his activist concerns to shape his disciplinary focus: he has always found deeper insights and motivations for research that engages political priorities. From the late 1980s his work in the UK was centred on the politics of the national conflict in Ireland; from the mid-1990s in Australia he wrote about social movements and globalisation, and what came to be known as the global justice movement; from the mid-2000s he became engaged with climate-change politics and mobilisation and with the concerns of this book.

Stuart Rosewarne is a political economist who has focused on questions of political ecology, from a broadly Marxist perspective, since the early 1990s, although he has had a long involvement in the environment movement that predates this engagement with socialist ecology. He has sought to project this academic pursuit onto an activist and political plane, through his involvement in teaching, in international liaisons, such as through his participation in the Asia-Pacific Non-Government Environmental Council, and with the journal *Capitalism Nature Socialism*, drawing on his active participation in tertiary education unionism to form the Trade Union Climate Action Network Sydney, and in regularly contributing opinion pieces in the media.

From 2007 the three authors have collaborated in various ways to develop their ideas about climate movement. From 2009 we became engaged in various debates at movement forums and within the FoE network over climate policy and the movement's response to the Australian Government's carbon trading scheme. In 2010 Goodman and Rosewarne edited a special edition of the *Journal of Australian Political Economy*, critically reflecting on the politics of climate change (Goodman & Rosewarne, 2010b). We have published similarly themed works in more accessible writing styles for Friends of the Earth's *Chain Reaction* magazine (Goodman & Rosewarne, 2010a; Pearse & Creenaune, 2011). These publications sought to link policy critique with questions of movement strategy. A common set of arguments in our contributions to these editions were critical of market-based policies and political strategies that did not take a critical position on growth and capitalist social organisation.

Outline of the book

In this boom we argue the 2007–10 period of climate movement prefigures what is to come: a growing appreciation of the inadequacy of the climate-change policies being formulated by major emitting countries; the comparative impotency of established peak environmental organisations to effect any substantive shift in the policy agendas; and the mobilisation of new climate movements and forms of campaigning that have confronted established modes of political engagement, and introduced a new momentum and dynamism into climate politics. In the Australian context, growing mobilisation on climate issues played an important part in unseating the Conservative Government in 2007. The incoming Labor administration ratified the Kyoto Protocol, stating that climate change was the country's 'greatest moral challenge', but shelved its carbon policies in the wake of the collapse at Copenhagen. Political conflict over climate policy precipitated leadership changes in both the main political parties, and continuing delaying tactics and efforts at burden-shifting under a new carbon pricing arrangement, legislated in 2011, only compounded the policy failure.

From 2007 the gulf between policy and awareness was widening, creating a sharp legitimacy crisis. In this fertile political context, a range of alternative channels for climate mobilisation began to emerge, to act as a counterpoint to established environmental NGOs. In developing this appreciation, the book reports on the 2007–10 climate action upsurge. In outlining key dimensions in the build-up to mobilisations, and during them, we draw out the distinctively personal transformative processes through discussion of the perspectives of activists as they engaged in the emergent movement. The accounts are set in the Australian context while necessarily reflective of, if not embedded in, the wider international context of climate-policy negotiations.

The book analyses the surge in climate politics that defined this period. In Chapter 2 it examines how the established non-government environment organisations engaged with climate-change concerns, which was bolstered with the establishment of several new dedicated climate NGOs. In highlighting how their lobbying efforts were concentrated on trying to progress policy action claims through conventional political channels, which invariably resulted in a pragmatic political agenda. In Chapter 3 we reflect on the catalytic effect this tendency had in impelling the emergence of a more provocative and radical approach to climate-change politics. This is captured in what we characterise as the 'climate action upsurge'. The distinguishing feature of this new political momentum is defined by a 'grass-roots', or 'bottom up', orientation of collective activism built around a solidaristic tradition of civil disobedience or non-violent direct action focused on material sites of carbon generation.

The study then moves to drawing on the interviews of those who participated and contributed to the 'climate action upsurge'. We explore in Chapter 4 the mobilisation of activists, reflecting on the distinctive personal rationale and motivational forces that brought climate action into the political arena. In Chapter 5, attention turns to the hopes and fears that impelled and helped sustain the involvement in the social movement of climate activism. Here we consider the collective resonance in the ethical imperative to act, and to mobilise. We chart the confrontation between the transformative realism of the movement, and the pragmatic utopias for constructing a low-carbon future. Chapter 6 moves to discuss the process of mobilisation, and experiments with direct action as they unfolded in the setting up of Climate Camps.

Finally, in Chapter 7 we document how participants explore the question of alternatives. Mapping alternatives to the status quo is the necessary corollary of the political project of critiquing the social causes and impacts of climate change as well as the rejection of what passes for climate policy. But what also emerges is the immense difficulty of strategising in the context of the urgency for action, and how to translate abstract climate science into concrete political objectives. We draw out the different emphases of the debate within the movement on the various pathways for building this future, from communitarianism to the more pragmatic economistic policy measures, through to state-based solutions.

While short-lived, the 2007–10 upsurge in climate movement politics was, we argue, hugely significant, although the dissolution of the movement also highlights the incredible challenge that confronts us. This, however, is not to dismiss the many visions, strategies and tactics that were developed during this period, which have had powerful generative potential. The movement's focus on the neo-liberalisation of climate policy has had an abiding effect in terms of foregrounding the injustice of climate policies. The 'climate justice' alternatives that emerged at this time have reframed the way climate change is understood, and approached, highlighting the collective power of climate activists. These advances will be critical for when climate is forced back onto the political agenda by the accelerating climate crisis, and by the ongoing failures of climate policy.

2 Climate Pragmatism

The environmental movement evolved as an increasingly robust political force in the developed world over the course of the latter part of the 1960s and into the 1970s. An environmental sensibility had emerged, evidenced in a host of grass-roots efforts to protect or conserve local sites or amenities. The notion that these campaigns constituted a 'movement' exaggerates the degree to which there was much coherence in the growing demands for environmental protection. However, as interest in environmental concerns strengthened, broadly focused environmental organisations, peak environmental non-government organisations, were formed to coordinate and afford support for advancing the different environmental causes. In large measure, this development was prompted by governments responding to popular pressure and legislating to set environmental standards, and establishing environmental agencies to regulate and monitor these standards.

Environmentalism in these early years was thus characterised by the combination of locally focused grass-roots activism and institutionalisation of the means for pursuing action to protect the environment. This was not without its tensions because, as the momentum and range of environmental claims grew in intensity, peak environmental non-government organisations came under increasing pressure to enhance their capacity to lobby state policymakers and governments, to professionalise and further institutionalise the organisations. Thus, while the impulse for action remained mostly grass-roots based, as environmentalism developed as a political force it tended to become more institutionally embedded for a range of reasons, advocating demands more removed from its grass-roots origins.

This would have considerable implications for how the environmental movement took on the challenge of climate change. Not unlike a number of environmental concerns, and Rachel Carson's efforts to expose the environmental dangers of DDT is among the most celebrated examples, global warming was an issue that was engaged by the scientific community. Up until the last decade or so, one consequence of the preoccupation of environmental struggles with local concerns was that climate change was generally not strongly foregrounded within the environmental movement, and nor was the movement particularly adept at driving climate change as a political cause.

Climatologists and physicists drove the debate. The broadcast of their concerns, especially in international forums over the course of the 1980s into the 1990s, that the increasing atmospheric concentration of greenhouse gas emissions would engender climate change, placed climate change as the premier environmental challenge on the global political agenda.

The environmental movement embraced the climate change cause, but principally as a global issue. Likewise, environmental non-government organisations took up the appeals of the scientific community, but rather than responding to a local constituency, their engagement was as much, if not more, formed with the context of climate politics being institutionalised within the United Nations framework. The organisations' involvement was propelled by the extent to which they were motivated by transnational links and frustrated by their efforts to champion the climate change cause within the national domain.

This had significant implications for the evolution of the climate movement. Climate politics has tracked an unusual and different trajectory to that which has tended to frame the other environmental focuses. This has tended to mean that climate politics has played out within local and national political arenas almost in a residual manner. The challenge confronting environmental movements has thus been how to respond strategically to this framing, how best to engage with and draw on the science, and how to effectively progress ambitions in and around international governance institutions, as well as with national governments, in the process of forging a climate politics.

The construction of the climate movement has understandably been a messy, and quite often fraught, process. The evolution of the climate movement has been contingent on the development of the broader environmental movement in all its complexity. The force of climate politics has been bound up with the organisational maturation of the environmental movement, although the forms of this politics have been sharpened by the international climate-change institutional developments, and especially those of the last decade. Some common patterns in the evolution of the climate movement and how climate politics has played out have been evident throughout much of the world, especially among the nations of the global North (Doyle, 2005), and the evolution of Australia's climate politics provides an intriguing illustration of the challenges and the potential promise of the environment movement's metamorphosis into a climate movement.

The setting of climate change politics

The 1960s marked a watershed in the place of the environment in politics generally. Issues of resource depletion, pollution, environmental degradation and the consequences of overpopulation were canvassed as challenges that had to be confronted. A surge in environmental concern throughout much of the world kept these issues alive, and one of the significant institutional outcomes was the many instances of governments establishing environmental protection agencies and departments to regulate human interactions with the environment. While the emergent environmental movements were primarily focused on local concerns, as were the government environment agencies, many of the issues were being canvassed internationally, and the United Nations proved a crucial forum in which these issues were further addressed. The 1972 UN Conference on Human Development set the ball rolling, and the UN forum thence also provided an arena in which environmental issues could be taken up. Threats to the earth's ozone layer and global warming were added to this environmental agenda, and it was the scientific community in canvassing these extra-territorial environmental concerns, rather than the environmentalists, which set this agenda.

The positing of the threat of global warming was the doing of science, of climatologists and other physicists. Science framed and acted as a catalyst in the debate on the imminence of climate change to become an institutionalised cause of concern within the United Nations. While the UN's World Commission on Environment and Development commonly referred to as the Bruntland Commission (WCED, 1987) identified global warming as one of the many ways in which the life-sustaining forces of the natural environment were being compromised, within a very short time climate change became the UN's pre-eminent environmental concern. This was especially the case following the World Meteorological Association conference held in Toronto in 1988, which set up the World Climate Programme and, under the auspices of the UN, and the International Panel on Climate Change that preceded the establishment of the United Nations Framework Convention on Climate Change in 1992 (Paterson, 1996).

An international-engendered discourse thus drew in UN member states to reflect on how they could contribute to addressing the climate change challenge. Somewhat surprisingly, and part of a broader project that had been prompted by the Bruntland Commission report, the Australian Government acted quickly in moving to map a gas greenhouse management strategy. This initiative could partly be attributed to the fact that the Australian scientific community had an established record in climate change research. Modelling in universities and other research centres, and particularly by the Climate Impact Group set up in the CSIRO in 1988, highlighted the vulnerability of iconic regions and particular key industries to the potentially damaging consequences of climate change (Pittock, 2006). The Government engagement was also the product of its ambition to assume a more prominent presence on the international political stage. The reputation of Australian research on climate change aided in this ambition, and the then Labor Government saw diplomatic advantage in projecting the image of being a global leader in the debate on mitigation of greenhouse gas emissions, and this opened doors for Australia to become an active participant in the Intergovernmental Panel on Climate Change when it was established in 1998 (Bulkeley, 2000).

The Government was also cognizant of the growing political force of the environmental movement. While environmentalism had, through the late 1960s and 1970s, captured the imagination of increasing numbers of people, who had joined community groups to lobby or taken action against the intensive logging of forests or mining projects, or urban development projects, these were essentially local in their focus and were not necessarily enduring. Nevertheless, they were symptomatic of the emergence of environmentalism as a more mature and robust political force. The convening of State-based conservation associations created conduits for many of the small local environmental groups. The establishment and strengthened organisation of national environmental non-government organisations, and most particularly the Australian Conservation Foundation, as well as some international environmental organisations, most notably Greenpeace and the World Wide Fund for Nature (WWF), setting up offices in Australia, and local chapters of FoE, consolidated the political momentum of the environmental movement into the 1980s. One of the clearest manifestations of this was the election of independent 'green' candidates in the Tasmanian State parliament, and the subsequent formation of the Tasmanian Greens, the first explicitly green party to win parliamentary representation in the world. Environmental organisations came to play a more strategic role on the national political stage, demonstrating what Doyle (2005: 2) refers to as 'a modern environmental sensibility' that had become evident in many countries.

The significance of this cannot be understated because it set the stage for the further institutionalisation of the environmental movement within the political process. In the lead-up to the 1990 federal election, the incumbent Hawke Labor Government set out to court the green vote and win the backing of peak environmental organisations. The green vote could obviously not be ignored. The Greens held the balance of power in the Tasmanian State parliament, and federal Labor's election platform committed a Labor government to an ambitious environment programme based on the Bruntland Commission's advocacy of 'ecologically sustainable development'. Following Labor's successful re-election, the Hawke-led Government sought to give voice to the environmental movement by engaging environmentalists in the formulation of policy. Modelling a framework on the tripartite collaboration with the union movement and business, in the ALP-ACTU Accord, the Government invited the peak environmental organisations to join state bureaucrats, business and union representatives and some other peak community organisations in a corporatist arrangement, the ecologically sustainable development (ESD) working parties, to map policies for a number of key industry sectors, as well as overarching policy frameworks designed expressly to meet the challenges of climate change.

The ESD process prefigured a distinctive phase in environmental politics in Australia. The movement, and peak environmental organisations more particularly, was placed in the position of having to consider their campaign and organisational fortunes in terms of the extent to which these were bound up with endorsing the election of Labor over the course of the political cycle. This was tied to the promise of government financial support. This funding would provide the means for enhancing the organisational capacity to become involved in policy debate, as well as supporting the expansion of campaign activities and the employment of additional staff, and assisting in professio-nalizing the organisations. It also served to further institutionalise the place of the environmental movement in national politics.[1]

The involvement in the ESD process provided an impetus, or entrée, for the environment movement to begin addressing the question of climate change, an issue with which it had not really seriously engaged. Certainly, Greenpeace had added the cause of climate change to its catalogue of environmental campaigns (Leggett, 1990), but climate change did not figure prominently as a campaign issue in a movement that was essentially formed around more parochial, albeit important, concerns. There was comparatively little engage-ment in environmental causes of a more international nature – the anti-uranium movement and the campaign for nuclear disarmament were exceptions (Doyle, 2000, 2005; Hutton & Connors, 1999) – and the environment movement in Australia was generally somewhat tardy in engaging with climate change poli-tics. Paradoxically, it was the Labor Government ESD initiative that laid the foundations for the movements' encounters with climate change politics, and it was the scientific community that provided the chief impetus for the policy debate.

In many respects, this mirrored the role assumed by environmental non-government organisations in other parts of the world. The Environmental Defense Fund and US Nature Conservancy in the United States were involved in an active dialogue with the Bush administration, and played a critical part in underwriting support for market-based approaches to mitigat-ing emissions, an approach that was to be the crux of the US administration's lobbying within the United Framework Convention on Climate Change (UNFCCC).

'Second wave' environmentalism in the making

Labor's invitation to the peak environmental non-government organisations to participate in the ESD working party process, of course, captured one sphere of the developing movement, and a small element at that. But the initiative did recognise that environmental concerns had become a *cause célèbre* and that there was a proliferation of campaigns that mirrored what was happening throughout much of the world. The 'movement' had estab-lished a vigorous public presence in domestic politics over the course of the latter years of the 1960s, through the 1970s and into the 1980s. It rivalled the labour movement in appeal, especially in the wake of the decline of the anti-war movement after the Whitlam Labor Government pulled Australian troops out of Vietnam in 1972, and attracted more participants and supporters than any other emergent social movement.

As many critics have observed, the environmental movement encapsulated a broad range of groupings, some formally constituted as non-government organisations and others, which accounted for the vast majority of those

lobbying and campaigning around environmental issues, less formally organised. Grass-roots campaigns were a feature of the revitalisation of this new
wave of environmentalism. The 'movement' was extraordinarily diverse in the
range of issues that was taken up, though they tended to canvass or campaign
around particular issues, and especially local concerns (Burgmann, 2003;
Hutton & Connors, 1999). This is not to say that environmentalism did not
canvass regional or even national concerns, or seek to launch national campaigns. But the parochial nature of the environmental movement tended to
reflect the fact that State governments retained constitutional authority over
land and waterways, and lobbying authorities or campaigning for government
intervention to secure environmental protections, or to achieve the conservation
of particular sites, generally meant calling on local government to act.

   In contrast with an earlier phase of environmentalism that was by and large
preoccupied with the conservation of native forests and ecosystems, and
especially in lobbying government to set aside areas as national parks, 'second
wave' environmentalism canvassed a broader range of environmental issues. It
also deployed a richer assortment of strategies in canvassing issues and in
pursuing different environmental causes. This new environmentalism drew on
a broader array of political traditions and pursued an extensive repertoire of
campaigns and tactics. This introduced a vitality and dynamism to the environmental movement which helped to engage younger activists in the cause.
The grass-roots nature of many of the campaigns also meant that they were
more open to attracting and engaging new participants. Likewise, the array of
different actions, which varied from lobbying and petitioning governments to
demonstrations, sit-ins and stage-managed stunts, civil disobedience and non-
violent direct actions and legal actions, also added to the dynamism and
appeal of involvement. Many of these grass-roots campaigns were not enduring, but in this vibrant political milieu there were many options available to
sustain participation in the movement.

   Of course, the assortment of causes and the different *modi operandi* of the
various campaign focuses make discussion of an 'environmental movement'
as if it were coherent and motivated by an agreed objective somewhat spe-
cious. 'Second-wave' environmentalism was in fact many environmentalisms.
The efforts to court the green vote prompted established political parties to
seek out representatives of the 'movement', which invariably meant engaging
with representatives from the peak environmental organisations, however
much these organisations were not constitutive of the environmental
movement per se.

   Organisational developments within the environmental movement also
contributed to privileging the position of the peak organisations. The State-
based conservation councils provided a forum in which various groups, as
members, could connect with one another and thus expand their horizons.
They facilitated networking, and this was regarded as a means of extending
support for, and participation in, campaign endeavours. There were a number
of concerted efforts to cohere the various environmental campaigns. However,

the peak environmental organisations assumed a much higher profile in their efforts to advance the environmental cause. They provided organisational and logistical support for some of the campaigns they considered to be among the most worthwhile, and helped to marshal wider involvement in these campaigns, and thereby to consolidate links across the movement.

This was particularly the case with the Australian Conservation Foundation, whose organisational and campaigning focus had been transformed. Established in 1965, the ACF national council had been dominated by scientists and businessmen, and its executive had pursued its objectives through similar conventional political channels to those that characterised the earlier efforts of conservationists. Success was contingent on the Foundation's executive members working behind closed doors, engineering personal approaches to bureaucrats and politicians, and thus wholly dependent on the goodwill of their contacts. This tended to make for a more cautious style of politicking that also kept the Foundation's members from any really active engagement in advancing the causes it had taken up (Hutton & Connors, 1999: 122). However, drawing on the more activist orientation of some environmental campaigns that had proved successful in their quest to protect particular sites, a growing core of Foundation members questioned this strategy of concentrating on the guarded private lobbying approach to advancing environmental objectives, and in a series of challenges beginning in the mid-1970s many of the established councillors were replaced by individuals who endorsed a more activist agenda, and the ACF assumed a more proactive stance in relation to its involvement in a range of environmental campaigns being undertaken around the country.

The ascendancy of the national framing of environmental causes, and thus the movement, was also evident in the reorganisation of the Tasmanian Wilderness Society (TWS) following the successful campaign to block the Franklin River from being dammed. The TWS had set up offices in several Australian cities to expand its membership and support base, and a national focus assumed much greater significance after the Federal Government intervened in this dispute to override the Tasmanian Government's approval of the dam project. The intervention had been possible because, breaking from conventional wisdom, the High Court had determined that the Federal Government did possess the constitutional authority to make laws pertaining to sites of international significance. Constitutional authority for matters relating to external affairs rested with the Commonwealth, and in listing the Franklin under the terms of the World Heritage Convention to which Australia was a signatory, the Federal Government was able to exercise its authority. With the Franklin saved, the TWS widened its sphere of concerns to join other wilderness campaigns across Australia, reconstituting the organisation as TWS.

The two peak organisations were not alone in ranging across a variety of environmental struggles, providing support to local grass-roots campaigns as well as taking the lead in some of these. Greenpeace and the WWF, while not representative organisations like the ACF or TWS, similarly engaged in a range of campaigns across Australia. Thus, by the early 1980s the environment movement assumed a more national character. There was also a common purpose that continued to define much of what these organisations were concerned with. The preservation of the natural environment remained their overriding preoccupation, evident in a host of campaigns, many of which involved partnering with sister organisations as well as grass-roots activists, to protect temperate and tropical rainforests along the Eastern seaboard and in Western Australia, to stop mining, including uranium mining in Kakadu, and sand mining on Fraser Island, and to protect the Great Barrier Reef (Hutton & Connors, 1999). The extent to which the peak organisations' more expansive approaches could give a sense of coherence and common purpose to the environmental movement was demonstrated in the decision by the ACF, TWS, Greenpeace and WWF to submit a coordinated response to the Labor Government's Ecological Sustainable Development working paper in 1991.

In the process, two crucial and related issues confronted the environmental movement: what sort of strategies should be pursued to achieve the desired outcomes, and how should the movement engage with the state? Many of the campaigns launched over the course of the 1970s and early 1980s were more activist-oriented than those that characterised the conservationist movements of a previous era. Blockades, civil disobedience and other tactics designed to disrupt or stop activities that threatened a particular environmental site featured in the developing repertoire of the grass-roots movement. These tactics reflected a more radical approach to advancing the environmental cause, one that was informed by understandings that environmental problems were systemic in origin. This often translated into questioning the legitimacy and challenging the authority of the state.

On the other hand, the increasingly significant role that the federal government assumed in environmental affairs not only reinforced the nation as the arena in which environmental politics would be concentrated. It also amplified the political import of the state. Debate on climate change made this all the more evident, and the Labor Government's efforts to engage the movement exposed the question of movement-state relations in quite striking ways.

Recasting the net: A 'third wave' environmentalism and engaging with climate change

The efforts by peak environmental organisations to enhance their position in the movement prompted some reassessment of their strategic focuses, which in turn resulted in some organisational restructuring. The ACF, for instance, prepared a Forward Plan in 1989 which was designed to map short- and long-term visions (Rosewarne, 1992). It sought to establish a more professional and businesslike profile, and lobbyists and researchers were employed to engineer this. As the foremost historians of the movement have observed, the organisation became more hierarchical and bureaucratic in the process, the leadership more aloof from its membership (Hutton and Connors 1999; Doyle 2000). TWS underwent a similar transformation.

The professionalisation of the peak organisations enhanced their capacity to make stronger representations to government. Labor's invitation to the ENGOs to participate in the multi-party discussions on ecologically sustainable development provided further scope for strengthening this organisational refocusing because the invitation came with the promise that the participation would be supported financially. The invitation to participate in the ESD process raised critical questions about the merits of this direct engagement with the government. There were obvious lessons to be learnt from the corporatist arrangement on which the ESD process had been modelled, the ALP-ACTU Accord, which had resulted in the trade union movement conceding some bargaining claims in return for promises on price controls and industry support that were never honoured. The ACF conducted an internal appraisal of the costs and benefits of participation in the ESD process and decided to proceed (Burgmann & Baer, 2012: 255–56). Other peak organisations were more circumspect. Of those invited to take part in the ESD discussions, FoE elected not to participate, Greenpeace withdrew before discussions got under way and TWS withdrew when the Labor Government passed the *Resource Security legislation* which guaranteed miners and forests secure access to resources. This left the ACF and the WWF as the remaining environmental organisations in the ESD process, and their organisational energies became concentrated on that process.

The principal objective of the ESD process was to consider how best to implement the recommendations of the Bruntland Commission (Rosewarne, 1992). Nine sectoral working parties were established – energy production, energy use, mining, agriculture, forestry, fishing, transport, tourism and manufacturing – and an intersectoral committee was formed with a view to providing complementarities and consistency across the sectoral groups. One of the corollaries was that this forced consideration of strategic responses for meeting the climate change challenge, and anticipated the formulation of *The National Greenhouse Response Strategy* in 1992.

The ESD working parties provided the first real occasion for serious reflection by the environmental movement on the climate-change challenge and possible policy options, and the ACF and WWF were placed centre stage in the ESD deliberations. However, by the time attention was directed to the actual subject, the shortcomings in the ESD process were already in evidence. Bureaucrats had taken charge of drafting the final policy recommendations and had removed much of any substance. The disproportionate representation of bureaucrats from the pro-business departments of Primary Industry and Energy and the Treasury, who supported the continued development of energy-intensive industries and the mining sector, was reflected clearly in the redrafting of *The National Greenhouse Response Strategy*. The

ENGO recommendations, which had received backing from some industry representatives and Government members, were sidelined, and the *Strategy* adopted a 'business-as-usual' approach. It included the caveats that, irrespective of an industry's contribution to the generation of greenhouse gases, a climate change policy should ensure that no industry sector or region should suffer any adverse effect or disadvantage from the adoption of the policy, nor should a policy compromise the continued growth of the economy or be implemented until other advanced industrial countries had done so. Moreover, the preference for policy based on market-based approaches signalled the increasing dominance of economic advice within the bureaucracy.

The tenor of the *National Greenhouse Response Strategy*, in fact, set the tone for policy considerations for successive governments. This reflected a more general retreat of government from committing to environmental agendas. The succession of the Labor Government's Treasurer, Paul Keating, to the prime ministership, underscored this retreat. The new Government determined to be a less environmental activist government, one that would not use its constitutional powers to override State authority in the interests of the environment (Economou, 1999).

The scope for environmental organisations to exercise any influence on environment policy, and the design of climate change policy more particularly, was to all intents and purposes extinguished. For the ACF in particular, the organisational refocus, by shifting resources to working within the corporatist framework of Labor's ESD process and away from campaigning, had effectively foreclosed recourse to returning to mobilise popular support for a policy of more consequence. With the Conservative parliamentary opposition even more pro-development than Labor, the ACF was more or less locked into supporting Labor for re-election in 1996. Labor's defeat at that election effectively guaranteed that any influence that the ACF could bring to bear on government policy was brought to an abrupt end. Further ignominy was added when the Conservative Government withdrew funding for the ACF. The Conservative Government, however, shifted most of the financial support dedicated to environmental NGOs to the WWF. Prior to the election, the WWF had weighed up the environmental policies of the respective parties and determined that a Howard-led Conservative Government could possibly deliver more than a Keating-led Labor Government, and declared its support for the Conservative coalition.

The change in government effectively marginalised the environmental movement from any real input in shaping government policy for the next decade. The political force of environmentalism was largely spent. The folly of investing in parliamentary politics was revealed with the election of the Conservative Howard-led Coalition Government in 1996 and its re-election on three successive occasions. The Government did seek to give the impression that it was not completely setting aside concerns about the environment by setting up the National Environmental Consultative Council, which brought together the peak national ENGOs with state-based conservation councils.

But it was evident that in broadening of representation of a range of environmental NGOs, the Government was set upon marginalising the lobbying power of the national organisations, and any influence was soon despatched with the dissolution of Council (Doyle, 2000). The Government shifted some environmental management responsibilities back to State governments and withdrew funding for those ENGOs that had not supported the coalition. This completely wrong-footed the movement. Doyle (2010) makes the point that the metanarrative of the environment was erased, and certainly climate change as a key political concern was forced from the political arena.

However, there were some concerted efforts to rebuild the movement's political stocks. In 1999 the ACF invited a number of different organisations to join in a regular forum to establish partnerships, share research endeavours and build organisational capacity. The heads of some 23 organisations, including national-focused organisations such as FoE, Greenpeace, TWS and the WWF, as well as State- and regional-based conservation councils and the nascent Climate Action Network Australia, first met at Mittagong. The so-called Mittagong Forum instituted regular meetings to promote greater collaboration and the sense of a common purpose. The focus on capacity building and leadership training reasserted the ambition to further professionalise the leading organisations of the environment movement. In 2009, the forum was disbanded in order to rebuild a 'more inclusive' network structure with a view to exercising more leverage with the Rudd Labor government after its election In November 2007. Divisions between member groups over the Rudd Labor government's proposed Carbon Pollution Reduction Scheme (CPRS) were a part of the impetus. The ACF, ACTU, ACOSS, and the Climate Institute came out in public support of Labor's national climate policy in April that year, creating tension between these groups and Greenpeace, FoE, TWS, Australian Student Environment Network (ASEN) and others. The Forum was replaced by the 'Future Forum' in 2011.

The environmental movement quite obviously faced difficult odds in seeking to recover political ground in debates around environmental issues, let alone climate change. The ACF floundered because its organisational focus had been defined largely in terms of access to government, with government funding to support this (Doyle, 2000). Although the climate figured prominently in Greenpeace's portfolio of environmental campaign focuses, it was not a member-based organisation so could not call out a constituency and, besides, its political stocks among the general populace had waned. TWS was not particularly focused on climate-change concerns. FoE was more engaged, although it did not have a wide support base, while the appeal of the WWF was questionable in light of its backing for the Conservative Coalition Government. There were also very few local or grass-roots environmental groups that had taken up the climate change cause. On the other hand, the business community, and especially energy-intensive industries and coal mining, realised what they stood to lose should a meaningful climate change policy ever be implemented. Business set its course by developing an extraordinarily well-funded campaign to lobby government, support those departments sympathetic to the continued development of industry, and sway public opinion (Rosewarne, 2003). Conservative economists within the bureaucracy, and especially within the Australian Bureau of Agriculture and Resource Economics, who would lead Australian officials in negotiations on the Kyoto Protocol, worked closely with industry associations to resist designing any agreement that would obstruct the continued growth of energy-intensive industries and mining.[2]

The Government's position had been made absolutely clear when the Bush administration announced that it would not ratify the Protocol. Howard declared that ratifying the Protocol would place key industries at a competitive disadvantage in the international economy, and the Government announced that it would not consider ratifying the Protocol unless a comprehensive global agreement in which all countries would agree to reduce emissions was resolved. Inaction was also justified on the grounds that Australia's emissions were insignificant compared with some of the developing countries, and China in particular, which were not subject to emissions-reduction targets. The Howard Government joined the United States Bush administration in moving to construct an alternative framework to Kyoto Protocol – the Asia-Pacific Partnership on Climate Change and Development – that emphasised the importance of technological solutions with no reference to emission targets (Christoff, 2005; Rosewarne, 2003).

Given this political milieu, and despite the negotiations taking place within the UNFCCC, there was nothing of substance proposed by Australian governments. The *Greenhouse Response Strategy* had set the tenor of policy prospects, business-as-usual policies, which were subsequently reiterated in Labor's *Greenhouse Challenge Program* and the Conservative Government's revamped *Greenhouse Challenge Program Plus* and the *National Greenhouse Strategy: Strategic Framework for Advancing Australia's Greenhouse Response*. These emphasised Australia's 'particular interests and circumstances' and the need to preserve the material significance of fossil-fuel-based industries in the economy. Rather than mandating emission-reduction targets, they embraced the idea of voluntarism and opposed any mandating of emissions targeting for industry.

Paradoxically, opinion polls indicated that a substantial majority of those surveyed were persuaded by the latest climate-change science and supported calls for urgent action to be taken to mitigate the potential damaging effects of greenhouse gas emissions. In an effort to be seen to be doing something concrete, in 1998 the Howard Government established the Australian Greenhouse Office within the Department of Environment to consult with various stakeholders and to formulate some policy proposals. The Office demonstrated almost no initiative. It released a number of discussion papers in 1999, the most noteworthy advocating an emissions trading system as the most efficient and cost-effective mechanism for meeting emission-management objectives.[3] Even representatives from peak industry associations expressed disappointment that the establishment of the AGO enterprise was a missed opportunity.[4]

The failure of the environmental movement to progress claims through the state contrasted with the effectiveness of business lobbying in underpinning governments' intransigence. Marginalised from the corridors of parliament, the peak ENGOs undertook a review of strategies with a view to refocusing their campaign efforts in order to recover their political stocks. Reflecting back on the experience in the ESD process when they negotiated across the working groups' tables with business representatives, the ACF began approaching businesses to explore promoting a number of environmental management initiatives that could be progressed through partnerships with business. While the initial encounters were not exclusively occupied with climate-change concerns, the arrangement served as a template for developing connections with the business community to focus attention on climate change. In 2006 the ACF formalised an arrangement setting up the Australian Business Roundtable on Climate Change with six large enterprises to undertake research on understanding the business risks and opportunities associated with climate change. It commissioned the CSIRO to quantify the impacts of climate change on Australia. The approach was designed to get business, and especially the insurance industry and some investment funds, to recognise that prudent business practice justified an assessment of the potential risks facing investments in the context of climate change.[5] Greenpeace, which hitherto had waged some high-profile protest actions against major corporations, made an about-turn and reoriented its climate change campaign around building partnerships with business. This by and large meant that the peak ENGOs conceded the policy parameters proselytised by the Howard Government, namely that greater reliance should be placed on technological solutions in the first instance and that consideration should be given to market-based approaches sometime in the future.

Climate change politics

In many respects, the state of play with respect to climate politics at this time was not unique to Australia. It reflected Anthony Giddens' claim that 'at present, *we have no politics of climate change*' (sic.) (Giddens, 2009: 4). The peak environment NGOs had taken the lead to place climate on the environmental movement's agenda. The focus has been almost entirely on winning government over to the cause of meeting the challenge of climate change, and this had proved a quite ineffective strategy. One consequence of being thrust back onto the back foot was a tendency to seize whatever gains appeared to be within reach. This, for instance, resulted in an acceptance of technological innovation as one route for addressing the climate change challenge. Another was to accept that an emissions trading system would be the core foundation of any climate policy framework. In both instances, the role of government would remain paramount. While they would have endorsed Giddens' contention that constructing a climate change politics would require adopting a long-term perspective, as well as the transformation of the state, like Giddens, there was no idea as to how this transformation could be effected.

In many respects, the forestalling of climate politics was bound up in the environmental movement's failure to move beyond an 'environmental sensibility'. The movement, and particularly the peak environmental organisations, embraced climate scientists' reports of the growing concentration of greenhouse gas emissions as being anthropogenic in origin, and simply added climate change to the list of the concerns that they felt compelled take up. The big difference between the threat of climate change and those issues that the organisations had historically dedicated campaign resources to fighting was that the climate change challenge occupied an entirely different scale. And Australia's place in the global energy-intensive industrial system that was driving climate change was of a quite different order to other environmental problems canvassed by the environmental organisations.

In so far as the emergent politics of climate change was defined in terms of the forecasts of climate modelling, the preoccupation with lobbying government to commit to mitigating emissions was always going to be caught up in debate about the veracity of the modelling and in arguments about the wisdom and potential cost of transitioning away from the fossil-fuel intensive carbon economy. This meant that the peak environmental organisations had to dedicate resources to relay the climate-modelling message that the threat of climate change was both real and urgent and to counter the propaganda advanced by energy-intensive industries and conservatives that fostered doubt and scepticism. It also meant that the efforts to win over public opinion had to translate into political pressure if there was going to be any likelihood of shifting government policy, and in the Australian context this had to be set alongside the reluctance of successive governments to adopt any measures that could possibly impede economic growth, and the continued growth of the resource sector and energy-intensive industries more particularly. The folly in this approach to climate politicking was made clear with the organisations' participation in the multi-party discussions initiated by the Hawke Labor Government. They invested unwarranted confidence in the possibilities of progressing environmental causes through the institution of the state that had made abundantly clear its commitment to underwriting the pace of economic growth, however much this was dressed up as 'ecologically sustainable development'. This precluded the possibility of addressing the climate change challenge as being systemic in nature, and their engagement was one that was in effect devoid of any real political purchase.

The climate change political project that had been spearheaded by the ENGOs withered. Hamstrung by the refusal of government to engineer any substantive measures and industry's resistance to adopting technologies to reduce the energy-intensity of their practices, the movement was left vulnerable to the prospect of either teasing out whatever gains could be secured or being cast into a political nether land. As we have seen, the efforts to progress the climate change cause through the state elicited not one tangible measure to mitigate emissions. Instead, the ACF and the WWF became locked into endorsing the position that argued the management of climate change was entirely consistent with the continued growth of the economy. On the other hand, in having entertained participating in and then pulling out of the ESD process, the TWS and Greenpeace stepped into something of a political void. In both instances, Labor's retreat from taking any consequential action on climate change and the Howard Government's move to ostracise the ENGOs from any real involvement in environmental deliberations served to compound the impotency of the movement.

The movement's capacity to progress the climate cause, be this through the instrument of the state or by challenging the thrust of state policy, was rendered quite ineffective. Paradoxically, while the state remained the principal instrument through which the movement endeavoured to secure some concrete initiatives to protect the environment, including measures to mitigate climate change, the state had also become a smaller and diffuse vehicle following the Keating and Howard Governments' moves to redesignate much responsibility for environmental management back into the hands of State governments, or by advocating the force of the market as a more efficient instrument for delivering environmental outcomes. This limited the ability of the movement to marshal resources of the diverse and fragmented grass-roots groups that were campaigning around a great variety of environmental issues and to fuse these to support the climate change cause.

This is not to say that there were not any serious efforts being made to revitalise the environmental movement and to mould the overwhelming sentiment of public opinion into a 'climate sensibility'. The 'Getting Together Conference', which brought an array of green groups together over a weekend in March 1986 to discuss strategies for consolidating the force of public opinion, was a start. But the fact that it was held on the same weekend as the Broad Left Conference, a similar event whose aim was to reinvigorate the political left, and that there was no dialogue between the two events, speaks volumes about the political malaise (Hutton & Connors, 1999). There were other positive signs that the environmental movement was exploring the different ways in which its political momentum could be resuscitated. The idea of alliances was tested, with the Rainbow Alliance formed in 1988, though the difficulty in sustaining such alliances was evident in the short life of this experiment.

The significance of these initiatives was that they led to the exploration of questions that were starting to be asked about broader social implications of climate change and which could provide renewed impetus for igniting interest in climate politics. The Alliance, for instance, took up the question of social justice which, along the way, aligned with some of the ENGOs' support for Indigenous communities' struggles to protect their lands from mining. 'In September 1993 the ACF, TWS, Greenpeace Australia, together with the Australian Greens and the Australian Democrats, launched a common position on ownership of land, the impact of dislocation on Aboriginal people, compensation and claims under native title legislation' (Hutton & Connors, 1999: 251). This, in turn, prompted further reflection on ideas of environmental justice which had been debated in North America and taken on board by the German Greens.

Inspiration was also drawn from the involvement in the annual Conference of the Parties (COP) the UNFCCC. The most significant movement development was the coalition formed under the umbrella of the Climate Action Network at COP8 in October 2002. This brought together over 300 organisations from 88 countries and mapped an ambitious agenda for promoting the climate cause. CAN set up a secretariat that coordinated the activities of member organisations to promote information sharing and networking, coordinating research and building the capacity of what had become a climate movement to mobilise public support and awareness and empower civil society and thereby enhance the climate movement's participation in international negotiations. While its core ambitions included the commitment to equity and justice, CAN was forced to work within the parameters being set by the UNFCCC.

The international debate on climate change in the lead-up to the negotiation of the Kyoto Protocol contributed to focusing the environmental movement on climate concerns. Several environmental non-government organisations, including the ACF, WWF, the Total Environment Centre and Greenpeace, ran campaigns on emissions reduction and energy transition. Some also moved beyond their traditional constituency in an endeavour to circumvent government reluctance to take up the issue. The ACF, for instance, commissioned research by the CSIRO and Allens Consulting to quantify Australia's vulnerability to climate change. A second report issued by the ENGOs sought to establish the business case as a prelude to organising the first Business Roundtable on Climate Change in 2006.

Riding the momentum of the global debate around climate change, several non-government organisations were set up specifically to champion climate change issues. The Climate Institute, the Australian Youth Climate Coalition (AYCC), and Beyond Zero Emissions (BZE) were notable additions to the ENGO network in Australia, supported by the donations of influential Australian philanthropists (Crikey, 2012; Pearse, 2011). The AYCC was formed by a set of student activists who had previously or were concurrently involved in the Australian Student Environment Network, and other NGOs such as the online campaign organisation GetUp!. The AYCC is an ENGO dedicated to mobilising youth support for climate action. It is modelled on the North American 'Youth Climate Movement', and mixes media representation by members of its board and social media campaigning with participation in grass-roots events, including the 'Power Shift' conferences first held in Washington DC in 2007. BZE is a small research organisation that has been influential in the public debate over transition to renewable energy. We discuss the role of these ENGOs in the new grass-roots climate movement in the following chapter. The Climate Institute, a non-partisan policy think tank dedicated to fostering a low carbon pollution economy, was established in late 2005. The Institute has produced numerous reports, including policy and climate science explainers, economic analysis of climate and energy markets and policies, analysis of public opinion and climate change, international negotiations, and other national responses to climate change. In the effort to influence public opinion and lobby for government policy, the Institute has worked with long-established and new NGOs engaging in climate politics, such as with the AYCC, the online campaign organisation GetUp!, WWF, as well as trade unions and the Australian Council of Social Services (Connor, 2010).

Interestingly, a lot of the organisational momentum drew inspiration and support from international connections. A strategy for engaging the public through work aimed at 'raising awareness' about climate change was based on a volunteer training programme modelled, for example, on Gore's film and advocacy tours. The 2009 CANA and Southern Cross Climate Coalition multimedia campaign targeting Australia as a 'dinosaur' blocking action on climate change adapted imagery taken from the CAN International stunts used at UNFCCC meetings.

Yet, as much as this surge of activity does seem to have shifted public opinion, the organisational emphasis and political culture of these new climate change organisations replicated the strategies and structures of the established ENGOs. They relied very much on expert advocacy and decision-making, and lobbying emphases remained the province of organisation leaders. Their model for engaging people remained largely passive. Street canvassers wring small but steady direct-debit donations from passers-by, online fundraising drives ask individuals to fund one-off campaigns, and websites hold strategically placed 'donate' buttons for interested members of the public.

In the mid-2000s, established ENGOs continued with the advocacy approach already established. The ACF, for instance, in its collaboration with the Business Roundtable, emphasised the merits of instituting a carbon price, promoting technological innovation and adaptation (ABRCC, 2006). Greenpeace also shared the confidence in technological innovation through its *Energy [R]evolution* report and policy advocacy. It did, however, distinguish its climate change campaign from others by campaigning against new sites for coal mining and coal power in the late 2000s. More generally, the surge in the organisational putsch underscored an emphasis on engaging business and advocating policies that could be reconciled with bringing broad-based pressure to bear on government, of pursuing what was deemed politically possible through conventional channels. This simply echoed the politics of pragmatism that had defined the efforts of the established ENGOs.

As much as these developments helped to revive the spirits of the ENGOs, the possibilities of achieving any progress remained frustrated by the Howard Government's continuing opposition to adopting any serious measures to mitigate emissions. There was some hope that this intransigence might be abandoned after the Business Council of Australia announced that it would support the introduction of an emissions trading system at its December 2006 council meeting, and the Prime Minister established a task force to consider this. More sympathetic to such a proposal, the Prime Ministerial Task Force reaffirmed the conditions that no such scheme should be adopted if it would erode the international competitiveness of energy-intensive trade-exposed industries or before other countries also committed to emissions trading. In the lead-up to a federal election in November 2007, the ENGOs once again faced the prospect of supporting the Labor Party, whose platform at least promised that if it won government it would take some action.

With the support of the 'green' vote, and in what has been dubbed the world's 'first climate change election', Labor was in fact elected to govern, although it did not have a majority in the upper house and relied on Greens senators to secure the passage of bills (Rootes, 2008). This held out the promise of marking a watershed in climate politics. The first act of the Prime Minister was to ratify the Kyoto Protocol, and the Government awaited the review of climate change the Labor Party had commissioned in 2007. Mirroring the Stern Review, the *Garnaut Review* recommended the introduction of an emissions trading system, and sought to allay business concerns by proposing a compensation package to protect the competitive position of carbon-intensive trade-exposed industries. It broke with the intransigent position of the Howard Government in recommending that the urgent need for action demanded that an emissions trading system be adopted as soon as possible. The Rudd Government proceeded to draft such a scheme, the 'Carbon Pollution Reduction Scheme'.

Meanwhile, the ACF tried to engineer a more strategic role in influencing policy design by forming the Southern Cross Climate Alliance in 2008, in conjunction with the Australian Council of Trade Unions, the Climate Institute and the Australian Council of Social Service. The union of the peak organisations, together with the independent research centre, was designed to present a united front of a constituency that had reasonably open access to members of the recently elected Government. The hope was that they would be able to exercise leverage with government and shift the debate on climate change to focus on the long-term economic, social-welfare and environmental challenges as Australia responded to climate change. The new wave of ENGOs also added their weight to this chorus.

While this marked a return to the politics of a previous period, in which peak environmental organisations focused all their resources on lobbying government, the effectiveness of this strategy was hampered by the fact that the Labor Government did not have the parliamentary numbers in the upper house to pass legislation without the support of independent and Greens senators. The influence of the Southern Cross Climate Alliance in shaping the design of the proposed Carbon Pollution Reduction Scheme was, at best, quite mixed, but in the end it did not matter. The Rudd-led Government failed to win the endorsement of the Greens, who regarded the compensation package for those industries and sectors which would be required to meet emissions-target obligations and participate in the emissions permit system, as being far too generous and believed that the proposed emissions mitigation targets did not go anywhere near far enough. The Carbon Pollution Reduction Scheme was withdrawn.

Paradoxically, following a federal election that returned Labor to office, governing only with the support of the Greens and independents, a subsequent and weaker proposal, the Clean Energy Future (CEF) Policy, was proposed. However limited, and faced with the prospect that this would probably be the last opportunity within the life of this Government to secure some action on climate change, the Greens voted in support of the bill. The Greens did so with the general endorsement of the peak environmental NGOs, and this could not have demonstrated more clearly the impoverishment of the environmental NGOs' strategy of concentrating their resources on lobbying government and trying to win business over to a more meaningful agenda. As Doyle observed for an earlier period, the frustration that this engendered fuelled the impetus for resurrecting civil disobedience and direct action as a means of trying to shift the momentum of the environmental movement and to deliver a climate politics (Doyle, 2000: 48). By 2008, a new wave of 'climate radicalism' had emerged in Australia, seeking to upturn the pragmatic logic of climate politics that came before it.

Notes

1 In fact, the Federal Labor Government had provided funding for environmental centres, the state-based conservation councils that acted as network centres for local environmental organisations, and national environmental organisations such as the ACF, as early as 1973 (Hutton & Connors, 1999: 123).
2 The Australian delegation that participated in the Kyoto UNFCCC deliberations, led by ABARE, joined the United States, Japan, Canada, New Zealand, Russia, Norway and the Ukraine, the so-called 'Umbrella Group', in pressing the case for differentiated emission-reduction targets for advanced industrial countries, and in a last minute stand-off successfully won support for Australia to be granted a growth, rather than reduction, target for 2012 of 8 per cent over 1990 emission levels.
3 The House of Representatives Standing Committee on Environment in 1998 recommended that consideration be given to introducing an emissions trading system.
4 This observation is based on interviews conducted in 2000 with officers of the Australian Industry Group and the Business Council of Australia, industry associations that represent, respectively, medium-sized businesses and corporations in a variety of industry sectors.
5 This initiative drew upon debates in Europe and North America in which climate-change risks were being taken up in risk-management assessments (Rosewarne, 2007).

3 Climate Radicalism

From the early 2000s, a network of NGO campaigners and popular intellectuals aligned with the global justice movement began critiquing international climate policy and calling for a more just and transformative kind of climate action than was offered by state and corporate elites. Engaging in the UNFCCC process, this radical fringe of civil society began articulating a set of critiques and principles for 'climate justice' that drew on environmental justice movements to initiate a marked and important shift in climate politics, one rooted in the praxis of climate radicalism.

What came to be described as 'climate justice' activism began as a series of group statements issued at movement conferences and workshops describing the climate crisis as an expression of global inequality, neocolonial and capitalist social/ecological relations. A small set of campaigners and popular intellectuals came together in the early years of the new millennium to cohere principles for a progressive climate politics, consciously defined in opposition to the technocratic and marketised policy cemented in the UNFCCC. Event organisers and popular intellectuals articulated a set of critiques of corporate, state and international institutional responses to climate change, and argued for a broad set of alternative political responses focused on elite consumption, North-South wealth transfers, and direct participation and sovereignty for communities in the global South.

The expression of these ideas as a popular protest movement did not occur until later in the decade, with climate activism taking to the streets in protests and direct action campaigns against the installation of new fossil fuel infrastructure. An upswell of collective mobilisations occurred outside UNFCCC meetings and at sites of fossil fuel expansion in Europe, North America, and Australia in particular. Here we trace the ideas to a flurry of mobilisations and, finally, to the particular experience of 'radical' climate activism in Australia. In narrating the story of the Australian chapter of this grass-roots mobilisation we outline how the principles of climate justice were tested in terms of their popular traction through a range of 'local' protest actions.

The years 2007–10 marked a crucial period for climate action, both internationally and in Australia. The distinctive politics articulated in struggles over climate change in Australia was an attempt to challenge the inertia of national responses to climate change. A critical catalyst in Australia was the failure of the Labor Government to embed a climate policy agenda that truly reflected what it had itself defined as 'the greatest moral challenge of our generation'. Kevin Rudd was elected in 2007 at least in part on the basis of his willingness to act on climate change.[1] However, the very limited commitments he announced dissatisfied the new movement. While the policy process remained tethered to pragmatist origins, the grass-roots climate movement was pursuing a broader agenda of structural change. In the process, a reconfiguration of environmentalism was underway. This redrawing of environmental politics was rooted in the effort to theorise and practise climate action.

In the rush of energy and enthusiasm in this emergent movement a break from politics and business as usual felt possible. Activists were engaged in a collective process of seeking to redefine what radicalism meant in the context of climate crisis. Put another way, climate radicalism was at large, confident, and spreading beyond the restraints of pragmatism. This movement extended the narrative of climate crisis into new political spaces. In Australia, activists were focused on the unique political economy of the Australian environmental crisis centred on a booming coal industry, and increasing dependence on coal exports. A striking feature of the early 2000s was the intensifying structural power of the resource sector. A mining boom took off from 2005, on the back of exploding commodities prices driven by increased Chinese demand for steel and energy resources. Climate activists contested fossil fuel expansion with numerous direct action protests and brought discussion about transition to renewable energy to the streets, beaches, and parks where groups began coming together. This upsurge of mobilisation reframed the strategic questions of climate action and contested the established strategies of the Government and peak NGOs by challenging the policy cycle.

What came to be a self-identified movement for climate action in Australia encompassed a plethora of local Climate Action Groups, an annual national Climate Action Summit, yearly Walk Against Warming events, actions expressing community demands for decarbonisation, and local direct actions – especially targeting coalmines, coal-fired power stations and coal export facilities. The movement reached its apex in early 2009, when direct action Climate Camps were planned in four locations in Australia, alongside more than 20 sites across the world. However, from 2010, in the wake of a failed international and national climate policy, signs of fatigue set in. Waning numbers at protest events, the institutionalisation of the movement into a wave of competing climate NGOs, the ongoing interventions of 'pragmatic' ENGOs and representatives from allied political parties and the seemingly impenetrable deadlock in federal politics over ineffectual carbon pricing very quickly dissipated the energy of the movement.

This chapter traces the lineages of the movement networks that emerged as a social force seeking radical political action for emissions reduction. We trace the linkages between globalist calls for 'climate justice' and the grass-roots movement for climate action in Australia. We show that climate radicalism emerged as a universal imperative to act, mainly on the basis of climate science, but also due to the growing evidence of climate change internationally and in Australia. A series of weather events dramatised the likely impacts – the European summer heatwave, Hurricane Katrina, drought-related food crises in the Horn of Africa and the longest and hottest drought in Australia's history. A wave of commentary followed the release of the IPCC's Fourth Assessment Report in 2007 and the related popularisation of Al Gore's *An Inconvenient Truth*, feeding intensifying debates about global climate policy and the process of negotiating a successor to the UNFCCC Kyoto Protocol, due to expire in 2012. Scores of journalists and environmentalists were writing books translating the science of climate change into popular narratives. Mark Lynas' book *Six Degrees: Our Future on a Hotter Planet* (2007), for instance, detailed the progressive impacts of climate change in order to give the public a sense of what two, three, four, five and six degrees' warming means in reality (Lynas dedicated a chapter to each successive degree).

Climate change was proceeding against a background of failing climate policy, opening a legitimacy gap in the climate debate. The radical climate movement sought to exploit this growing political crisis, critiquing failed policies and arguing for societal transformation to meet the climate threat. The global political context set the terms for the movement, but the claims and mobilisations were embedded in specific circumstances. One of the difficulties for the movement, as we illustrate in this book, was to balance the universalising and embedding tendencies, both not to impose abstract imperatives and not to lose sight of the climate context. Like all universalisms, climate radicalism is born out in the local, social and historical conditions in which activists find themselves embedded. In the particular sites of struggle the project of radicalism must be translated and enacted by 'local' social forces. Here, we introduce these radical agendas and political traditions produced by movement groups contesting fossil fuel expansion and climate and energy policy in Australia.

Origins of 'radicalism'

The story of climate radicalism is far from a linear evolution of social forces. However, one the most salient points of origin for present-day climate activism begins with the environmental justice movement in North America in the 1980s. Through this movement a line of antagonism was drawn between minority communities and polluting industries encroaching on the poorest neighbourhoods of the US. The imposition of industrial and nuclear waste facilitates in poor, predominantly indigenous and ethnic communities in the US came to be recognised as a civil rights issue by community activists. Movement intellectuals like Robert Bullard and Benjamin Chavis communicated compelling evidence for the relationship between marginality on the basis of race and class with the imposition of toxic industries across the US

(Bullard, 1983, 1999a; Chavis, 1987). They coined a new vernacular for grass-roots opposition to the patterns of pollution and inequality. State and corporate entities imposing toxic waste depositories on black and Hispanic communities were charged with 'environmental racism' – defined as 'any policy, practice or directive that differentially affects or disadvantages individuals, groups or communities on the basis of race or colour, whether the differential effect is intended or unintended' (Bullard, 1999b: 33–34).

In the late 1990s, global warming came into the frame of environmental justice through movement leaders such as Tom Goldtooth of the Indigenous Environmental Network (IEN) and anti-corporate organisations active in the global justice movement. The idea of 'climate justice' was first enunciated by San Francisco-based NGO CorpWatch. In a 1999 report titled *Greenhouse Gangsters vs. Climate Justice* (Bruno et al., 1999) the authors were mainly concerned with the oil industry, its global reach and the corruption of political processes where it operates. Illuminating the link between climate change and local struggles against Big Oil in the US and Africa, the report signalled a new global dimension to environmental justice politics. The clash between agents of the globalised 'hydrocarbon economy' and communities organising to achieve social justice/environmental protection had begun. CorpWatch presented the World Bank and international financial lenders as hypocrites for funding fossil fuel projects in the developing world; they argued against UN policy for pollution trading and for the alignment of workers and communities to struggle for a just transition away from fossil fuels.

From the early 2000s, a series of workshops convened by NGOs involved in the global justice movement cemented the political and epistemic basis for climate justice. These meetings often paralleled the UN process in civil society gatherings outside official proceedings, but involved the process of developing shared critiques of international institutions. Declarations were premised on a critique of the logic and structural form of institutional responses to climate change through the UNFCCC and World Bank Group. At the Johannesburg United Nations World Summit on Sustainable Development in 2002, activists articulated 27 'Principles of Climate Justice' (CorpWatch US et al., 2002). The statement was signed by a group of 14 Northern and Southern NGOs, including CorpWatch, FoE International, Greenpeace International, the IEN, and the Third World Network. The principles took the 'Environmental Justice Principles' developed at the 1991 People of Color Environmental Justice Leadership Summit, Washington DC as its template, demonstrating the wider lineage.

The idea of ecological debt underpinned the claim that Northern states and corporates 'owe the rest of the world as a result of their appropriation of the planet's capacity to absorb greenhouse gases.' Stronger involvement from affected peoples in the South was seen as a priority, to allow local control, local sufficiency, and conservation. NGO campaigners had closely followed Northern country pledges of climate finance, the design of finance mechanisms and rules for the protection of local people's rights, where grants and loans for climate 'mitigation' and 'adaptation' have started flowing. Commodification and corporate influence on climate finance were rejected, but market-based policy was accepted provided they conformed to 'principles of democratic accountability, ecological sustainability and social justice'. Corp-Watch India convened a similar summit attended by 1,500 international activists from 20 organisations, and mostly local activists, fisherworkers, Dalits and indigenous groups in New Delhi later that year (October 26–28, 2002). The final statement of the conference rejected market mechanisms and technological fixes as 'false solutions' (CorpWatch India, 2002).

By the mid 2000's climate policy for carbon trading and carbon offsets has become a focus of a vocal group of mostly Northern academics and researchers in the small critical NGOs. A new market in tradeable rights to greenhouse gas emissions (measured in equivalent tonnes of carbon dioxide (tCO_2.e)) is the direct consequence of most international and national climate policy.[2] The carbon market was being instituted at great pace, on the back of multilateral finance, to trial carbon offset programs in developing countries, linked to the commencement of the EU ETS in 2005 (Newell & Paterson, 2010). The carbon market trebled in size and profitability starting from a value of US$7.9 billion in 2005 to US$100.5 billion in 2008, mostly from EU trading and parallel activity in offset markets (Linacre et al., 2011: 9). With market expansion came intense debate over market regulation in the EU, and unrest in Southern communities where offset projects were undertaken.

As new experiments in marketised climate policy began in Europe and South and Southeast Asia through the UNFCCC CDM, the critique of carbon trading was developed in more concrete terms. For instance, the Durban Climate Justice Summit held in South Africa 2004 gathered representatives from 20 organisations from Europe, the US, Latin America, India and Africa. The resulting Durban Declaration on Carbon Trading outlined the various ways in which emissions trading both undermines existing sustainable practices and contributes to climate change, highlighting the irony that with the 'process of creating a new commodity – carbon – the Earth's ability and capacity to support a climate conducive to life and human societies is now passing into the same corporate hands that are destroying the climate' (Carbon Trade Watch et al., 2004). The Declaration attracted support from a further 163 organisations, and given the growing importance of emissions trading and offsets in the Kyoto Protocol, and with the EU ETS about to start in 2005, its message has had a strong influence in networks.

The arrival of the carbon market sparked campaigning across North and South. In the far-flung cities of London, Barcelona, Brussels, Durban, Jakarta, Asunción and San Francisco, academics and NGO researchers including Larry Lohmann, Oscar Reyes, Tamra Gilbertson, Kevin Smith, Patrick Bond, Simone Lovera, Kate Dooley, Tom Griffiths, Chris Lang and others started putting considerable energy and resources into documenting and reporting the social and environmental impacts of the EU ETS, the CDM and the UN negotiations of forest offset policy called Reducing

Emissions from Deforestation and Forest Degradation in Developing Countries (REDD+). An explosion of public and private investment into trial REDD+ programs was spurred by a landmark decision to negotiate greater inclusion of land carbon sinks into the post-Kyoto agreement within the UN in 2005. The result had brought campaigners for forest and indigenous people's rights into the fold of climate politics and experimentation with new translocal solidarities. For instance, in our involvement with FoE we have contributed to criticisms of Australia's Indonesian REDD+ program in alliance with FoE Indonesia (Wahana Lingkungan Hidup Indonesia, WALHI) and an affiliate group in Kalimantan, Yayasan Petak Danum (YPD).

Campaigners and researchers in the climate justice networks have produced numerous reports, websites and short films aimed at communicating the problems with emissions trading to the broader public, and to government officials in policy review processes. They translate complex carbon trading policy into relatively plain language and imagery, seeking to bring the social and ecological impacts of the carbon market to life. For instance, CTW and Larry Lohmann of the Corner House have written definitive reports challenging neoliberal economic theory and flawed practice of carbon trading in the EU and in international offset programs (Gilbertson & Reyes, 2009; Lohmann, 2006). Heidi Bachram from CTW (then an affiliate of the Transnational Institute) produced a film called *The Carbon Connection* (2006), which presented a video exchange between local communities living near a BP an oil refinery in Grangemouth, Scotland, and a monoculture tree plantation funded by BP through the World Bank Prototype Carbon Fund[3] in Sao Jose do Buriti, Brazil. Bachram's film travelled through movement networks, as an online resource and in film screenings hosted by community groups (for instance, FoE screened it at a small gathering in Sydney August 2008). The story of carbon offsetting illustrated the compounding inequalities of pollution and commodification of CO_2. A few years later, Annie Leonard's *A Story of Cap and Trade* (2009) communicated the established critique of carbon trading in a ten minute cartoon.

In December 2007 the Climate Justice Now! coalition was founded by movement organisations attending the Bali Conference of Parties to the UNFCCC. CJN! membership consists of over 700 NGO and grass-roots groups, including a range of Southern and Northern-based NGOs and social movement organisations who have played a central role in global justice movement networks, such as Focus on the Global South, the International Forum on Globalization, La Via Campesina, and the World Development Movement, as well as signatories of previous climate justice statements. The network sought to carve out new strategies that were distinct from the incrementalism of the Climate Action Network (Bond, 2012). Rather than campaign on the technocentric terms of the UN and national governments, this network was opposed to fossil fuel dependence, marketised climate policy and technological fixes like 'clean coal' technology (CJN!, 2007). Members of CJN! focused energy on building a popular movement through the creation of alternative dialogical spaces and collective protest, notably civil disobedience in the form of counter summit protests. The largest of these was the Reclaim Power protest outside the failed UNFCCC negotiations in Copenhagen 2009.

Convening workshops to deliberate over the claims of climate justice became an ongoing tradition across the 2000s. Also at Bali in 2007, another climate justice network of NGOs working in the Asia-Pacific region established a process for the Peoples' Protocol on Climate Change (Asia Pacific Research Network, 2007). The Protocol rejected 'market mechanisms that impose the cash nexus on ecological priorities', and was critical of technological fixes. It asserted People's resource sovereignty, and the need for affected peoples to be involved in climate policy, stating that the 'climate change crisis is not simply about adaptation and mitigation, but changing the whole economic framework into one of eco-sufficiency and sustainability.' Other People's statements followed CJN!, the most notable of which is a statement released from the World People's Conference on Climate Change and the Rights of Mother Earth held 19–22 April 2010 in a sports field in Cochabamba Bolivia (PWCCC, 2010). The People's conference was the last major transnational gathering of movement groups seeking to build climate radicalism before the Arab Spring, anti-austerity mobilisations in Southern Europe and Occupy movements displaced climate justice as a focal point for radical agendas (Müller, 2012).

The creation of People's Protocol processes and the knowledge produced through media and critical scholarship opened several lines of discussion and debate in the broader climate movement, centring on issues of economic growth, ecological sufficiency, technology, markets, sovereignty and climate debt. Importantly, whilst the reading of climate change as systemic and the political critique of climate policy has been articulated as a set of coherent principles, the production of climate justice in social movement mobilisations varies significantly across local and national spaces. This is particularly relevant to the organisation of protest movements against fossil fuel expansion through collective mobilisations such as direct action Climate Camps from 2006 (see below), and other local and national campaigns against coal, oil and gas across the world. There is no coherent 'climate justice movement', but rather 'a range of overlapping, interacting, competing, and differentially placed and resourced networks concerned with issues of climate change and justice' (Routledge, 2011: 387). This became most clear in the late 2000s when groups began waging both local and national campaigns against fossil fuel expansion.

Through the Australian example, we illustrate that collective understanding of 'climate injustice' and the forging of solidarities are necessarily produced in place-based struggles like those waged over coalfields, export ports and the electricity grid of Australia. Thus the universal of climate justice is constituted by movements through a variety of interconnections within multiscalar activist networks as well as the particular political, economic, cultural and ecological relations they seek to shift. These local struggles are not discrete 'building blocks' that aggregate into global universal demands (Featherstone, 2005). Instead, they are best understood as generative sites of contestation that necessarily (re)negotiate the question of global climate justice within the structural and political/cultural landscapes of national economies and polities. The Australian climate action upsurge illuminates the possibilities and tensions in the project of climate radicalism when it hits the ground.

Climate radicalism upsurge

In Australia, the grass-roots 'climate action movement' emerged as a visible social force in 2006. Popular concern about climate change had reached a peak across the country, as it had in most affluent countries. With this wave of awareness, over 80 small community groups sprung up along the east coast, primarily in NSW and Victoria. These groups often brought together people who had little or no prior engagement with political activism. Activists with longer histories in environmental and/or other anti-capitalist and social justice organising in Australia worked alongside, and sometimes within, groups formed by this new movement. Student networks and environmentalists with experience in the forest and anti-nuclear movement also oriented to the climate problem.

The swirl of connection and collaboration fostered through the new climate movement promised something different in environmental politics, a new radicalism and new visions for transformation. The emergent climate radicalism in Australia was characterised by a clear-sighted view of the severity of the climate problem. With a national annual Walk Against Warming initiated from 2005, and pressure for climate action in the run-up to the 2007 federal election, there was growing public awareness of the climate crisis. In 2008, a new vernacular of 'climate emergency' and rapid transformation was articulated, particularly by environmentalists and researchers in Melbourne. This evolved into a process of popularising the idea of rapid transition to 100 percent renewable energy by 2020.

The emergent movement was heavily science-based and focused on domestic transitions. The growing popularisation of green industrialism coincided with the minerals export boom, and with a string of new and expanded coal mining regions. The combination of rising climate activism and the booming coal sector produced a burst of civil disobedience and community organising across the Hunter Valley coal chain to the north of Sydney, connecting mines to the world's largest coal port. Activists building opposition to port expansion sought to demonstrate the possibilities for global and local climate justice (Evans, 2010). Whilst collective attempts at building a broad civil disobedience movement on climate change did not eventuate, small but persistent direct actions spread to the coalfields of the La Trobe Valley Victoria, the Darling Downs and Brisbane coal export port.

A self-described climate movement became a semi-formal network of individuals and groups, knitted together through participation in an annual
national Climate Action Summit first convened in 2008, and also through
protests and public events that occurred on a State or local level and through
discussions on a number of cross-group e-lists. The network is made up of
what came to be known as community Climate Action Groups (CAGs), socialist
organisations such as Socialist Alliance and Solidarity, members of a national
network of student 'enviro collectives' meeting yearly through an annual Students
for Sustainability conference, and other groups such as Rising Tide Newcastle
and the national FoE federation.

Protest activity of all groups spiked across 2008 leading into 2009. Direct
action protests targeted 'root causes of climate change' in coal hotspots across
NSW, Victoria, Queensland and Western Australia. Thirty direct actions at
coal ports, power stations and mines occurred over 2007–10. They were
organised by Rising Tide, FoE groups, ASEN and Greenpeace. In parallel,
dozens of human signs were organised as finales to large protest marches, and
by CAGs to protest events engaging school groups. Modest and large groups
of people spelled out slogans on beaches and ovals. Most messages were cries
for urgent energy transition: 'Clean Energy for Eternity', 'Solar Not Nuclear',
'Climate Emergency!', 'Cut Carbon Now or Never', 'Halt Climate Change
Now!', '350' and 'Climate Change – Our Future Is In Your Hands'.

NGOs such as Greenpeace and the State-based Conservations Councils
have participated in the movement since it first took off. For instance,
Greenpeace and the autonomous group Rising Tide worked closely together
on the Anvil Hill coal mine campaign in 2005, and Greenpeace funded the
first Camp for Climate Action in Newcastle 2008. Greenpeace and the NSW
Nature Conservation Council (NCC) were active in supporting the formation
of local CAGs in Sydney. A dedicated campaigner at NCC hosted an online
platform for connecting and coordinating movement groups. Activists from
FoE have been heavily involved in the movement, as collectives engaged in
direct action protest, and organisers became involved in cross-group projects
like Climate Camps. In less formal ways, individuals on the payroll of NGOs
participate independently. They consciously assert they have taken their
'NGO hat off' in order to engage in grass-roots organising. NGO workers are
often also formerly or concurrently autonomous activists in Rising Tide,
ASEN or FoE. They are often described as the 'doers' of the movement, for
their roles as facilitators and strategic thinkers (Ruth 2008b).

In parallel with the grass-roots movement, and drawing on it, a number of
new climate-focused NGOs were created between 2005 and 2010: the
Australian Youth Climate Coalition, the Climate Institute, Beyond Zero
Emissions, Safe Climate Australia and 100% Renewables. These had the effect
of institutionalising large sections of the grass-roots movement into organisations constituted as not-for-profit companies, usually with a small, self-selec-
ted board employing staff to coordinate large contingents of volunteers and
supporters, often through social media. With the exception of the Climate

Institute, these groups have a close engagement with both the CAGs and the peak ENGOs. BZE and AYCC are highly visible at movement events, and are led by prolific public speakers. These organisations routinely rehearse narratives of hope about the possibility for transition to a zero carbon economy and the power of the youth climate action movement respectively. At the same time, a large number of locally based CAGs became more directly involved in local actions to reduce greenhouse gas emissions, inspired and in some cases affiliated with the Transition Towns movement.

As regards the emergent 'radical' climate NGOs, BZE was the first to explicitly campaign for the models it had devised. BZE is part think tank, part lobby group, part education initiative. The small number of paid staff, with university researchers and a volunteer network has dedicated themselves to communicating the feasibility of decarbonisation:

> Our goal is to transform Australia from a 19th century fossil fuel based economy to a 21st century renewable powered clean tech economy. Through the Zero Carbon Australia project BZE is researching climate solutions that are in line with the science.
>
> (BZE, undated)

Their ecological imaginary is modernist and technocentric, but radical in its ambition. BZE staff and volunteers give polished PowerPoint presentations on their vision for decarbonisation to corporates and politicians at movement events. In 2009 their vision was formalised in a 'Zero Carbon Energy Plan' detailing the technical and economic viability of a transition to 100 per cent renewable energy in 10 years (Wright & Hearps, 2010). BZE is located in the professionalised culture populated by energy and climate experts. For instance, Hugh Saddler, Mark Diesendorf, and Richard Dennis (2004), and Sven Teske and Julian Vincent (2008) have written similar reports costing clean energy scenarios for WWF and renewable industry associations and Greenpeace. However, where they differ from previous reliance on expert reports is in seeking to organise supporters to promote their models. Over time, BZE coordinating staff have been employed to support small volunteer groups in Melbourne, Sydney and Brisbane. These employees and their supporters campaign for decarbonisation armed with the BZE plan and imagery of solar and wind power on a grand scale.

The AYCC is another new and visible climate ENGO that emerged in the late 2000s with the self-appointed task of mobilising youth. Headed by a small group of ambitious Generation Y campaigners, the AYCC also mix the professionalised model of campaigning with grass-roots participation. AYCC members are highly visible participants in the movement, often wearing bright blue organisation T-shirts armed with well-produced pamphlets and policy asks that more or less align with other CANA members and the Greens. The AYCC is overseen by a board, and like BZE hires coordinators to mobilise volunteers through social media, and through 'Power Shift' conferences, stalls on campus and rallies. AYCC ran a 'Youth Decide' online poll in 2009, where individuals voted online for a transition to renewable energy and international cooperation, and organised a flash mob of 1,000 activists in the lead-up to UN negotiations in Copenhagen. The group has been widely revered for its capacity to mobilise large numbers of youth. In 2009, the AYCC claimed a database of 50,000 people and over 2,500 active volunteers. AYCC has also stimulated debate and critical attention within the movement. For instance, in mid-2009, debate ensued after the AYCC was criticised by an autonomous activist for its acceptance of corporate and state funding and representation at its Power Shift conference (WWF, Westpac, PacificHydro and State governments donated to the conference).

CAGs, NGOs and other groups have also participated in 'global' co-ordinated campaigns and actions such as Walks Against Warming as part of the Global Climate Campaign[4] and Bill McKibben's 350.org movement organisation. Pragmatic climate advocates, coordinated through the 'peak' body, Climate Action Network Australia (CANA), have sought to recruit CAGs to their approach to climate policy. CANA is funded by big-brand NGOs, yet as a 'peak' it seeks to be seen to constitute and represent the climate 'sector'. Accordingly, from 2009 it sought to open up to 'the grass-roots', allocating places for two grass-roots representatives in its steering committee and providing free or discount admission for CAG members to attend CANA's national meeting. For some years, CANA has sought to integrate its national conference into the yearly movement-based climate summit. This has not occurred, as conveners of the climate summit have sought to retain an autonomous movement convergence, although the two events have been held sequentially to enable crossover. Greens are also active in the movement – both local party members and sitting MPs are highly visible in climate movement events, from strategy meetings to protests. Finally, a set of academics and popular intellectuals are aligned with the movement.

Amongst the set of self-identified 'usual suspects' in Australian climate activism, membership in groups affiliated with FoE and the Newcastle group Rising Tide is common. In Australia, Friends of the Earth is a small NGO, largely volunteer-run with a few paid workers mostly in the FoE Melbourne office and occasional paid work in other collectives when fundraising is successful. The organisational structure of FoE and its member groups is less formal and more fluid than other ENGOs. There are varying degrees of organised recruitment methods across the network, and few nationally coordinated campaigns. FoEA had a part-time Climate Justice Campaign Coordinator from 2007–10, liaising with local groups working on a range of national and transnational campaign areas including climate-induced displacement, biofuels in the Asia-Pacific, Australia's carbon trading policy and the AusAID REDD+ program, population debates, coal expansion in Queensland and rising sea levels on the east coast. Member FoE groups are located in Brisbane, Sydney, Wollongong, Melbourne and Adelaide. FoE

Sydney and FoE Melbourne activists were engaged in the organisation of significant conferences for the climate movement (the Climate Movement Convergence Melbourne 2008 and annual Climate Action Summits), as well as Climate Camps in NSW and Victoria. FoEA is part of FoE International, an international federation of groups spanning 71 national groups. FoEI navigates a transnational identity across Northern and Southern groups, which has involved differences in ideology and strategy in relation to climate politics (Doherty, 2006). The transnational federation stands out in the field of large transnational ENGOs, in that it is explicitly seeking to address environmental issues through a critique of neoliberalism and commitment to environmental justice.

The Rising Tide collective is a member group of the UK and North American networks, first formed in 2000 in the UK to organise mobilisation against the UNFCCC meeting at The Hague. The Rising Tide network is anti-capitalist, and describes itself as organising for 'social justice, community autonomy and sustainable living' (Rising Tide International Network, 2011). The Australian chapter, Rising Tide Newcastle, formed in 2004 in order to resist the Carr Government's plans for a new coal fired power station in the State of NSW. This first successful campaign was titled the No More Polluting Power coalition. With groups across the state, they used a mix of public protest, civil disobedience, strategic litigation and engagement in department consultation processes to discredit the decision. Following success in this campaign, the group has led community opposition to projects across the Hunter Valley coal chain. The second major campaign for Rising Tide targeted the proposal for a mine at Anvil Hill that was to be the largest coal mine in NSW (estimates for the mine production were 10.5 Mt of domestic and export grade thermal coal annually over a 20 year period). The campaign failed to stop the mine,[5] but it did start the discussion about the environmental and social costs of coal mining in the Hunter and its relationship to climate change.

Rising Tide has instigated numerous small and large direct action protests since 2006. Along with activists in their extended networks, Rising Tide organised the first Camp for Climate Action in July 2008, targeting the construction of a third coal-export terminal at the port of Newcastle. This protest, held at the end of the four day event, was the largest single direct action protest event of the climate movement in Australia, with around 1,200 people participating in a rally where around 40 people occupied the train line into the Carrington Coal Terminal for five hours. Between 300 and 500 people camped two kilometres from the coal terminal at a local sports ground in Wickham, Newcastle. In 2009, Climate Camps were held in the La Trobe Valley Melbourne and Helensburgh NSW. Switch Off Hazelwood targeted the Hazelwood coal fired power station, contesting the State Government's decision to extend its lifetime. In Helensburgh NSW the Climate Camp targeted extension of an underground coal mine producing coking coal for steel production. This camp elicited a counter protest from local residents. Tensions in this engagement were considerable for activists seeking to argue for a 'just transition' away from steel production and 'green jobs' for displaced workers (see Chapter 6).

Groups and individuals attending or organising Climate Camps and other direct action events are often immersed in activist networks and traditions of radicalism (autonomism, socialism, community organising and indigenous rights activism). In public contestation, autonomous groups in Australia articulate anti-capitalist positions with the language of social justice. 'Climate justice' has been expressed as solidarity with those most affected by climate change and fossil fuel expansion in rural communities and the South, a critique of 'false solutions' such as biofuels and carbon capture and storage (CCS) and, in the case of FoE, an opposition to 'market solutions' and the emissions trading scheme announced by the Rudd Government in 2008. Most commonly, anti-capitalist radicalism is associated with strategic focus on civil disobedience to halt emissions reduction.

A shared worry for climate activists who attend and organise direct action protests is how to build the popular appeal of radicalism within the climate movement and broader public. Few CAG members and only small numbers of local residents engage in civil disobedience and Climate Camp events. Direct action mobilisations are challenged as a means to reach outside what one participant in Climate Camps called the 'ghetto' of radicalism (William, 2009). The annual Climate Action Summits are the gatherings that cast the widest net in terms of bringing these individuals and groups together each year from 2009–12. Around one third of the Summit participants represented a CAG group (made up of three to twelve core members). Most of those attending are 'networked' in some way. Summits are a key site where the social, political and affective bonds are created and on display. These events draw 200–400 people over two to three days. A strikingly older demographic (50+) is visible at summits, of attendees who participate in one of the more than 80 CAGs that formed across 2005–8. They are most often new to political activism.

Lined up against the foyer walls at the summits are fold-out tables attended by members of CAG, socialist, autonomous collectives and a few NGOs. In varying combinations they might display photos of actions and offer e-list and petition sign-up sheets, books for sale, magazines, reports, issue briefings, zines and pamphlets for the next critical protest or public meeting. Leading climate science and policy experts enter the Summit for a spell to give short lectures, as do Australian Greens MPs and NGO campaigners. Each year a group of organisers take on the role of convening the summit from different groups across the country. Together they have been coordinating event logistics for weeks in the lead-up. In plenary sessions, 'organisers' are rarely the expert speakers but are likely to introduce, facilitate, and summate proceedings, announce housekeeping information and be running in and out of the door, mobile phone in hand.

Summits are places of knowledge exchange, report-backs from numerous fronts of campaigning, and celebration. All-in plenary sessions have been lively, particularly at the moments when the movements debated common

political positions and attempted to create an official national network structure. By 2010, key political campaign themes were carved out as: 100%
Renewables, Coal, Green Jobs, and Climate Emergency. The Summit had
been established at a state level in NSW in 2008 as an attempt at movement
building, and initially was designed as a deliberative consensus-forming process. Yet even in the early stages local groups were already, for the most part,
anxious to preserve their autonomy. As a result, decisions made at the first
national Climate Summit in 2009 on policy, campaigns and network structure
were unevenly implemented. As activists gravitated to the various climate
NGOs – discussed below – which had their own decision-making structures,
the Summit began to operate more as a talking shop than as a decision-
making body for the movement. The Summit retained a more informal networking and dialogic role, as a forum for campaigners to establish new
agendas and to work together (in some ways akin to the World Social Forum
model). In 2013 it still attracted upwards of 150 activists and remained one of
the lasting legacies of the upsurge in Australia.

Clearly, though, from 2010 the movement had suffered a series of setbacks,
and the number of people engaged in public contestation began to decline. In
order to understand this process of demobilisation, there is much more to say
about the project of climate radicalism, its potentials and dilemmas. From
here, we sketch the contours of climate radicalism in Australia, with its particular focus on urgent action to enable a transition away from fossil fuels.
Finally, we introduce the role of civil disobedience in the movement through
Climate Camps and a range of smaller protests as a focus for radical praxis.

'Emergency' NGOs

As noted, from the mid 2000s climate change became something of a popular
cause célèbre, with numerous commentators and activists discovering its
importance. Their chief preoccupation was to popularise the latest science and
translate it into policy. In Australia, David Spratt and Philip Sutton's book
Climate Code Red: The Case for Emergency Action (2008) was particularly
influential amongst climate activists. In it they argued that global warming is
much more serious than conservative estimates of the IPCC and other official
reports. They made the case for 'emergency action', imploring the new movement in Australia to assert rapid social, technological and economic transformation as not a radical, but rather a sober response to a pressing problem. The
political task taken up by these men was to explain and legitimise the climate
science that focuses on tipping points and feedback loops in the climate system.
As John Urry observes, climate science had been drawn out of the laboratory
(Urry, 2011). Whilst scientists have been subject to intense scrutiny, science is
nonetheless the primary epistemology through which society debates climate
change (next to neoliberal economics). Celebrity scientists and expert advocates
such as Lynas, Spratt and Sutton have become popular prophets of climate
change, providing proof that apocalypse is nigh, but can be prevented.

The process of mobilising a 'climate movement' involved building political leverage from the prophecy of climate chaos and reams of science reportage. Movement activists put considerable effort into explaining the science of climate change. Science in effect had a legitimising effect for the new climate radicalism. For instance, one of the most famous images of the second Climate Camp in the UK at London's Heathrow Airport features hundreds of people standing in a field holding a banner stating: 'We are armed only with peer reviewed science'. In turn, the new climate radicalism was based on the insistence on the need to transition to a completely decarbonised economy-society.

In Australia, the climate action movement mobilised for the Federal election in 2007 to unseat the Conservative Coalition Government. But with Labor installed under the leadership of Kevin Rudd, it became progressively disenchanted and critical of the slow, moderate plans for emissions reductions. The consensus was that the 450 ppm target (giving a 50:50 chance of staying below 2°C of warming) laid out in the IPCC reports, UN negotiations, and federal climate policy advice authored by Ross Garnaut in 2008, was unrealistic. Some CAGs focused on calling for cuts of as low as 285 ppm (pre-industrial levels), and others 300–350ppm – roughly equivalent to 1.5 degrees warming (NASA scientist James Hansen is the attributed the authority behind this number). Heated debates over what demands to make in terms of targets erupted on e-lists and in meetings.

Contention over emissions targets is expressed as a proxy for negotiation of the tension between radicalism and pragmatism. Asserting the imperative for urgent action and deep emissions cuts distinguished the grass-roots from professionalised ENGOs. An early example was the debate over the movement's standpoint on the Rudd Government's emissions reduction target of 5–15 per cent below 2000 levels by 2020, which was announced in December 2008. CANA coordinated 55 NGOs and community groups to sign a joint open letter calling for a new target of 25–40 per cent below 1990 levels by 2020 (Shalhorn et al., 2008). The argument that satisfied most, but not all in the 'grass-roots', was that whilst there was no agreement on what the emissions target should be, there was agreement on what it should *not* be.

There have been related disputes over the role of gas, clean coal, and biomass in future energy scenarios, which has been a hot topic that has produced sharp disagreement in the movement. When BZE arrived as a new intellectual force in the movement, their model for a 100 per cent renewable energy grid by 2022 was contested by a number of movement academics and individuals arguing that some inclusion of gas as a transition fuel offered a necessary and pragmatic pathway away from fossil fuel dependence. When the BZE report (Wright & Hearps, 2010) was released, a small group of vocal campaigners in the movement began debating what this meant for the movement's vision and goals. In online discussions between activists, detailed figures for solar thermal capacity, the emissions profile of natural gas and the assumptions of scenario models were entangled with reflection over the deteriorating national climate policy debate. There was a questioning of national campaign demands, for instance, over the extent to which a demand for 100 per cent renewables should be favoured over more negative campaigning against new fossil fuel extraction and burning.

While activists debated technologies, the national debate shifted markedly away from emissions reduction, as the Conservative opposition abandoned its bipartisan support for pricing carbon and instead adopted a 'direct' incentives-based approach. The 'great big tax on everything', as the carbon price was described by the Conservative leader of the opposition (Green, 2010), had become a political liability for the Government, and was considerably watered down through a plethora of subsidies and offsets. The Government had moved progressively closer to a policy of favouring gas as the new 'transition' fuel, and in this was followed by some key environmental agencies, such as Environment Victoria – which caused a furore within the climate movement in 2010 when it endorsed a new gas-fired power station to replace Hazelwood, a coal-fired power station in Victoria and the single biggest greenhouse gas emitter in Australia (EV, 2010). Opposition to EV's strategic call for gas was described by a Melbourne activist as the most important rift in the movement that year (Courtice, 2010). This moment of contention and many more like it illustrate the complex co-production of expert knowledge and antagonistic politics. 'Technical' debates about so-called transition fuels like gas were a key subject of political discussion within the movement. Further, debates over gas reflect a series of tensions that played out over the period over the relationship between the strategic decisions of ENGOs and grass-roots campaigning.

Direct action

In parallel with the emerging project of 'radical' green industrialism, the Climate Camps and other direct action events built by networks in and around Rising Tide and FoE were aiming to popularise and legitimise the strategy of civil disobedience. In practical terms, the first layer of people that this sought to mobilise were the newly formed CAGs. The Climate Camp model, derived from the UK, had been taken up by activists in more than twenty mostly Northern countries around the world, including Australia's first Newcastle Climate Camp and, in 2009, another three camps in Helensburgh NSW, Morewell Victoria, and Adelaide South Australia, plus a further 15 worldwide. These were not moments of large-scale mass mobilisation: even the largest Camps in the UK attracted no more than 3,000 people. In Australia, as noted, the Newcastle Camp attracted 1,200, and the two major Camps in Helensburgh and Morewell were attended by approximately 350 to 500 people. Yet the Camps did attract considerable attention, especially in the UK where they were policed with violence, as highly symbolic interventions into the climate debate that highlighted the continued expansion of fossil fuel industries. Despite their marginality, the Climate Camp mobilisations suggest the flow and exchange of ideas for collective mobilisation through the interconnections between various activist projects, alliances and association in networks. They also offer a highly resonant experiment or laboratory for the climate movement – and hence our focus on activists involved in them for this study.

The Climate Camp as a concept originates from global justice movement mobilisations against the Gleneagles G8 in Scotland 2005. Hori-Zone, the 'eco-village' made up of autonomous neighbourhoods beside the Firth River in Stirling outside the Gleneagles summit, is a direct predecessor to the Climate Camps. Activists in the Dissent network created plans to hold an out-door protest event on climate change. The first Camp for Climate Action was organised as a week-long action camp outside Drax coal power station in Yorkshire, the UK's largest single source of carbon emissions. Yearly camps have been organised along four principles: education, direct action, sustainable living and building a movement to effectively tackle climate change. The camp targeted Heathrow Airport in 2007, Kingsnorth power station in 2008, the European Climate Exchange in London during the G20 meeting 2009, the UK's biggest coal fired power stations at Ratcliffe-on-Soar in Nottingham in 2009, and finally the Royal Bank of Scotland in Edinburgh in 2010.

Climate Camps are a form of strategic direct action geared to movement-building. Camps are spatial interventions mounted as close as possible to the physical site of large-scale carbon emissions. Activists' reflections on this strategy at the Ratcliffe-on-Soar Climate Camp 2009 illustrate that the intended effect of these mobilisations is to materialise the climate problem.

> Climate change is abstract – about the weather. We wanted to create symbolic moments of tension to break through this. This was the reason why the first camp was at Drax, Europe's biggest coal-fire station. Saying we'll shut it down was central to this idea.
>
> (CfCA Nottingham, 2009)

The Camps express the autonomous politics of the global justice movement that spawned it. Camps are based on principles of ecological sufficiency in the processes of provisions (food, equipment, energy for the camp and so on). They create a temporary community organised as local 'neighbourhoods'. The camps combine daily practices of consensus decision making, workshops on climate issues, strategy sessions, and training in non-violent direct action (NVDA), culminating with a series of direct actions against expanding fossil fuel installations. As such, they create power as ideological and cultural counter-sites, designed to unmask and contest plans to expand carbon-intensive infrastructures and industries and model direct democracy and sustainable living.

Beyond these two main examples from the 'radical' climate movement – the emergency frame and the direct action frame – there were numerous other experiments and interventions. Several sectors began participating in debates about what would constitute the required radical climate action. One example is the trade union movement, which began its own internal debate about how to engage union members with climate issues, which in some contexts overlapped with the broader debates in the climate movement. Likewise, two socialist organisations developed their own critiques through a string of public conferences centred on climate change, focusing on climate crisis as a crisis of capitalism, and injecting a focus on the social injustices of both climate change and climate policy. Other sectors also became more engaged, notably the overseas development and social welfare sectors. Overall, from 2006 this broad array of initiatives began to draw critiques of climate policy into the political field, offering a means of deepening public engagement with the issue.

Radicalism in retreat

The peak of climate movement activity in 2008–9 was followed by a trough in 2010 after UNFCCC negotiations in Copenhagen faltered, the global financial crisis advanced and the national debate over climate policy took the air out of the broader agenda the movement had begun to articulate. In domestic parliamentary politics, two party leaders were deposed by their members in the midst of disputes over the CPRS. Malcolm Turnbull's support for the ALP's carbon trading policy put him at odds with conservative elements of the Liberal Party, who remained sceptical about climate change, were opposed to regulation and had perhaps read the imminent signs that UN negotiations would fail to boost, let alone retain momentum toward fresh international commitments beyond 2012. The Labor Party's proposed Carbon Pollution Reduction Scheme (CPRS) was voted down in Parliament twice. Rudd was unseated from the leadership in April 2010 by the Labor party's right-wing faction when his consistently high public approval ratings dropped.

Certainly part of this drama was Rudd's poorly executed attempt at progressive tax reform for the resource sector through the Mining Super Profits Tax (not designed as an environmental tax). The largest mining companies and industry associations waged and won an advertising war against this tax and the carbon trading scheme before it. The CPRS promised little to no reduction in greenhouse emissions due to its low cap and weakly regulated carbon offset rules (Rosewarne, 2010; Spash, 2010). Mining and energy companies that were deemed 'emissions-intensive trade exposed' (EITE) made numerous threats of closure and capital flight. By the end of 2009, the CPRS committed over AU\$9 billion compensation to polluting industries in the form of free emissions permits and cash. The Greens opposed the scheme, claiming it was 'worse than doing nothing' (Milne, 2009).

The NGO response to the CPRS, however, was split. In July 2008 a coalition called the Southern Cross Climate Coalition (SCCC) was formed by the ACF, the Australian Council of Social Service (ACOSS), the Australian Council of Trade Unions (ACTU) and the Climate Institute. The coalition described themselves as 'dedicated to leading debate on a fair response to climate change policies' (SMH, 2008). In 2009, the group publicly backed the CPRS. In a private meeting with Climate Change Minister Penny Wong, a group of

NGO directors were offered an a second conditional emissions reduction target of 25 per cent below 2000 levels 'if the world agrees to an ambitious global deal capable of stabilising levels of GHGs in the atmosphere at 450ppm' (the government had already announced a 15 per cent conditional target if a global agreement fell short of 450ppm, but major economies committed to contraining emissions). Senator Wong established this modus vivendi with the NGO peaks at a private meeting in May 2009, securing their support for the up-coming CPRS (Roberts, 2009).

By contrast, the climate movement engaged briefly but critically with the emissions trading debate during 2009. At the national Climate Action Summit in January 2009, the movement network committed to ensuring the CPRS would not become law (Climate Action Summit, 2009). At the same time as the SCCC announced support for the CPRS, 66 CAGs, the Conservation Councils, FoE, Greenpeace, TWS and GetUp! criticised the low emissions cap, free permits, unlimited trading in offsets (outsourcing emissions reduction) and no room for individual action (Climate Action Groups, 2009; Faehrmann et al., 2009). This opposition was expressed in small protest actions outside federal Member of Parliament offices (23 March) and a direct action in June at the Tomago Aluminium smelter outside Newcastle. The Rio Tinto owned smelter was scheduled to receive over $250 million in free permits in the first year of the CPRS.

There was little traction from these brief interjections, and no coherent campaign against or for the CPRS from the grass-roots movement groups. Within movement networks people were shuffling positions. The most common direction seemed to be to take a place outside of the debate. Some individuals and a few groups wrote letters to the directors of SCCC encouraging them to reconsider their support for the CPRS. Socialist Alliance and Solidarity were on the front foot, with calls to oppose the scheme in a coordinated campaign. A letter to the Greens was also circulated by FoEA which affirmed support for their opposition to the bill's passage through the Senate. FoEA left CANA that year, mirroring the decision of FoEI to leave CAN International in 2010.

At the Climate Action Summit of March 2010 the climate movement network voted on proposals for the movement's focus in its election campaigning using a modified consensus procedure. The group voted in favour of a proposal to support a 'carbon levy' made by a former FoE campaigner and soon to be Green Party staffer speaking at the conference. In January that year the Greens had announced what they called a political 'circuit breaker' in the form of a proposal to Labor to agree on a fixed carbon price for two years before transition to an emissions trading scheme (Taylor, 2010). There was some ambivalence about this strategy at the time, evidenced in other decisions taken by the movement during the summit debate. At the same time, attendees did not agree on a vote over the proposal to call on Labor to negotiate with the Greens on a carbon levy. The motion was not carried as it failed to reach the weighted majority of 75 per cent, with people arguing that it would mean the movement was backing a political party (thereby comprising its political independence) and that the strategy would lead to an emissions trading scheme.

In practice the movement endorsed carbon pricing – albeit second time around in 2010. Support for a carbon price had become a near consensus 'Plan B' position across the movement. Negotiating a carbon price would then become the basis for Green party negotiation with Labor at the end of 2010, leading to the installation of a carbon trading scheme in 2012. Abruptly, facing the prospect of aligning with the conservative Coalition against carbon pricing, the 'radical' critique had imploded and the movement backed the status quo delivered to them by the ALP-Green coalition.

The overall feeling within activist circles across 2010 was fading energy and a fragmenting sense of common purpose. Autonomy from political parties and from large 'brand' NGOs had been seen as important to both autonomous collectives and CAGs. However, it was imperfectly realised and hotly contested within the movement. Tensions arose between elements of the grassroots as well. There were considerable tensions, for instance, over what autonomy or non-partisan status of movements groups should mean in practice. A major line of dispute in movement network discussions was over the role of political parties in the movement (the Greens and the Socialist Party). In 2009, a heated debate occurred with limited resolution over what critics called *entreeism* by socialist organisations into autonomous activist spaces, CAGs and the Climate Action Summit process.

The cloudy sense of how to proceed after 2009 and divisions over strategy reflects challenges of collaboration within the movement and the difficult political terrain. The movement also found itself operating in the context of the failure of international negotiations at the UNFCCC the growing influence of climate denialism and a consolidating global financial crisis.

Conclusion

Over four years the climate movement network instituted itself, congealed, and ultimately differentiated through processes of internal and external debate. Here we have introduced the movement and explored the contours of the emergent new climate radicalism. We emphasise that climate activist praxis is dialogic and dynamic, developing its own values, knowledge and visions, not contained by fixed, pre-existing approaches. However, common motifs arose in the processes of forming, experimenting and defining 'the climate movement'. Across the period of political experimentation we analyse, a number of common themes were visible: Climate science as an epistemological foundation for radicalism; systemic diagnoses of the climate problem; populist calls for urgent action; technological optimism; political pessimism; and a moral stance on the need for wide sweeping reform.

These ideas were recurrent, co-constitutive and sometimes conflicting. For instance, climate science is taken up as a neutral basis for defining the task of climate radicalism. The movement's investment in developing a vision for decarbonisation is also constituted through the expert advocacy of engineers and economists. Climate activists were actively translating climate science into political contexts and strategic and visions for wide sweeping change (contra Swyngedouw, 2010).

In climate activist praxis there are certainly populist elements, but these lack coherence and are overwhelmed by a larger story of embedding political claim-making. In the following chapters we explore a variety of tensions that played out over the short period of mobilisation this book is dedicated to. For instance, the tension between activists' calls for urgent action and anti-systemic critiques opened up a set of questions about the means of political and social change: the role of prefigurative autonomous organising, professionalised advocacy and, more generally, whether and how the state might be transformed for the required structural change. In the contest over national carbon trading policy that engulfed climate politics in Australia from 2009, familiar strategic divisions emerged between socialist organisations, peak NGOs and other groups. Yet at the same time, as revealed here, there were also new alignments and models for values, political action and strategy, suggesting possibilities for future climate movements.

Notes

1 Industrial relations was a defining election issue during the 2007 campaign. Climate change was at least a secondary cause behind Howard's election loss (Rootes, 2008).
2 We use the terms carbon trading and emissions trading interchangeably. However the latter is the more accurate term, as emissions trading encompasses a range of different greenhouse gasses, not solely carbon.
3 The World Bank Prototype Carbon Fund was a public/private initiative for demonstration projects that sequester or conserve carbon in forest and agro-ecosystems in developing countries.
4 The Global Climate Campaign organised a Global Day of Action on Climate Change to coincide with the Climate Conference (First 'Meeting of Parties' to the Kyoto Protocol) in Montreal, 28 November to 9 December 2005. The international NGOs supporting it included FoE International, Earth Rights International, Global Women's Strike and the European Green Party. In Australia, participating organisations were: the Arid Lands Environment Centre (Alice Springs), the Australian Greens (Green Party of Australia), Cairns and Far North Environment Centre, Friends of the Earth Australia, Nature Conservation Council of New South Wales, Conservation Council of the South East Region and Canberra, International Socialist Organisation, Australia, and Queensland Nuclear Free Alliance.
5 On 7 June 2006, the NSW Planning Minister Frank Sartor approved the mine. He stated that the mine would make no overall difference to climate change because if it was not approved another mine would spring up in another location, and this would slow down the economy of NSW without good reason (Sartor in Trembath, 2007). As part of this campaign, Rising Tide won a court case 'Gray v Minister for Planning'. Peter Gray – a member of Rising Tide – challenged the validity of the decision by the NSW Director General (DG) of Planning to accept the

environmental assessment (EA) of Centennial Coal for the Anvil Hill mine. Gray argued that since Centennial did not include an assessment of the impacts of burning the coal (Scope 3 emissions) on the environment, the EA failed to comply with the direction from the DG in the EA requirements to include a 'detailed greenhouse gas assessment'. He also argued that the DG failed to take into account ecologically sustainable development principles, and that this contravened the Act because ESD principles were included in the objects of the NSW *Environmental Planning and Assessment Act* 1979. On 27 November 2006, Justice Nicola Pain decided in favour of Gray, establishing that State governments should take into consideration the downstream emissions of projects being assessed under Part 3A of the Environmental Planning and Assessment Act (see Evans, 2010; Rose, 2007).

4 Living in Climate Crisis

In this chapter we begin to explore the lifeworlds of climate activists in order to generate insight into the process of becoming engaged in the climate movement. Why and how do people become involved in climate activism? How do they come to experience and understand the climate crisis and what forms of participation do they undertake in building 'radical' climate politics over time?

In July 2008, interviews began with 25 people connected to the climate movement. All participants attended protest events, and at least one Climate Camp in Australia. In a sense, they inhabited the radical edge of the broader network described in Chapter 3. However, their political backgrounds are quite diverse, illustrating the varying degrees of involvement in movement networks that occur, and the interconnections between more professionalised campaigning and 'the grass-roots'. This group was a mix of seasoned NGO workers and community organisers, a sitting member for the Australian Greens party, students, forest activists, a landowner and two coal miners from the Hunter Valley, an indigenous activist and people newly recruited to climate groups with little prior experience of social movements. Speaking to them at this time, we gained a keen sense of the excitement, and a little frenzy, as networks were rapidly built from old and new alliances. The first conversations Pearse had with them were often just before, or at, a Climate Camp in NSW or Victoria, or at the 2008 Students of Sustainability conference in Newcastle.

In these first discussions with activists, our inquiry into their motivations for participating in the movement was often met with passionate responses and a sense of possibility for change. Connecting to the climate crisis is an affective process of coming to terms with the problem and its incredibly challenging political dimensions. In these conversations, it became clear that activists were connecting to the climate crisis in more than one temporal and spatial plane, often oscillating between concerns for inequalities of the past, present and future. In the first instance, climate action is expressed as a deeply held moral commitment based on a sense of obligation to those more vulnerable: people in the global South, future generations, and the non-human world. Activists describe experiences of ethical and affective connection with the climate problem as catalysts to their involvement in the movement. In their reflections on how and why they are involved in climate action, activists make universalist claims, often pronounced in the form of responsibilities and duties to act.

Importantly, the collective urge to mobilise a climate movement was articulated in different ways. Beyond a general sense of historical responsibility for climate change, activists are engaged in a search for the most powerful locus, or more rightly loci of political community and praxis. This is a considerable task. The temporal and spatial scale(s) of climate responsibility are multiple and thus challenge historical categories of social and political action – territoriality, sovereignty, polity and citizenship (see Dobson, 2006; Hayward, 2006). Whilst the moral imperative behind climate action is often expressed in sharp, pithy terms, the forms of praxis activists deploy are as hybrid and contested as in any social movement (Chatterton et al., 2012; Reitan & Gibson, 2012; Saunders, 2012). Within the climate movement differences between individuals and groups are visible as political tendencies. These include variants of autonomism, socialism, and liberalism (Reitan & Gibson, 2012). Activists assert political orientations as both ideological and cultural patterns within the broader network.

We stress this point in order to contest the critical appraisal of climate movements as a conduit of a post-political condition (Schlembach, 2011; Swyngedouw, 2010). In a strand of this argument, Catney and Doyle (2011: 176) have waged a critique of the ways in which the environment/welfare nexus is experienced and understood in Northern environmentalism (in the singular). They argue that there is a trade-off between the 'politics of the now and the politics of the future' in the practice of civil society, and there is a propensity in Northern environmental politics to privilege the future 'post-political' citizen in their ecological imaginary over the present citizens of the global South. They further assert that Southern environmentalism is by contrast oriented toward the historical conditions producing unequal environmental risks and power in the present.

In contrast to this conceptualisation we argue there is a more complex picture, particularly at the level of the lifeworld. Activists in Australia often (but not always) come to know the climate crisis in ways that subvert the dominant forms of abstraction the above authors are critical of. In the everyday, climate activism is a creative process of experimenting with new ways to critically comprehend and act in the world. Climate activists commonly describe moments of exploration, critical reflection, as well as contestation over the form(s) of praxis they enact.

We follow the roads into climate activist networks within and across these differences. The personal and collective process of mobilisation is punctuated of social learning and identity formation. The rhythms of learning and experimentation are deeply personal but do not occur in isolation. The experience of collective energy for climate action was produced by the broader confluence of events that promised a reinvigorated climate politics in the mid-2000s. Our focus in this chapter is on the lifeworld, however embedded in the narratives of mobilisation, and immersion into activist counter cultures are illustrations of the dialectical play of these 'local' experiences with historical forces. Activists join groups posed against a series of others: capitalism, its carbon-intensive industries, the governments that prop them up as well as other movement groups. Importantly, the process of engaging in any social struggle is not linear. We illustrate the creative process of experimenting with activist praxis over time.

Climate connections

In conversations between 2008 and 2010 participants were thinking through the meaning and utility of their actions whilst they navigated various modes of activist praxis. It is here that we see the intersection of how activists go about creating change and what their motivations are. Instead of accepting the forced choice between the *how* and *why* of movement activity, activist identities are formed at the intersection of these lines of inquiry (Farro, 2004). In other words, groups and individuals define themselves by who they are and, at the same time, what they do.

The process of becoming an activist likewise involves moving from a passive understanding of the world to a critical consciousness. Paulo Friere described the dialectical play between coming to know one's self as living *in* and *with* the world as an agent in its making (Freire, 1970). Friere's term *conscientização* – 'conscientisation' – captures the process of learning. Activists develop a critical comprehension of the world through their experience of the world around them, rather than through abstract theory. Agency stems from the interwoven elements of being conscious of the world and acting upon it. By participating in social movements, activists become beings of relation. Liberation comes from moving through admiration of the world as object to understanding one's self as subject of historical processes and an agent of collective action (Freire, 1995[1970]: 73).

By 2008, the increasing consensus of scientific models of anthropogenic climate change, and the communication of this message by popular figures and a confluence of disastrous weather events across the world had served to concentrate people's attention on the need for more decisive action. Ruth, a social worker and member of Rising Tide, articulated a keen sense of ecological exhaustion in Australia and across the world.

> I mean the Murray-Darling basin is on its last legs. So many examples throughout the world just show that climate change is not a myth. It is a reality. We need to be acting now. We can't wait until 2010. We can't wait until 2015. We need to be doing things now.
>
> (Ruth 2008a)

Ruth and her husband Robert are from the Hunter Valley. After being influenced by their daughter's views on global social and ecological justice issues in the mid-2000s, they became involved in Rising Tide, occasionally the

Greens, and financial supporters of TWS and Greenpeace (Ruth & Robert, 2008b). As the climate movement began to spring up in the region, they were drawn into the Anvil Hill campaign and then into the 2008 Newcastle Camp for Climate Actionand other protest events building opposition to coal export expansion in Newcastle.

Samuel, a climate campaigner for a State conservation council commented that he had had a sense of the 'disconnect' between the message of climate science and the policy response for some time. However, he felt that the high stakes of the climate crisis were being illuminated with the new weather, fermenting the idea of radicalism:

> Hurricane Katrina in the US or the recent weather events in Burma. I mean that's really dangerous. That's really mass devastation ... The urgency of the situation and the science of climate change is demanding a really strong and maybe even really radical response.
>
> (Samuel, 2008a)

Cathy remembered 'always having an environmental sort of conscience, probably from lots of bush walking and spending time in the environment'. She had been a supporting member of TWS and the ACF, but her involvement in the climate movement was something new.

> I never bought the ticket and blockaded down in Tassie or never really stepped up into a major activist thing ... it just didn't touch me that much that I needed to get more active.
>
> (Cathy, 2008b)

Cathy was a founding member of one of the new CAGs being formed, often by individuals who were quite new to activism. In 2006 she had more time and made contact with a woman known to her through her children's school. Sally was forming a CAG in their suburb through a public forum put on in partnership with the Conservation Council.

> It was an emergent period where I was sort of coming out of that really labour intensive period with the kids and then incidental conversations with mums at school and then this follow-up meeting after the forum [Sally] went to, and I asked her without knowing her that well, but just said, 'What was that?' and so I went along to the next meetings.
>
> (Cathy, 2008b)

For Cathy, it was Sally who provided her with important knowledge about the coal industry and its links to climate change.

> She was really well informed and was saying to the wider group, 'Let's write letters, because they've just approved another mine.' And I'm

thinking, 'But this is climate change, what are we talking about coal mines for?' And I didn't get that, and then after talking to her and finding out 40 per cent of our greenhouse gas emissions are produced by coal fired power and all those things, it was like, 'Oh my god!' I just couldn't believe it. I thought, 'Why don't I know about this?' I mean everybody needs to know about this, and that's terrible.

(Cathy, 2008b)

Cathy's group became a well-known CAG in NSW. They campaigned in their local area to raise awareness about climate change and its causes, as well as produced an online campaign focused on Federal climate policy. The 'Turn the Tide Kevin' campaign called on the Federal Government to peak carbon emissions by 2010. This kind of ambitious emissions reduction demand was common in public claims from CAGs and other grassroots organisations in the new climate movement network.

Radicalism sprung from the closing temporal gap between present and future. Claire, a climate justice campaigner at FoE, described the incredibly short timeframe in which wide-scoping change would need to be realised.

We have a very, very small window of opportunity in which to act and make really very deep reductions in our emissions, um, before it becomes permanent and irreversible.

(Claire, 2008a)

Claire was among a handful of new climate change campaigners to emerge in the smaller ENGOs working with the new grass-roots network. Interestingly, this sweeping sense of urgency and proliferating activity was a surprise to some. Rosalind is a graduate student who had returned to Australia in 2008 from a trip to Mexico and Venezuela, where she had participated in Zapatista communities and a World Social Forum. She was struck by the dramatic reorientation of social movement groups to climate politics in Australia.

I was quite startled to hear that climate change was the big thing that everyone was doing. And yeah, to be honest, when I first heard about it I didn't really feel that excited by it. I guess coming from a place where ... groups are coming together to form a new way of doing politics is all quite revolutionary. And coming back and going, 'Oh, climate change.'

(Rosalind, 2008c)

Rosalind's reaction to the arrival of climate change campaigning reflects the challenge of connecting climate change with the practice of 'global justice' politics. Rosalind did find an inroad to the issue. When she settled back into life working in a small social justice NGO, she began to get a sense of the possibilities for climate radicalism.

I think the opportunity that I see in it, and what excites me about doing anything on climate change, is the opportunities to radically restructure the way that we live. And that it challenges people on those core assumptions that need to happen.

(Rosalind, 2008c)

Like many others, Rosalind came to see climate change as an issue that 'has major impacts on the global South as always, who are least responsible for it' (Rosalind, 2008c). In turn, she proposed that climate action in Australia begins from recognition that activists are implicated in a carbon intensive economy-society in which they live. For her, climate action has an element of solidarity with peoples most impacted by climate change (Rosalind, 2008a). Claire came to a similar set of conclusions. She commented that at one point she 'realised that social justice and environmental sustainability were inextricably linked' (Claire, 2008b). In practice, this inspired her to focus her campaign work on climate-induced displacement in Pacific Islands with FoE at that time.

George, a coal miner from the Hunter Valley who participated in climate movement events in the gaps between his full-time shift work echoes this sentiment, albeit with a different kind of frontline viewpoint.

We are responsible for their fate [those] ... thousands of people that are out in the Pacific Ocean ... [whose] homes are slowly being inundated by rising sea levels ... And I believe that we are morally bound to do something about it.

(George, 2008b)

He couched his sense of obligation as a consequence of his participation in the coal industry. When he elaborated on his connection to the climate crisis George reflected on his time working in Papua New Guinea (PNG) on the infamous Ok Tedi gold mine. When the mine was under construction in 1982 the tailings dam failed, and BHP decided to send the mine waste directly into the creeks that run into the Ok Tedi and Fly Rivers. By 2000, more than 250 tonnes of wastes had flowed into the rivers, contaminating drinking water and local agriculture and killing the forests along the flood plain.[1] And over the same period in his home town in the Hunter Valley, he witnessed dramatic changes to the land and threats to the health of local communities as open cut coal mining displaced agribusiness in the region.

I feel as if for those years of destruction that I did on the end of a scrub pulling chain, pulling a thousand acres every two or three days, I owe back to society.

(George, 2008b)

His good friend Gary often tells a poignant story in the same vein. Sitting in George's backyard after the first Climate Camp in Newcastle, he related a scene in his life that gave impetus to his split from the coal industry and his decision to take a deeper step into the environment movement. In 2005, Gary travelled to South America and found himself on an island in the south of Chile travelling with locals to see glacial waters.

> I went down with this bloke I met on the bus, and he was manager of a salmon farm, and we went down with his cousin. We went further down to this long fiord where the glaciers come down to the sea. And the glaciers are littered with ice. And we went down there and we had a look at this glacier and you could see it moving. And through a three-way conversation, me talking to the bloke in broken Spanish, and him talking to me in broken English and his cousin talking the local Indian dialect, basically he asked me what I did for a living. And I said, 'I'm a coal miner.' And he looked at me and he said, 'Where is your heart?' He said, 'Your coal is killing us.' And lots of people say, 'Well, what did you say?' Well really, what can you say? What can you say? That's the truth. And sometimes the truth hurts. So yeah, I came back home and I knew then I was going [from the coal industry]. It was too much.
>
> (Gary, 2008b)

Gary left his lucrative job in the coal industry and began participating in a wide range of campaigns collaborating with many groups in the movement, including Greenpeace, Solidarity, Socialist Alliance, and Rising Tide. He and George became important figures in the movement in this period of mobilisation. As trade unionists from an industry driving Australia's considerable national and international carbon footprint, Gary and George's dissenting words carried much moral and political weight for activists.

> And now we see the future prospect of our climate … That's the cause of it: coal fired power stations and the use of coal and fossil fuels. We've got to stop that, collectively as a nation, as a state, as a local area and globally. We've got to stop that for my kids, for their kids and for your kids and for everyone's kids; for the bloke in South America. We've got to stop it.
>
> (Gary, 2008b)

Gary's refrain illustrates the way intra- and inter-generational justice sit together in climate activists' understanding of the crisis. People with children were particularly likely to express concerns for the future generations. For instance, Vicky, an occasional participant in Melbourne environmental justice networks, talked about her concerns for her young child. She described being more interested in climate campaigning now she is a mother, driven by the uncomfortable thought of 'having a son growing up in a world that is potentially not going to be able to support his survival, or at least going to make it really difficult for him to survive, or his kids to survive.' (Vicky, 2009).

Multiple explanations for the climate crisis were offered by activists, with a mixed set of ideas about society-nature. Reading climate change as a systemic problem is a shared perspective. However, there are a number of ways they express this. Taken together, these articulations of the crisis convey its complexity. Humanity's hubris and cultural disconnection from 'nature', capitalism, population growth, patriarchy and colonialism were all described by activists in different amalgamations. The variance in ideas about climate crisis reflects both different political traditions and personal history.

In conversations about how they understand the crisis, there was certainly discussion of humanity in the singular. For instance, Cathy argued that the climate crisis is human nature out of control.

> I think humanity has to take a good long, hard look at itself and find a new way of existing on the planet ... We've lost contact with, the unconnectedness with, um, nature and with things that really, the systems that really exist to keep the world going.
>
> (Cathy, 2008a)

Frequently activists lament society's disconnection from the non-human world. Sarah, a local resident of Newcastle, reflected many times in conversation on the impact of climate change on the non-human world, frustrated with its persistence.

> Well the whole idea I guess that our actions, as in our society, are changing the Earth. We are going to have an impact on animals ... it's like this ignorance or maybe ambivalence or something there, that is so frustrating to see.
>
> (Sarah, 2008b)

She placed a great deal of emphasis on the need to 'reconnect' to the non-human world and discover a simpler, more sustainable way of living (Sarah, 2008a, b).

Refrains about human disconnection from nature were not expressed as a self-evident condition. Participants shared a range of explanations for the 'systemic' origins of climate change. All participants were clear that lines of responsibility did not fall evenly across society. Lillian is a member of a socialist organisation active in the climate movement. Climate change is one of a range of issues she and her group engage in. She spoke routinely about the centrality of the state and capital in producing the climate crisis.

> It's big business, its corporations that have caused [climate change], and their backing by the state.
>
> (Lillian, 2009)

Lillian argued for the need to understand the climate crisis in terms of the structure and organisation of the economy.

At least in terms of individual views, the role of capital is widely recognised by activists from other groups in the movement. Susie, a student environmental activist, mixed a neo-Malthusian concern with population with an anti-capitalist reading of the crisis when she reflected on its causes.

> ... population growth and consumerism in Western countries, and, yeah, um, trade and economies that are based on mining and ... capitalism [laughs] – all these big words.
>
> (Susie, 2009a)

Finding the language to articulate the systemic origins of climate change was often challenging. Offering a hybrid set of ideas was common. Vicky argued that the lineages of global climate injustice trace the historical intersection of capitalism, colonisation and patriarchy.

> It's part of a whole epoch of patriarchy. And denial of nature, denial of humanity, denial of animalism, denial of the fact that we live and die really.
>
> (Vicky, 2010)

She traces her outlook in part to university courses in women's studies, and their focus on questioning social structures (Vicky, 2010). There were in fact a number of critical political traditions drawn on in these discussions, which spanned Marxism, anarchism, feminism and critiques of (neo)colonialism. For one participant, colonialism was close to home.

> I think there's a parallel between genocide and ecocide. And the indigenous people who are grown up in this country for such a long time, we know what this land needs, we know how to take care of it. But we haven't got any access other than what's determined by the invaders and the state.
>
> (Jimmy, 2010)

Jimmy is an indigenous man from the Krautungalung people of the Gunnai Nation. He grew up in the expanding brown coalfields of the La Trobe Valley, Victoria. His father worked for the State Electricity Commission, and he recounts how parents were strong, politically minded people (Jimmy, 2009).

A number of activists spoke in quite romantic terms about the Earth. Kylie is a geology student who describes the origins of her activism with reference to the respect for nature she developed at a young age on long drives and camping trips with her family. She commented that in her teens and early twenties, overseas travel as a volunteer and studying geology made her realise how fragile life on Earth is.

> Like, the Earth itself is going to be here, it's going to a be a big rock, but the life, the outer skin of the Earth, is such an amazing and really important thing. Like, we haven't found it on any other planet ever. Obviously not in our solar system, but we haven't found it in any other

solar systems. And it's just, we've got such an amazing opportunity here. We can't destroy it.

(Kylie, 2009b)

Kylie's insights into the climate crisis speak directly to Chakrabarty's call to 'scale up our imagination of the human' to contemplate the universal history of life on the planet (Chakrabarty, 2009: 206). At the same time, Kylie was critical of the ecological exhaustion propelled by consumer society.

I also see consumerism as a really big thing. The fact that we have this linear system where we take stuff out of the ground, we make stuff, we use stuff, we use stuff, we buy stuff, and then we just dump it. And it's a very linear thing. And you look at the Earth system – it's not a linear system. There is no system on the planet that is from A to B. It's all circular. And we haven't been able to create a system that fits with that.

(Kylie, 2009b)

Numerous activists who cite a respect and love for nature were keen to illustrate that the social and political dimension of their critical consciousness stemmed from social learning. For instance, Josh, a campaign worker focused on the NSW southern coal fields for a peak ENGO, began his account of becoming an environmental activist with his experiences living on the edge of a national park.

I always had a fairly good understanding of how a forest worked, and, ecology that didn't necessarily give me any social consciousness.

(Josh, 2009)

He attributed his social consciousness to exposure to activism at technical college.

[There] were a lot of activists in the inner city at that time in the late Eighties, who could afford to be full-time activists and live in the inner city, so ... I guess a social awareness arose from having my sandwiches with a lot of people from different backgrounds.

(Josh, 2009)

Similarly, Alistair, a campaigner at one of the leading ENGOs in Australia, spoke about the role of other people in enlivening his critical understanding of the world. One pivotal influence was a housemate studying environmental philosophy.

So every day we would sit down and say, 'So what did you read today?' and, 'What are you thinking about?' We'd have these fantastic conversations, so I think over a couple of years while I working full-time as an engineer in a blue collar factory in Brisbane, I was on this sort of amazing intellectual journey of discovery on weekends and in the evenings. And didn't have much time to do stuff, but I guess my ideas about the world really developed far ahead of my actions. I was working 60, 70 hours a week.

(Alistair, 2008c)

Alistair read the work of Earth First! founder David Foreman and social ecologist Murray Bookchin, and was becoming inspired by the radical environmental movement in North America. His decision to engage in activism and make a swift move out of engineering came during a period of reflection instigated by a family member passing away.

I looked at this crate of industrial filters that were going to the Roxby Downs uranium mine, that I'd helped make. Well I'd made the machines that made them. And the next day I handed in my resignation and went forest blockading basically. Just decided I wasn't going to do things that weren't aligned with my values, and make a contribution to the world that I'd be happy reflecting on when I was on my death bed.

(Alistair, 2008c)

Jimmie's perspective on coal and climate crisis links to indigenous political activism, a tradition he traces back to the first colonial encounters in Australia.

I didn't learn anything until I left school and started learning from people like Gary Foley and the late Dr Bruce McGuiness, Aboriginal activists who very much similar to what I'm doing now, they were doing for the generations before me. Then you go to William Coopers, and the Fergusons and it goes right back to the beginning, to the Pemulwuys and the resistance fighters. I'm at the end of that line right now. And it's a proud history.

(Jimmy, 2009)

Talking to Jimmie at the Switch Off Hazelwood camp, he explained the intersections between his life, colonial history and fossil fuel expansion.

I've got a personal connection to this particular area, and the La Trobe Valley itself, which is probably one of the most disgusting places on earth in terms of its pollution. Apparently 17 million tonnes of CO_2 are going into the air out of this one particular building behind me here, Hazelwood power station. Victoria's got a disgusting record on the environment; it's got the highest rate of species depletion in the world, Victoria. It's got no land rights legislation; it's not got native title legislation.

(Jimmy, 2009)

Jimmie illuminates the site of the camp as a meeting point between the historical forces of colonisation, and the imposition of emissions-intensive industries.

The expression of personal connection to histories of social injustice in these stories speaks to Chakrabarty's climate problematic. Rather than displacing the 'social' justice questions, Chakrabarty argues that there is a second necessary mode of conceiving climate change that must be held at the same time. We need to 'view the human simultaneously on contradictory registers: as a geophysical force and as a political agent, as a bearer of rights and as author of actions.' (Chakrabarty, 2012: 14). This is no easy task, he admits, given our limited phenomenological capacity to experience ourselves as a geological agent (Chakrabarty, 2009: 221–22). Harriet, an organiser in Climate Camp events, and member of various autonomous activist collectives, spoke to what this might involve in more simple terms.

> [We need to] have a bit more imagination and empathy and understanding of what it's like in other parts of the world or for other species that are already feeling the effects of climate change.
>
> (Harriet, 2008a).

Susie, an engineering student active in ASEN, argued that 'when people go "oh who cares about the environment?" really you're saying "who cares about society?"' (Susie, 2009b). For Susie, concerns with the uneven impacts of climate change and polluting industries like those in the Hunter Valley also illuminate the human fragility climate crisis indicates. She commented that having these concerns 'means that you're not only helping the environment in general, but really you're trying to help the human race.' (Susie, 2009b). Susie's slippage between differentiated impacts of mining and climate change with the common threat to humanity mirrors Chakrabarty's dual imperative to think at the level of justice and species. Bifurcation of nature and society persists in activists' appraisal of the climate crisis. Or put another way, it is a dualism that is difficult to transcend analytically and politically.

Climate activists experiment in creating new publics, new spatialities and new solidarities. Political agency rests upon the production of social and socioecological ties. A 2008 communiqué from FoE climate activists describing why they chose to name their new group Six Degrees illustrates the challenge and reflexive praxis involved in building a politics that bridges the many fractured lines of the climate problem.

> The name Six Degrees stands for what lies ahead, both the immense challenges the earth is facing and the opportunities this presents for transformation. Six degrees is the worst case scenario predicted for global temperature increase this century; it's a trajectory we're still on and a future we are staring in the face. But six degrees is also the connection between us all, non-human and human; six degrees of separation,

between those on the frontline and those most responsible, between those just learning and those already coming together to forge alternatives and take action in solidarity with those affected. It is the six degrees of connection between those of us around the world who are working together for climate justice.

(Six Degrees, undated)

In a thoughtful campaign on coal expansion in Queensland, Six Degrees activists went on a 'listening tour' in coal affected communities across the east and inland areas of the state. In July 2008, Queensland Premier Anna Bligh announced $15.6 billion in public funds for infrastructure to meet the Government's coal expansion target of 370 million tonnes in export annually over 20 years. In this context, the group was seeking to build bridges across the divides that commonly occur between urban activists and regional communities. The group took seriously the diversity of perspectives of coal communities concerning the benefits and impacts of coal mining. This is illustrated by their documentation of the tour (FoEB, 2008). The experience of the tour fed into their campaign work with a local farmers group in Felton Valley, west of Toowoomba. The other focus of Six Degrees from 2008 was to contest the Brisbane coal export port expansion with small direct actions and media stunts (Rhianna, 2010).

This is one example among a number of different ideas held by activists about how best to build alliances and a social base with power to address climate injustice. Returning to the stories of personal motivation and mobilisation for climate action, we introduce the different political traditions of the movement below through activists' reflections on the process of conscientisation.

Embedding: Experimentation, praxis, contestation

Engaging in activism is a process of immersion for many. Activists experience an iterative process of conscientisation that involves first encounters with quite foreign social spaces, followed by experimentation and debate, which shifts and sometimes refines political praxis. Climate activism involves routinised forms of interaction including inter- and intra-group meetings to make decisions and/or undertake shared projects, production of social media, and considerable time spent on email exchanges where debates are waged and callouts for group mobilisations are spread. Collaboration and direct democracy is put into practice through all sorts of labour (most often unpaid) focused on the strategic and affective bonds of the movement.

Embedding in social movements occurs over time. Individuals vary in the extent to which they are embedded in the movement activity (Stryker, 2000). At the Climate Camp in Helensburgh NSW, Rhianna, a FoE activist who had travelled inter-state to be at the camp, reflected on the process of becoming immersed in the radical climate movement politics.

I think a lot of people at Climate Camp have made that journey. You don't just meet someone on the street and say, 'Oh, I'm concerned about climate change,' and the next week they are going to lock on to a coal fired power station.

(Rhianna, 2009)

She talked about the ways in which she and many others in student activist networks were becoming part of a movement through participating in collective meetings at first, then activist collaborations and national gatherings like Students of Sustainability (SoS).

Stories of entry into activist spaces for the first time were depicted as daunting by some, including those who became the most embedded in movement networks. When describing her first experiences in activist meetings, Rosalind related that she 'found the face of activism somewhat alienating' (Rosalind, 2008c). Beatrice's first steps into activism were similarly tentative and characterised as uncertainty about what activism entails. She described her first experience in a student environment collective meeting.

I went along with a friend and we were both not really sure if we really liked the people and the ideas behind them – we found it a little bit odd. I was really ambiguous about what I thought they were doing and whether it was what I sort of wanted to do, and whether it was really effective.

(Beatrice, 2008)

One of the participants echoed Beatrice's experience when she described the Climate Camp in Newcastle. When Sarah came into contact with established groups from all over the country she was struck by differences between her local neighbourhood and these groups at the camp.

I realised that our group was a bit of an outsider, and I think there were other ones as well. The core groups seemed to be really well organised and clear on their roles ...

(Sarah, 2008b)

Beatrice discussed how she became involved in movement networks as a process of learning the language and modalities of activism, moving from a sense of disconnection to embeddedness in activist cultures. Interestingly, both Rosalind and Beatrice talked about the fundamental role activism came to play in their lives.

I [don't] identify as, you know, 'I am an activist', but more just that's what my life is about – is wanting to see radical change. And whatever I do in my life, I want to feel like I'm doing whatever I can to do that and whatever is true to what I believe. And so I guess that meant that in terms of what work I did, and what life choices I made, that shifted quite dramatically I think.

(Rosalind, 2008c)

Beatrice and Rosalind reflected at length on how it felt to become immersed in activist practices. She noted that non-hierarchical group structures and democratic decision-making were once foreign concepts. However, through practice over time, these means of organising collectively became a central focus of her praxis. She became embedded in the networks of autonomous activists in Sydney, made up of small collectives such as the student environment collectives at each of the university campuses, an anarchist bookshop and community hub, FoE, food cooperatives and various projects people come together to do.

Susie, a student activist, talked about the role of ASEN training camps in giving her an understanding of climate, nuclear and forest issues. She described the impact of being encouraged to actively contribute in meetings and training conferences.

> They kept asking for ideas and it made me think more about, 'What is my theory of change?' and, um, got me to actually put my ideas into action.

(Susie, 2009b)

In her turn of phrase, Susie signals a 'theories of change' workshop that is commonly used. The workshop is derived from the *Resource Manual for a Living Revolution* (Coover et al., 1977), a text from the US Quaker movement used in Australia as far back as the Franklin Dam campaign. The workshop involves reflection on how activists understand power and the mechanisms of social change. Individuals are asked to reflect on their understanding of power and the process of change in relation to specific problem, in order to foster the capacity to recognise and articulate their political praxis, and understand difference in perspectives. What kinds of politics arise from this form of praxis? Differences in political analysis are navigated in these sessions with a kind of radical pluralism. An excerpt from the ASEN training manual encapsulates this.

> ... we are all theorists and we are all creating change. A radical process of theory is about reflecting on the world in which we live and our actions to change it, what is and is not effective, and then discussing these ideas with others and drawing out common themes and ideas – this discussion, based on our real life experiences, is the basis of theory. In this radical idea of us all being theorists, theory is not static and still – it constantly needs to be reflected upon and changed, based on new experiences. This is the message of praxis – theory, action, reflection, in a never-ending circle ...

(ASEN, 2008)

In another vein, training workshops focus on the nuts and bolts of campaign planning. Facilitated workshops and strategy sessions held in ASEN, other autonomous activist groups, as well as NGOs, involve deliberating together on the focus and strategic aims of the group. Facilitators guide groups through a process of 'cutting the issue' into smaller issues (from climate change, to energy, to coal and renewables, cancelling-out the systemic contexts), mapping 'critical paths' to change decision-makers' minds, identifying SMART (specific, measurable, attainable, relevant, and timely) goals. These sessions of facilitated group deliberation prize clarity of purpose and delineation of roles and doable tasks for individuals and groups above all else. Underpinning this approach is the assumption of radical pluralism, where the focus is on coalition-building through practical action, not through shared political analysis.

In contrast, the traditions of socialist organisations and the one or two anarchist collectives that have participated in the movement place a more central emphasis on the process of developing shared critiques of a given issue, for instance, energy privatisation, public investment in renewable energy, and the carbon trading scheme. Solidarity and Socialist Alliance both produce magazines. Longstanding members become skilled at writing, web design and, hopefully, the art of persuasion through considerable time spent running information stalls on campuses, conferences, talks, rallies and more. The effect is a constant flow of political analysis spread within and outside their membership. Group meetings are likely to centre on a topical political development, be well advertised to potential members and serve as a place to develop and master their shared views on issues of the day. In movement networks settings, this cohered political position is brought to bear in the form of well-rehearsed interventions by socialist activists. The spirited exchanges this makes for can be daunting to other climate activists (Cathy, 2008b). Lillian, a socialist activist, is aware of this sentiment, but maintains that debate about movement priorities, and broader meta-political and substantive questions about the roles of the state in climate action, is an essential ingredient of a progressive climate movement (Lillian, 2009).

The participatory character of student environment networks involves a mix of informal and organisational methods. The first experience of student environmental activism is often sitting in on a collective meeting where climate campaigns focused on renewable energy and efficiency measures on campus are often developed. Students have also been key participants in direct action events like Climate Camp and smaller actions throughout the year. The ASEN and individual 'enviro collectives' on campus have a yearly turnaround of relatively formal roles facilitating network activity. Susie described the feeling of stepping into greater involvement through one of these roles.

Um, well, probably when [Alison] asked me to do convening, I was like, 'My God,' and then I thought, 'Oh, I'll just learn how to do it.' Yeah, but

I'd only been to the collective a few times, and I was like, 'Oh, okay, I don't really know that much,' but if she hadn't asked me I would have been, like, cautious. It just gave me a reason to put myself in the deep end, get involved and learn the way ASEN was structured, that was exciting.

(Susie, 2009a)

Alison was a very active organiser in student networks involved in the climate movement. She convened the national network in 2007. That is, she held a part-time paid position that is focused on facilitating collaboration between student environmental groups across the nation. She relates the importance of two learning experiences that shifted her trajectory toward climate action.

A couple of years ago I went, 'Right, climate change – it's really building into a movement over here, I really, really want to be part of that.' And there are a couple things that happened, I think it was 2005–6 where one was a workshop on theories of change ... I visioned the world that I wanted to live in and articulated, you know, how I thought change was made and politics around that. And then a couple of weeks later, I went to a talk given by a guy called Hermann Scheer, who is called the 'Father of the German renewable energy policy'.

(Alison, 2008a)

Herman Scheer's talk instilled Alison's sense that renewable energy could be a catalyst for change. And she said this brought her to a new personal and political trajectory. Alison set herself three goals.

And so those three things were: supporting young people to become social change makers, trying to develop a direct action movement against coal in Australia, and developing renewable energy cooperatives.

(Alison, 2008a)

In turn, Alison was inspired by the energy coalescing around the Newcastle Climate Camp, and became a key organiser for the camp over 2008.

As soon as I heard about Climate Camp, that's why I jumped on board. It's like, 'Yes, this will build the direct action movement around coal in Australia,' and I think that's really important and essential to stopping climate change.

(Alison, 2008a)

Goals change over time. At the end of 2009, Alison had shifted emphasis to the third goal of building renewable energy cooperatives, after completing her studies and taking time away from activism to reflect and recover from what she counted as five years of being very involved in it (Alison, 2009). There are ebbs and flows in the energy and enthusiasm for movement participation. People move in and out of periods of intense activity, and they shift their political focus.

Experimentation is a central feature of how activists define their activity. For instance, when we met Angus, a student who recently graduated with a degree in engineering, he was heavily involved in a Climate Camp logistics group (a sub-group of the Climate Camp Organising Collective). He was instrumental in providing electricity, lighting and other infrastructure for the camp. Having just finished university, he saw the project as a way to test his capacity to 'do activism all the time', as well as assess Climate Camp as a method for creating change. The combined elements of direct action and sustainable living appealed to him and his skills.

> I thought, 'Oh, this is a good way to see how to test this approach to helping the environment in general, and is it going to work for me.' So yeah, I was excited enough when I heard about [Climate Camp] to go to some all-day meetings. It wasn't too long before I realised I'd had enough of all-day meetings [laughs] and just stopped going to them. But you know, all credit to people who kept on going and organised some things that had to be done in meetings. But for my part, I thought it was more important I do the things I said I'm going to do, instead of going to meetings.
>
> (Angus, 2008b)

Angus talked about the potential for originality and creativity involved in his participation in social movement as a key source of inspiration. He seeks out the creativity and sense of efficacy involved in creating something that would otherwise not have happened.

> You feel a bit more assured that you're making a difference, I guess. So one example is something I was involved with quite heavily was restarting the Nunnery Bike Club in Newtown. And I got a lot of satisfaction out of seeing what we were doing and seeing what was happening. And we all knew that if we didn't do it, it wasn't going to happen. It's not like getting a job at BHP where there's a position that someone's designed that hopefully you can do an okay job of. You might do it better than the other person, but it doesn't really matter does it? Someone will do it.
>
> (Angus, 2008b)

For Angus, the fact he and others are creating something that would otherwise not exist gives it meaning and value. He is drawn in by the process of learning and problem-solving, working with others who are there of their own volition, and seeing the direct results of their work. His reflection here became more prescient the last time Angus was interviewed. He had just made a decision to end his participation in the energy cooperative he had founded because Federal renewable energy policy had weakened the ecological impact his work was doing.

The policy change in particular that has pretty much made me now unable to continue from an ethical point of view is one called the Solar Credits legislation, which is part of the Renewable Energy Target (RET) which was passed four months ago. It basically gave a special handicap for photovoltaic systems to earn more certificates against the 20 per cent target than what is actually produced by their electricity. So, essentially it means that you put in all these systems, the 20 per cent target is achieved on paper, but you really only have less than that. So the handicap was a factor of five, you can put in 4 per cent solar panels throughout Australia and they'll tick it off as the 20 per cent target having been reached.

(Angus, 2009)

In Angus' example, we see the political economy of climate and energy policy filter to the level of individual political agency.

There is a great celebration of diversity when activists reflect on their praxis. Many activists work with a range of groups at any one time. Gary's participation in numerous groups is an example.

Really it is a learning curve. I like to have fun, I like to work with all different ways. The Greens are a necessary part of it. Because like it or lump it, we need representation in government. Greenpeace – we need them, because they have their own way of doing things. I've worked with Greenpeace. I'm learning, I'm working with invariably younger people, and they are the future and I like that.

(Gary, 2008b)

Miriam works with a handful of different autonomous collectives, and values the variety between them in terms of both the political focus and type of affiliation. Autonomous collectives can take the form of close affinity groups, open collectives or networks. The degree of organisation is often reflected in whether there is a group name, and/or routines of communication instituted (e.g. meeting space, website, e-list, Facebook account).

I also quite like working with a few different groups at the same time, because they keep each other in perspective. So, like, a group like Rising Tide for example is quite organised in a lot of ways. And there are other groups I work with, like the really loose group of people in Newcastle campaigning against the intervention in the Northern Territory, and that's also non-hierarchical and have lots of things in common but it's a much looser group that's probably a bit more chaotic. And yeah I really value the contrast between those two ways of organising – even though they have a lot in common, they feel quite different to me.

(Harriet, 2008c)

Radical pluralism extends to professional campaign work also. The celebration of a diversity of methods to produce change was common. For instance, Samuel sees no tension between the mixed forms of praxis he employs as an advocate at a conservation council and as a participant in autonomous groups.

> There's a lot of different techniques that we use to create change and I think we need all of those. And I think there are none that are invalid and I think it's exactly that diversity of techniques that will allow us to reach the broadest audience possible which is what we need to do to achieve what we want to achieve with climate change.
>
> (Samuel, 2008a)

Collaboration was highly valued by all. At the same time retaining a sense of autonomy was important. For the new CAGs being 'nonpartisan' and independent from the major NGOs and political parties was a key political claim. Cathy talked about how she came to this conclusion in the early days of forming her local CAG. The group debated how campaign activities would relate to priorities of the Greens and NGOs supporting them to build their group. The group's conclusion was that "we want to be separate, we want to be on our own..". When communicating this, she felt professional campaigners she worked with 'totally got that and let us be what we wanted to be and making our own decisions, it was great.' (Cathy, 2008b).

A dedicated layer of activists become organisers that have both professional and volunteer roles in the movement. A number of the very involved climate activists combine paid campaign work in an NGO or union with unpaid participation in an autonomous collective, socialist organisation or CAG. Often, climate activists who work in paid positions have come through ASEN, or the forest movement, practising autonomous methods, and shifted to part- or full-time campaign work.

Alistair reflected on his decision to take a paid campaigning position in affective and political terms:

> I decided that I need to earn a living, I wasn't going to be either using my savings or on the dole. So I did a bit of market research, set up a recycling business up in Brisbane. I did that for about four to five years, and it's still going and employs about seven or eight people. I was really working on a broad revolutionary strategy of trying to fund environmental campaigning and activism that was about stopping bad things from happening, at the same time as trying to create an alternative economy and political institutions. I guess which is that anarchist dual strategy of social change. And then I kind of got a bit worn down by working in sort of grass-roots, you know really long term, long slog campaigning I guess. And then I had an opportunity to come and work with ENGO ... I've been working with ENGO since then, which is less

about the building alternatives and more about campaigning to try and
shift values and stop the worst excesses of the industrial system, and from
killing the planet.

(Alistair, 2008c)

The decision to join ENGO was not taken lightly by Alistair. In his words,
the best approach as an 'social change agent' is to make an 'assessment about
what suits your own skills and experience and passions'.

Beatrice had her own experience within an ENGO before she took a more
radical turn. She talks about her tandem participation in Sydney University
Environment Collective and her media internship as a time when she weighed
up the relative merits and disadvantages of both styles of organising. In contrast to the university collective, where she was exposed to consensus decision-
making, anarchist and socialist politics, the ENGO work seemed less
encompassing.

> I think I was really aware of it as a job. Like people had pretty typical
> homes and families that they went to afterwards and they came to
> ENGO nine to five or whatever, and then went home. And you know
> there's this kind of separation of activism from the rest of your life, and
> activism as like a job.
>
> (Beatrice, 2008)

After the internship she chose to become more involved in state student networks and a climate justice radio programme instead. Importantly, embedding in activist networks itself produces new forms of politics. Over time,
activists often change and refine their ideas about how to build change. Many
described it implicitly or explicitly as a journey from relative naivety to a
more well-defined form of radicalism. For Rosalind, this involved shifting from
faith in institutional reform to an autonomist focus on building alternatives
and opposing state and corporate power.

> [In the beginning] my approach to wanting to see change in the world was a
> much more institutional approach and a power-based approach. Like 'I just
> need to become the president of the United States, and then it will all be okay.'
>
> (Rosalind, 2008c)

Ben, a union organiser and member of a socialist organisation, described his
shift from aligning with anarchist praxis to socialism. Contestation over ideas
and strategy was central in his experience of this change.

> The conversations [I was having at that time] were, it was around the
> idea, okay if I am an anarchist and want to take myself seriously, well go
> and build an anarchist group, build something that can make a difference.
> And then I started to think about well what sort of organisation would

you need to, you know, make a difference in the world. What sort of organisation would you have to build? And I guess the more I thought about that, it was very similar to the, you know what I thought the ISO idea was of socialism from below. Or what I thought of at the time of as anarchism with a plan.

(Ben, 2009b)

Ben was a paid organiser in a national socialist organisation for a short time before a major split occurred within it. These events, among other life changes, led him to shift away from socialist politics and towards union organising in his workplace, before returning to a reunited socialist organisation later on. In hindsight, Ben described the time away as a process of shifting how he thinks about social struggle, as well as the everyday strategies of organising.

I think after having gone through this process ... [of] trying to break out of having simply a propaganda routine where people did stalls and talked about socialism rather than, you know, throwing themselves into struggles.

(Ben, 2009b)

What Cathy, Alistair, Ben and Beatrice's trajectories show is that political praxis in the movement is an ongoing process of critical reflection and contestation.

Conclusion

The journey in climate activist networks is an intensely personal process. Activists use experiences of moral shock to explain the instigation of their participation in action. The climate crisis is a profound challenge to society. In narrating how they have come to understand the problem, we can see activists engaged in a challenging and creative process of coming to understand and act on the issue. Their stories sought to explain shifts in thinking, feeling and occasionally a new life trajectory. Immersion in movement cultures involves experimenting with new forms of praxis, and becoming involved in new social relations. Activists thereby forge communities with their own language and vision for the world, that takes time to learn, and to adjust to.

There are different approaches to political organising in the traditions of autonomous networks, socialist groups, professional NGOs workers and the new community CAGs. In the period of mobilisation we are looking at, a great deal of collaboration between different groups went on. The critical reflections offered by participants about how to organise together in the context of political diversity illustrate that personal and collective reflexivity is central to creating effective alliances as well as personal sustainability in activism.

The ebbs and flows of individuals' participation in the movement trace with broader political cycles, periods of critical analysis, and strategic (or not-so strategic) realignments and demobilisations. These also reflect personal trajectories, where individuals shift between a sustained commitment and periods of more distanced individual and collective inquiry, or complete rest from the labour of activist praxis. In the next chapter we take up the question of hope in climate action, and how activism produces a sustained movement over time.

Note

1 BHP Billiton attempted to pull out of the project following revelations about the scale of the impacts, but at the behest of the PNG Government the mine was kept open and Ok Tedi shares were transferred to a trust to fund development projects in the Western Province. Legal proceedings between indigenous people and BHP Billiton resulted in an out-of-court settlement for compensation and remediation in 1996, but a new case in PNG's national court calling for compensation for ongoing impacts was launched in 2007. Extension of the project to 2025 is currently being debated (see Low & Gleeson, 2002; Santow, 2013).

5 Hope

In creating a language for climate politics, climate activists directly engaged with the question of hope. With advancing climate change they found the hope for a 'safe climate' becoming increasingly illusory. For most, the best that could be hoped for is that dangerous climate change does not gain its own 'runaway' momentum. Given the scale of the challenge, interviewees oscillated between despair and hope. Here the movement becomes the hope against hope, as the vehicle for change. As the crisis deepens, the movement assumed greater significance. Here, the pessimism of the intellect strengthened the optimism of the will in a dialectic where the one demands the other. The logic recalls Mike Davis' (2010) rereading of Gramsci for a climate age, where the political imagination assumes a centrally significant role. This political imagination for the climate age had its foundations in an ethical sense of purpose, of humanising climate change. Here we found activists defining and asserting explicitly ethical foundations for their collective action. These ethical principles translated values into political practice, through the movement. As such they were a form of relational ethics, involving an engaged ethic of 'care' rather than some logic of duty. In our interviewees we found activists elaborating these dispositions, in a passionate assertion of the necessity and legitimacy of direct climate justice.

Hope, we may say, is the central fulcrum for social movement mobilisation. Here we can interpret social protest as moral protest, as 'the ability to provide a moral voice' that is both public and collective (Jasper, 2008: 5). Personal outrage is greatly magnified when expressed in a collective setting, and directed at wider publics. Human agency – what Jasper calls 'creative artfulness' – is founded on the resulting process of collective interpretation, where social issues are evaluated and diagnosed against shared values. Echoing our discussion of Elias in Chapter 1, this process puts protest movements 'at the cutting edge of society's understandings of itself as it changes' (Jasper, 2008: 13). Direct action climate activists, we would suggest, have sought to rise to this creative challenge of constructing an imagination for the climate era. As Jamison states, the climate justice movement remains in the early stages of developing its knowledge base, and it is still unclear how its knowledge claims will develop (Jamison, 2009). This chapter explores the emergent frameworks, centring on ethical precepts developed by the movement. These, it is argued, have the capacity to distribute a broader social imaginary, constituting a new set of meanings for living with climate change.

It is often stated that 'radical' politics is centred on protest and resistance, and often lacks a broader 'project' for transformation (Castells, 2004). The imaginative struggle for such movements is to derive widely shared values and translate them into political strategy and programmes that can inspire millions of people to overthrow the status quo. An historical parallel to the emergent climate age may be the industrial era, when societies underwent substantial transformation and in the process generated new social movements founded on new values. One example is the socialist movement, which centred its appeal on the positive values of equality and solidarity, and mobilised them against structures of exploitation. The ethical appeal of socialism was – and is – centred on these embedded values. A further parallel can be found in the early struggles for self-determination amongst colonised peoples, where the positive ethical value of human dignity was mobilised against colonial domination. We might anticipate a similar ethical appeal emerging from climate politics, capable of mobilising millions across the globe for climate justice. In this Chapter the discussion revolves around these questions, pointing to emergent possibilities.

Under advancing climate change, climate movements are moving more explicitly into developing ethical foundations for action. Instrumentalism certainly remains central as it is often assumed that people need to vest their hopes in climate stability if they are to take action. Our interviews revealed that for activists dangerous climate change was already with us, and their priority was to imagine how runaway climate change can be avoided. In this context, some climate campaigners argued that the climate movement had to deliberately accentuate the positive. At a 2008 UK Climate Camp workshop, for instance, attended by one of us, the point was made very clear: we all know there is little in the way of hope, but if we want a movement we must use the language of hope. In this context activists arrived at what may be called 'strategic climate action', a position that represses the reality. Activists may have found themselves welcoming climate policy initiatives that, while inadequate, at least signalled a willingness to address the problem.

In this study, we found activists producing different motivations for action. Rather than false hopes, we saw an emerging model of ethical action where climate mobilisation did not necessarily depend on mitigating climate change, although it certainly hoped for this. It was grounded in a much more durable motive, one that said quite simply this is the right thing to do. Here, climate mobilisation became an intrinsic necessity, an end in itself, regardless of any anticipated outcome. Climate mobilisation thereby affirmed self-respect and human dignity and, as such, made a claim to be all-enveloping, a movement that was everywhere, embedded in the emergent universal subjectivity of life under climate change. Significantly, this ethical motivation was not articulated 'for itself', but for humanity in general. Against accounts of movements as self-expressive manifestations seeking sectional autonomy, ethical climate action produces a universal humanism. From this perspective activists could realistically despair at the inbuilt logic of climate change, and at the same time vest hopes in mass action to create new possibilities. Regardless of whether these are realised, climate action remained the right thing to do. The difficulty, as we shall see in Chapter 7, was how to translate this ethical appeal into political strategy, to operationalise these metapolitical appeals and gain mass political traction.

Through these ethical translations, we argue, climate activists were producing a new language of climate protest. The identity was universalist and, reflecting the enormity of the problem, the scope was maximalist. In this respect, climate action is not confined to the environmental movement, and, as reflected in the interviews discussed here, it had little to do with traditional conservationist forms of environmentalism. Climate action was more concerned with human rights and social justice. With failing climate policy, as noted, the climate movement adopted an increasingly radical stance. Activists often positioned themselves as part of a deliberately countercultural force for broad-scale transformation beyond consumer capitalism. In doing so, as noted in Chapter 3, the movement linked together the lineage of radical ecologism and environmental justice with the counter-globalist upsurge of the late 1990s and related themes of global justice.

In the interviews, we were witness to a struggle for language, and through this an emerging movement frame. Climate change is especially hard to engage with in terms of its simultaneously all-encompassing and personalised scope and requirements. Activists struggled for an approach grounded in full apprehension of the climate crisis that could express and produce a deep sense of engagement. As such, the interviews took us well beyond the perhaps anodyne truisms, confronting us with the intensely personal process of climate action, as a generative exercise of the political imaginary. Throughout, we found climate activists self-consciously engaged in the intellectual process of generating new visions and new models for action in the context of climate change. The initial interviews were designed to elicit perspectives on how people understood the impacts of climate change, its causes, and how to solve it. The follow-up interviews, sometimes several of them, held after Climate Camp, then explored the question of motivation and inspiration in terms of hopes and fears.

In what follows, the perspectives are outlined in this order, from impacts, causes and solutions, to fears and hopes, so as to reproduce our deliberate effort at using the interviews to stimulate a process of reflection, of moving towards questions that are most difficult to address. The difficulty arises at least partly because activists are still developing the language and concepts to enable us to address them: as activists wrestle with these difficulties we see the new frames for action in development, offering real possibilities for transformation.

Interpreting climate crisis

The language of climate politics begins with the question of interpretation: how is the crisis to be understood in terms of impacts, causes and possible solutions? The understandings of climate change that activists arrived at in turn had a critical impact on their interpretation of political prospects. In terms of impacts, it was notable that most interviewees stressed the human impacts of climate change, with only a few mentioning implications for species survival. Ben (2009b) was blunter than most, answering the question with 'Ah ... how serious? ... what happens when a billion people run out of food?' In addressing human impacts there was a strong awareness of stratification. There was uniform consciousness of 'living in a high emitting country' and, as Rosalind (2008a) put it, the need to take 'responsibility and action to be in solidarity with people who are going to be a lot more affected by climate change'. Echoing the sentiment, Robert (2008a) acknowledged 'we've got a bit of a buffer with our affluence so we can absorb a little bit of it', unlike others. Without effective action, Rosalind (2008a) anticipated 'more repression and millions of refugees', with 'fortresses' and a 'more repressive environment'. Lillian (2008a) stated clearly that 'it is going to hit certain layers of people and not others'. The main examples people used to illustrate the impacts were social examples. Lillian cited the impact of Hurricane Katrina in New Orleans, with others citing Cyclone Nargis in Burma, and the impacts of flooding in Bangladesh. The loss of Australian icons, such as the Barrier Reef, the Tasmanian forests, or native species, were only mentioned once. This suggested a strong environmental justice theme among those interviewed, as against a more conservationist approach.

Along with its human impacts, the sheer scale and all-encompassing character of climate change is a major factor. Lillian noted how many different aspects of society are affected by climate change, as both the 'biggest' and 'hardest' thing for activists to deal with. The scale of the problem is magnified by the 'vested interests and the barriers to change' that for Samuel (2008a) were 'so much bigger than really what the environment movement has dealt with'. For virtually all the interviewees, climate justice was also understood in temporal terms, as intergenerational. This was highly immediate. Rather than seeing themselves as having an abstract responsibility to future generations, activists talked of the fearful legacy they would leave to their younger friends and family. George (2008b) put it in terms of parental duty: 'I have two young sons and it's my duty as a parent and a father that when I depart this earth, that I hand over to them a world that's better than it is now.' Several of the older interviewees reflected, with regret, on their own generation, one that, as LR stated, lived a 'charmed life', yet now leaves a 'burden for future generations'. AH stated frankly: 'We've stuffed it up. We need to do something now to redeem it, so that they can have a future.' The imperative was both personal and universal: 'For my kids, for their kids and for your kids and for everyone's kids.'

The question of responsibility to children was especially powerful. Vicky (2010) stated that her son will 'grow up in a world which I can't necessarily imagine, that could be absolutely horrific ... it's not only that I don't matter, it's that my kids' future doesn't matter.' The question of what the future holds is also a prime concern for younger activists. As Kylie (2009b) stated, 'This is our future. And we should stand up for our future. Um, I'm only 21 ... I don't know whether I can morally have children if the future's going to be this bad.' In this context, climate activism becomes a form of redemption. Vicky (2009) said 'I need to be able to look my son in the eye when he's grown up and say "I tried really hard" and I think that's one of my major motivations.' Not acting for climate justice becomes a denial of humanity. Perhaps the most powerful statement of intergenerational justice came from Jimmy, who argued that parents who deny climate change renounce their child's existence: 'these people don't care whether they're your parents or not, they don't care it seems, they're just taking your future.' Later, he asked, rhetorically:

> If they love their children they will stop the destruction of the planet. How much do they love their own children? Doesn't sound enough [be] cause they're not giving them any future.
>
> (Jimmy, 2009)

Several interviewees stated that they believe theirs is the last generation that could prevent runaway climate change. As Gary (2008a) put it: 'It's now or never ... We're not going to get another chance.' George's metaphor calls us to put on the brakes: 'It's a downhill run from here and it is getting steeper and steeper. We have to act now before it's too late' (George, 2008a). This hope of averting runaway climate change is shared by all interviewees. Yet the danger signs are already present. Claire (2008a) said 'climate change is already dangerous. 150,000 people die a year due to climate change', adding, 'we have a very, very small window of opportunity in which to act and make really very deep reductions in our emissions before it becomes permanent and irreversible.' Robert (2008a) wondered whether the impact of dangerous climate change is enough to force action, saying 'the thing that scares me is that, um, it's not perceived at the moment as dangerous'. Ruth (2008a) agreed, predicting

> a period of absolute misery for the great proportion of the Earth's population. I just don't think that that can be avoided. There's a window of opportunity, but you do wonder is it possible for the world to see this?

Angus was similarly sceptical, and added a dose of irony:

> I don't think we're anywhere near getting anywhere ... if I was going to bet money, I don't think we're going to win. And there's not much point winning any money if we don't win [laughs].
>
> (Angus, 2008b)

Interviewees positioned climate change within an overarching explanatory frame of disconnection and alienation from ecosystems. Disconnection of society from ecology was a systemic problem, expressed in consumer culture and possessive individualism. Alienation was expressed in two ways, in the capacity of vested interests to maintain fossil-fuel dependency, and in the disaggregation and stratification of communities. For all interviewees, ecological disconnection was driven by materialism. For Cathy (2008a) it was 'part of human nature ... a disease called materialism'. A capacity for consumerist self-delusion, perhaps false consciousness, was emphasised by others. For Margo (2008a), 'humanity has this incredible ability to just think things will go on forever'. Gary agreed, arguing, 'We've gone along with this idea that nature will provide, it certainly will, but there's a limit' (Gary, 2008a). Angus emphasised the myth of modern necessities, of 'people using a lot of energy for what they think is daily life' (Angus, 2008a). Several interviewees were more specific. Robert, for instance, said 'being human we get caught up with, you know, needing another car and needing new clothes and a bigger, better house, and the list goes on and on' (Robert, 2008a).

For most interviewees, the virulence of consumerism arose from the specific kind of society we live in. They argued, as Claire did, that 'if we are to address it, then we actually need to address the whole system' (Claire, 2008a). For Alistair, we 'have a whole culture that is incredibly dependent on fossil fuel use' (Alistair, 2008a). From this perspective there was a strong emphasis on the deep-seated nature of carbon-intensive consumerism, reaching into everyday lifestyle and culture. Sarah expressed a shared frustration with the deliberate 'ambivalence' of everyday consumerist rhetoric, which implicitly tells us,

> 'Oh it doesn't matter, you're not going to be alive, you're not going to be able to care, it's all about money, it's what we can get now' ... that whole rolling, gathering, getting bigger, bigger and bigger, destructive ball of consumerism.
> (Sarah, 2008a)

Ruth expressed her personal complicity, of knowing that society is 'on the edge of a cliff' while being 'caught up in its day-to-day lives', on a 'treadmill ... hooked by all the advertising' (Ruth, 2008a).

Everyday disconnection from community, locality and ecology was seen as central. In terms of disconnection from ecology, several interviewees talked of children not understanding where their food comes from, for instance believing that milk comes from a carton rather than from a cow. Sarah articulated a powerful sentiment, expressed by many:

> If you were to ask me what are the greatest joys that I could have, it would be picking a strawberry that had been in the sun, warmed by the sun, that I'd watch grow. This beautiful red piece of food, so simple, and that taste of it. And now how many kids or how many people get to experience that simple, simple joy? It's like you go to a big air-conditioned

fluoro lit, homogenised, supermarket laid out the same, holding the same amount of food and you buy a plastic packet of non-tasting, artificially grown things.

(Sarah, 2008b)

The importance of this, as Cathy (2008a) put it, was that 'We've lost contact with ... the systems that really exist to keep the world going.'

The resulting alienation was expressed in a mixture of complicity and blame. Some interviewees are quick to acknowledge that they benefitted from carbon-intensive development. Angus, for instance, stated 'I'm not afraid to say that it's just ordinary people like you and me that are responsible for it' (Angus, 2008a). Others stressed the deep power differentials and uneven responsibility. Consumerist consciousness is all-pervasive. As Robert (2008a) noted, 'everyone's apathy is a little bit to blame and, you know, I'm to blame as well.' In this context, Harriet blamed 'all of us ... our over-consumptive lifestyle, our addiction to fossil fuels, our unwillingness to engage with the seriousness of the problem' (Harriet, 2008a).

Beyond a generalised sense of complicity there was a strong emphasis on how carbon emissions are stratified, with clear winners and losers. Margo (2008a) argued that the problem lay with the carbon-intensive 'lifestyle that largely people in western democracies, and to some extent, with um, middle-class and upper-class communities in developing countries, have adopted'. Gary (2008a) linked responsibility to per capita impact and the inequity that 'some people are using more than their share of the resources ... at the expense of other people in the world.' Despite this, 'people have the hide to criticise because they're using too much: they're on about two bucks a day, we're on hundreds of dollars a day. Just disgraceful.'

Rather than blame elite consumers for emissions, several interviewees cited corporate promoters and their beneficiaries as key drivers. Cathy (2008a) talked of the need to focus on the political process and a 'quarry view of economics' that delivers corporate influence. Some wanted to directly target the high emitters, citing specific companies, political parties and government departments, and individuals in those institutions, as directly responsible. For Alistair, it was a question of power and relative impact:

the chief executive officers of Exxon Mobil, Shell, Texaco, those kind of companies and the big coal companies, bear far more responsibility than the average parent who drives a four-wheel drive.

(Alistair, 2008a)

In Australia the coal industry was seen as the key perpetrator, both in terms of direct emissions and in terms of corrupting the political process, creating, as Alison put it, a 'major failure of our current economic and political system' (Alison, 2008b). In the final analysis, Sarah argued, with political institutions bound and gagged by the fossil-fuel industry, 'it has to come down to individuals, because we can all do something' (Sarah, 2008a). From here, activists invoked a collective responsibility for mass action, not to reduce personal emissions but to target perpetrators.

The key problem for all interviewees was fossil fuel dependency, especially coal dependency, both in terms of the export trade and domestic coal-fired electricity. There was deep scepticism of any effort to sequester coal-related emissions. Technology was only embraced when it was thought to have the effect of reducing the extraction and combustion of fossil fuels. In terms of a positive agenda, perspectives centred on technological solutions, on reduced consumption and growth rates, on collective action and deepened community capacity. Each of these, in different ways, could offer a means of reconciling society-ecology disconnections. The first strengthened society's ability to harness forces of nature, through a form of 'thick' ecological modernity, which has regard to side effects. The second sought to regear society in accordance with ecological limits, a form of ecological sufficiency. The third put faith in the mobilisation of collective action and community embeddedness, as a means of generating new capacity to transform relations with ecology.

Virtually all interviewees voiced an unqualified faith in renewable technologies, an 'energy revolution' as George (2008a) puts it. Alistair charted a 'clean energy future',

> something that people can get inspired and excited by because so often the issue gets framed as either we cook the planet or we have to go and live in a cave and eat lentils.

> (Alistair, 2008a)

The technological solutions are presented as practical and available. For Robert (2008a), Australia had easy access to sources of solar and wind power, which pointed to 'political obstacles' forcing renewable technology offshore, to China and the US. Cathy (2008a) wanted the government 'to embrace the technologies that we have right here and now', with strengthened forms of social provision, such as through public transport, that could already address issues of both equity and climate.

For most interviewees, though, technological solutions were only a small part of the answer, and had to be combined with efforts at reducing or reorientating consumption. In tension with the call for new forms of renewable technology, there was a strong element of voluntary simplicity in the effort to connect with community. Robert, for instance, spoke of a holistic model of sustainable lifestyle, centred on the virtues of physical labour:

> Just go and do a good day's work and you know, learn simple, basic skills that satisfy people. Good physical work when required won't hurt you, it will make you more healthy.

> (Robert, 2008b)

Sarah (2008b) likewise asked,

> When are we going to go back to simple stuff? Have little community groups, go back to community gardens and more schools growing gardens.

A key element was a reengagement with nature, in recognition of its wonder. As Sarah said, 'I think people have really lost and are encouraged to lose sight of the simple things of life. Just appreciating nature and what's in nature. The amazing things that we live alongside.' Similarly, Cathy argued

> humanity has to take a good long, hard look at itself and find a new way of existing on the planet ... building an awareness of larger systems and appreciate what we have.
>
> (Cathy, 2008a)

A key theme here was the issue of ecological limits and the extent to which prosperity and abundance were socially defined and constrained. There was a widespread insistence that ecology does not limit happiness. Angus believed that

> we can achieve a stabilised society and environment based on what our actual resources are ... we can live a peacefully, happily fulfilled life without you know burning massive amounts of fuel, creating carbon dioxide, driving around in cars and all these things that people seem to feel are connected with happiness.
>
> (Angus, 2008a)

Echoing the aspiration to a redefined prosperity, Ben mobilised a wider understanding of the impacts of unequal accumulation:

> I think if you have a democratic system in which wealth was shared there would be no reason that you couldn't have improved living standards alongside protecting the environment which sustains us all.
>
> (Ben, 2009a)

Unique amongst non-indigenous interviewees, George referred to indigenous knowledges as a source of inspiration in this regard: 'You have to take a page out of the book by our, the traditional owners of this country, how they've managed and looked after what they had' (George, 2008a). Central to sufficiency was a critique of growth, yet only a few interviewees confront this issue directly. Discussing the obstacles, Angus highlighted the central paradox, that 'people are still fixated with the idea that growth is good, and anywhere where there is growth in the economy there's growth in emissions' (Angus, 2008b).

Climate change was often seen as requiring reconnection with community as part of the decarbonisation process. Several interviewees embedded possibilities for sufficiency in localisation and community connectivity. Alison charted a vision for

> ... communities that are much more self-sufficient than they currently are ... local sourced energy and food, where there's local governance systems, where you know people take enjoyment out of each other's company and you know working together and there are less cars and more public transport, there are kids playing in the street.
>
> (Alison, 2008a)

Other interviews charted a less romanticised vision, of a 'value-based lifestyle' for Robert, or in Ruth's case, the need for a 'well-being manifesto', but the concerns were similar (Ruth & Robert, 2008a). There was self-conscious validation of efforts at local sufficiency, understood by several interviewees as a means of community self-protection. Beatrice specifically cited the need to strengthen adaptive capacity: 'we need to work really hard at building communities and supporting people in our communities and internationally because I think we almost can't escape the fact that there are going to be intense impacts even if there are lots of changes to how things are done' (Beatrice, 2008). Community-based production systems were seen as a necessary coping mechanism. Harriet argued that

> One of the really important things that we need to do is start setting up systems where we're better able to cope ... recently I've been thinking about that more on a community level, and getting people to think more in terms of community and their neighbours and local food and consuming less resources because at some point all those resources aren't even going to be available to us.
>
> (Harriet, 2008c)

Robert was also developing practical models for sustainable living through a permaculture centre, so that 'if society is still around to live that life in years to come then these sort of ideas will become more and more necessary ... we would like to be part of the education of that new lifestyle [to] teach people in community living, even like a transition town' (Robert, 2008b). Other interviewees had a more open-ended definition of community, arguing that self-protection and self-sufficiency should be rejected in favour of solidarity and connectivity. Rosalind, for instance, called for 'community governance, not self-sufficiency', that would involve forms of inclusive localisation underpinned by climate justice, and 'solidarity with places which for whatever reason, be they environmental or historical, aren't able to transition so easily' (Rosalind, 2008c).

While there was a strong commitment to just solutions to climate crisis, across all interviewees, there was lack of clarity on how that can be defined, or pursued. Most interviewees focused on ensuring that polluters pay for the transition to a decarbonised society, and several had strong critiques of existing climate policy. As discussed in Chapter 7 there was a surprising consensus among interviewees that government was the key means of addressing climate justice. Yet, given the manifest inadequacy of government responses, hopes are vested in the climate action movement. Rosalind, for instance, believed that 'through our dissent, through our organising, [we should be] making it political suicide for governments not to take seriously climate change and to do something about it' (Rosalind, 2008a), while the solution may rest with a form of transformed government that could only be achieved through the mobilisation of a climate action movement. As Rosalind insisted, with failing international negotiations and derisory government initiatives, there was nothing that can act as a proxy for popular mobilisation: 'I only trust myself and people to make this happen' (Rosalind, 2008a). Angus made the point clear: 'even if it wasn't our fault, we're still responsible for fixing it 'cause no-one else is going to do it ... whether it's our fault or not, we're going to have to deal with it now' (Angus, 2008a).

Pointing to the mobilising effects of climate change, a number of interviewees articulated a double-sided or dialectical understanding of climate crisis, as both destructive and transformative. A crisis situation can transform possibilities. As Robert (2008b) argued, it 'can flick the switch in people's minds to say it's time we lived differently'. Rosalind agreed:

> I don't think we've even had this kind of challenge before. Or this opportunity to radically restructure the entire way we do things.
>
> (Rosalind, 2008a)

For Rosalind, climate change creates an imperative for change: in the context of runaway climate change 'it becomes very easy to talk about alternatives' (Rosalind, 2008c). Reflecting this, Harriet (2009) argued that the movement needs to develop a much wider agenda of social transformation, that 'the climate change movement really suffers almost from being the climate change movement rather than this really broad movement that's trying to have a safe and just society on this planet'.

From despair to hope?

The climate action movement, like all movements, is embedded in activist subjectivities. As noted, the motivation of activists to take action was often assumed to revolve around the nexus between anger and hope. What was very clear here, was that hope was only part of the story, with despair and anger figuring at least as large. Involvement in the movement became a powerful antidote, as a means of reconnection, and as an ethical force for renewal.

Given the apparently unremitting logic of climate change, despair at the current trajectory towards runaway climate change was a major theme across all the interviews. All the interviewees embraced climate science as offering irrefutable evidence of this trajectory. The hard certainty of science prompted a deeply affective crisis that for some produced nightmares and depression. Alistair reported that 'everyone I have spoken to' who reads the latest climate science has become immobilised by fear, like a 'rabbit in the headlights' (Alistair, 2008c). He 'could hardly get out of bed' when, after a bout of reading climate science,

> I spent a couple of days almost in foetal position just feeling quite over-whelmed about, um, the climate impacts. I was just reading too much climate science.
>
> (Alistair, 2008a)

The despair was most intense where the likely victims were personified. As Ruth (2008a) reported, 'I have nightmares thinking about what my young grandchildren, thinking about what their world will be like when they're my age. If there is a world they can live in when they're my age. It scares me.' Vicky likewise despaired for her child's future, saying, 'when Copenhagen came I spent the whole day crying' (Vicky, 2010). Alison went so far as to name the condition: 'I went through climate depression, which I think should be a clinically diagnosable illness' (Alison, 2008a).

Vicky was wrestling with the future, through her imagination of what kind of a life her child will have to live:

> Capitalism, it is dependent on being able to treat people like slave and treat nature like a resource, it can't exist without it ... I can't think of any time where a society like ours has managed to change the road when you're this far down it. So, no, I see apocalypse. And hopefully something good comes out of that. And like I said I hope that either my son survives it, or his kid survives it. I don't think it's that far away.
>
> (Vicky, 2010)

Given an understanding of climate science, and having gone through 'climate depression', many interviewees found themselves in a world apart. Society's complicity in climate crisis, and the resultant widespread efforts at avoiding the issue, despite knowing the impacts, became a major cause of frustration and anger. For Angus (2008b), prevalent apathy was predictable. He argued very powerfully that climate action within a carbon-intensive society was a logical fallacy: when people's lifestyles depend on carbon emissions, how can people be expected to take meaningful action on climate change?

Others saw less of the irony, especially when confronted face-to-face with those refusing to apprehend the need for change. Indeed, the greatest anger was reserved for those who wilfully refused to take action despite knowing and accepting the likely impacts of their actions. The deliberate refusal to accept responsibility was very confronting for many of the interviewees. One form of refusal was expressed as a kind of strategic hopelessness. Claire (2008b) talked of coming into contact with people who know that things are not right, and they know that things need to change, and they know that we're heading for really drastic changes to our planet which may make it unliveable for humans,

but who then strategically exit from taking action by choosing to 'feel like it's too hopeless'. Beatrice (2008) reported the 'disheartening and depressing' impact of meeting people 'that don't think it's significant or happening or whatever': here it was the exercise of hierarchy to silence or marginalise that was most frustrating, where 'they act like they think you're an idiot … [with] all the confidence that comes with power.'

But perhaps most revealing was the performance of ambivalence that Sarah so vividly outlined:

> that whole ambivalence about you know 'oh the power stations are going to run anyway, so I'm going to use the electricity, I may as well put my air conditioner on, even though I can open the window and get that nice summer breeze'.

(Sarah, 2008)

There was a deep understanding of how consumerist ideology maintains itself (not least because climate activists live in that same world). This exchange between Sarah and the interviewer, which followed from the discussion of air conditioning, is very telling:

> Sarah: And I guess for other people not to even think about it, not to try and do something … We know now. Ignorance is not an excuse. Isn't that just illogical?
> Interviewer: Or as you said, "open the window".
> Sarah: But we still get the whole "keep your house cool" thing.

(Sarah, 2008)

Anger at society's wilful ignorance was embedded in generational stratification, where the last generation to live under a stable climate refuses to take action, despite the crisis into which many young people have fallen. Ruth stated, 'I look at my own kids, and they know, and they're doing what they can, and I see their despair, and I see them and others falling into depression, and that really upsets me' (Ruth, 2008b).

For several interviewees, the question then became one of managing despair and anger, of not letting it immobilise, but at the same time, not denying the plausible realities. The emotional self-awareness spoke to the gulf that opens up between climate activists and the rest of society: there was a need to harness one's emotions so as not to self-exclude. Sarah had to self-consciously repress the frustration: 'The whole yeah, laziness and acceptance of people is infuriating for me. So I'm like I said, I've got to try and keep it in check, otherwise it would really overwhelm me to a destructive point' (Sarah, 2008b). Similarly, Alistair spoke of 'going through a period of thinking "maybe I'm just despairing too much about climate change"', and then thinking,

> I was too angry to do my job properly because I just couldn't exercise effective judgement because I just wanted to, you know, lock up coal industry executives. And I was just so angry about climate change. And, you know, a bit of anger is good, but it often can cloud your judgement as well. But then I've managed that effectively.
>
> (Alistair, 2008c)

Alison (2008a) articulated a similar need to manage engagement, in this case to lift 'this huge pain and burden of the world on your shoulder', to enable recuperation and maintain engagement. For others, managing despair and anger was a tactical necessity. For Ruth (2008b), it was a matter of accentuating the positive, 'trying to focus on the half-full glass rather than the half-empty glass', to motivate action. She added, 'why focus on the things that you can't do anything about?', and Robert (2008b) expressed a similar sentiment, stressing that 'the way to help the most people, was to be optimistic and to do what you can'. These concerns were reflected in Alison's comment that

> I just don't really let myself think about failure. Yeah there's a very, very likely probability that we're going to fail but there's absolutely no point in dwelling on it because, you know, I'm doing as much as I can at the moment.
>
> (Alison, 2008a)

Aside from managing despair to maximise mobilisation, several of the interviewees spoke of having arrived at a self-conscious state of balance, a 'combination of despair and hope', as Beatrice put it. The two 'need go together so you don't go crazy' (Beatrice, 2008). For Claire they were locked into each other:

> Interviewer: So it sounds like you oscillate between having hope and not having hope ...
> Claire: Oh, gosh. I mean it happens pretty regularly, those oscillations.
>
> (Claire, 2008b)

An important aspect of this position was a concern that climate action may not succeed. Beatrice put this in the form of an imperative to realise 'that you know, as hard as we work at activism, we're probably not going to be able to do enough', rather than trying to just ignore that and thinking, 'no, no, no, we can stop this, we can stop this'. For Beatrice, this position emerged out of a period of reflection, sometimes painful:

I think there is a lot we can do in terms of changing our behaviour and others' behaviours and that kind of thing. But I think realising that we probably aren't going to be able to do enough to stop everything, while that's quite a painful thing to realise, you know because I've felt that for a long time, but it's only recently that I've started being really open about the fact, that I don't think we're going to be able to do enough in that regard.

(Beatrice, 2008)

Yet action to minimise impact, even if limited, was not lacking in instrumental purpose. One of the key features of climate science was its dynamism, reflecting ecological interconnectivity and also the sociopolitical feedback loops that lend a degree of openness to possibilities and potentials. There was always uncertainty over the future, not least because societies are reflexive, and permanently act on themselves, redefining the future. In this context, as expressed in Beatrice's confidence that 'there is lots we can do', action could unexpectedly change outcomes. Beatrice, for instance, later insisted that climate mobilisation was creating new alliances, such as between farmers and environmentalists, and creating 'hope from hopelessness' (Beatrice, 2008).

Taking her position further, Alistair (2008a) used the metaphor of cancer: 'if you're diagnosed with cancer or if your partner or your mum or your dad is diagnosed with cancer you don't just say "oh well I'm not sure we can cure this, I'm not sure we can save them, therefore I'm not going to do anything". You do what you can.' Doing what you can is life-affirming and is guided by the hope, perhaps a hope against hope, but also a certainty that doing something will alleviate suffering and offer at least the possibility of cure. Climate agency became an expression of humanism.

Hope and reconnection

Any hopes of addressing climate change rested upon hopes for mass connection with movements and mobilisation. Disconnection from ecology, locality and community was answered through the construction of new ways of living. A starting point was to live in ways that are more critically aware of power structures, dominant interests, and the implications for ecologies. It also meant gaining a greater appreciation of the intrinsic value of ecological systems, as against circuits of money and commodities.

Most interviewees gained their hope from social connectivity and the power of the movement. Ben (2009b) stated, 'how much hope you have comes and goes, and it comes and goes with the movement'. This was perhaps one of the clearest statements of the centrality of mobilisation, and was reflected in many other comments from the interviewees. Beatrice felt 'hopeful and energised now knowing that people can support each other and put energy into supporting each other with all the stuff that's going to happen' (Beatrice, 2008). Claire also found great strength in the movement:

> I think just being involved in campaigning and activism in itself gives hope; and being surrounded by and working with other people who are really dedicated to creating a better world. That inspires me with hope constantly.
>
> (Claire, 2008b)

For Margo, involvement in the movement was quite simply 'good for my soul and I do draw great strength from that' (Margo, 2008a). For Samuel (2008b), helping people take action, and see them becoming more radical,

> 'really inspires me and I guess that's what gives me hope'. Alison (2008a) expressed this as a great love for climate activists, saying 'they are some of the most inspiring, bright, brilliant, strategic thinkers ... and that's a pretty fantastic feeling to have, so that's one of my sources of hope.'

The Climate Camp held in Hellensburgh had been especially significant for Alistair. The need to rethink tactics at the mine site, and the decision to focus on individuals declaring publicly why they were there and why they would try to walk onto the mine site to close it down, was seen as very effective. For Alistair, this use of public testimonials was symbolic but very powerful, especially when a seventy-year-old grandfather with his son and grandson walked to the fence:

> It just reminded me of how much passion there is, and how much hope there is and how much inspiration there is in the climate movement and how people are willing to really stand up for their convictions. And so I found it pretty inspiring.
>
> (Alistair, 2009)

William said simply: 'I believe in the movement, the movement, the movement. Because what else is there?' (William, 2009). Reflecting this, several interviewees saw the movement as having a precious status, reflecting its pre-figurative radicalism. Here there was a strong sense of the historical significance of direct action, no matter how marginalised. William (2009) stated, 'It's a kind of politics and a kind of way of being that I want to keep alive for its own sake.' He saw his involvement in the movement as keeping 'a candle in the window trying to keep another form of life alive that isn't dominated by bureaucracy, market and capital'.

The key issue here was the capacity of the movement to produce the knowledge that is required for transformation. Margo (2008b) noted that with climate change there are no precedents: 'It changes our world in ways that we can't understand ... but we understand enough to know that we have to change.'

Answers came from the process of collective action: LD had 'real hope that people have the capacity to act for not only themselves but for the greater benefit of the community and to come together and to be more imaginative and visionary'. Likewise, Lillian (2008b) had 'hope in the social movements to be able to develop a collective power and analysis of what needs to be done'. Margo, also, voiced a deep faith in the creative power of popular movements, but at the same time revealed the absence of strategy: 'so where my hope comes from is from people … you never know how you're going to get the breakthrough. You just keep going and you hope that the great spirit of humanity will find a way' (Margo, 2008b). Alistair put it simply, inadvertently highlighting the tautologies: 'I have hope in the sense that if I and you and others work to make that happen, we'll make that happen and we have to' (Alistair, 2008c). Kylie (2009a) agreed: 'being around a lot of other people doing things gives you more hope because you don't feel alone, you don't feel as though there's only a few of us in the world trying to fight this …'

Faith in the movement points to ethical foundations and the extent to which climate mobilisation was rarely, if ever, purely instrumental. For most of the interviewees there was clearly a strong ethical foundation for action where, effectively, the climate action movement becomes an end in itself. This was not a mode of cultural identification that pursued autonomy for its own sake, but rather was open-ended and universalistic, asserting an underlying set of human values that obtained whether or not runaway climate change was avoidable. From this perspective, activist agency could become its own justification: climate action against fatalism becomes an issue of personal integrity, a way to remain sane.

That said, most interviewees stated that they would not be involved in climate action if they thought runaway climate change was unstoppable. Kylie is straightforward:

> There would be no point if I didn't have hope. I think already it's like there's going to be devastating consequences, but I think it just depends how bad it gets, and we really need to push it, push the government, push world leaders, who have the power to do major changes, so that it doesn't get any worse than it already will be.
>
> (Kylie, 2009a)

At a personal level, hopeless activism was an impossibility – 'I don't see why I'd bother going out and rallying or sending letters or doing all that sort of thing if I didn't truly believe that it would do something.' Yet, when pressed, Kylie acknowledged the ambivalences. She was asked 'But will it do enough?', and she replied:

> Well it will do as much as it can, and I think that's the point you've got to get to, whether it's enough or not … I think if it achieves anything, then it's a plus … it's kind of hard to wrap your head around.
>
> (Kylie, 2009a)

Samuel (2008b) had a strong faith in the ability of the movement to shift power-holders, stating that elites were already on the defensive, seeking ways of maintaining the fossil fuel sector as the movement became more powerful. Cathy stressed the diversity of movement mobilisations, with 'all these little ripples throwing these little stones everywhere ... I think they are seeing a million ripples from many different sectors' (Cathy, 2009).

When asked 'so if we work on it fast enough we can prevent dangerous climate change?', Cathy responded 'Well I guess if I didn't believe that I wouldn't be here. So, I believe that we can do it' (Cathy, 2008a). When pressed, Cathy's optimism was more strategic, expressed in her statement 'if you don't hope for better, then you don't have a hope in hell' (Cathy, 2009). Her position was also grounded in human rights:

> I think people are really beginning to connect human rights and climate change – hallelujah ... where we can actually say 'I do have responsibility ... [given that] the continuation of export coal means the death of millions of people around the world'.
>
> (Cathy, 2009)

Again, Rosalind was ambivalent, sharing Cathy's sentiment: when asked 'Can we prevent dangerous climate change?' she replied,

> Yeah! [laughs]. We sure can. Um, yeah I totally have hope. Like I think if I didn't I wouldn't do anything. Oh maybe I would because you've just to, you know, it's a way to, at least not sit back and watch it all unfold. I think we can prevent it, but I don't think we can rely on governments to do it for us.
>
> (Rosalind, 2008a)

The combination of instrumental hope and expressive action was shared by most interviewees. Angus declared: 'Seeing as we're looking at we're probably going to fail, then I think you've got to be able to say "I tried somewhere"' (Angus, 2008b). For Gary (2008b) 'it's not easy but what keeps me going is the fact that I know for the benefit of everyone that what I'm doing is right. And that's why I'm doing it.' Again, there was a sense of collective responsibility for future generations: George asked,

> What do we do? We are responsible for their fate. And I believe that we are morally bound to do something about it.
>
> (George, 2008b)

Even if climate action fails, the act of trying was regarded as necessary and positive. Samuel argued,

> so when, if the Arctic does completely collapse and all of these terrible things happen and we are getting to 3 billion refugees and people

starving ... I think it still would have been positive to work against those things happening even if we're not successful.

(Samuel, 2008b)

Again, the tautologies were there to be played with, and Angus was more willing than most to engage with them:

I think if we don't win there's no future for anyone. So there's nothing to be gained by giving up ... You would want to think that you tried. And I suppose that there's various levels of dangerous, catastrophic, irreve sible climate change. So every time you do anything, you win. It's just a pity that you're probably not going to win enough [laughs].

(Angus, 2008b)

The sentiment could be seen as almost that of an agnostic, of lacking certainty and placing bets both ways. But the ethical force has a purpose, as noted, to reconnect with ecology, to heal the metabolic rift. This expressed an understanding that human society is constituted with ecologies, and rests on a deep regard for the world we live in as the foundation for our existence. Alistair (2008a), for instance, explained his understanding of climate action in terms of a love for the world, arguing

if you love something, you should defend it', and adding 'whether or not you believe we can prevent dangerous climate change, I think we've got a moral obligation to try.

Kylie shared this sentiment, but gave it a different complexion, where love for the world is itself generative:

the world is amazing and I think that gives you hope, I think that gives you hope in the sense that it's something you don't want to lose as well. So it really gives you something to fight for ... .

(Kylie, 2009a)

Vicky (2009) put it simply, and perhaps most modestly:

I can't change the world. All I can do is try really hard. And that as long as I try really hard, I can look myself in the mirror.

Kylie (2009b) agrees that passivity leads to guilt:

I just couldn't sit by and know that this is happening and just not do anything. I just thought that was just immoral pretty much not to do anything. To be aware and not do anything.

The sense of identity, of self-regard, sustained by climate action, was a measure of the depth of feeling. For Harriet, not being involved in climate action was unthinkable:

> Regardless of how enormous and terrifying the problem is, it's really important to keep active on it. Partly just because I would certainly find it a lot more difficult, and my mental health would be a lot worse if I wasn't trying to do anything about it; I'd just feel a bit like I was in denial if I was aware of this enormous problem that was threatening to change everything about life as we know it on this planet, and not doing anything about it, I would find that really difficult.
>
> (Harriet, 2008c)

This statement is remarkable for its honesty: in acknowledging that climate action is an antidote to what Alison called 'climate depression', Harriet allowed us to understand the depth of feeling at play. Fatalism, and 'not doing anything about it', destroys activist identity, and negates climate agency.

Ethical action of this sort is a demonstration of the power of society's reflexivity, of climate agency in this case, suggesting an autonomous capacity of society to act on itself, for itself. The parallels with traditions of liberal civil disobedience are there to be drawn, where passivity and compliance in the face of an injustice is itself a crime. Direct action becomes redemptive in this sense, as a form of symbolic self-sacrifice in the Ghandian tradition. Angus had a strong appreciation of this, arguing: 'I think you can hold some hope, or some kind of reminder that we are in control ... we do have the power of veto, we can just go down and stop it.' The principle that it is our society, that ultimately we all own, and all have the right and responsibility to act on it, comes into view with climate action. In so far as climate-intensive industries violate those responsibilities, we all are required to take direct action to shut them down. Angus made an appeal to activists:

> [to] remind yourself that it is your coal, and your coal trains; it's on your train tracks that go past your town so you know that it is possible, and it was shown that it is possible – you can walk on and stop it.
>
> (Angus, 2008b)

From this perspective, climate action was mass reflexive ethical action. As Angus argued, 'I think there's enough people to stop the problem considering that people are the problem. So there's by definition plenty of them [laughs].'

Conclusions

Climate movements – and the activists involved in them – were developing their own means of conceptualising and exercising climate agency. In key respects this involved a re-interpretation of existing categories of social life.

Engaging with the science of climate change forced activists into a context which was simultaneously metapolitical and immediately personalised. Understandings of how to interpret and act on climate change reflected the extent to which climate crisis produces a crisis of political interpretation, and of the very language of politics. We found climate activists refusing to deny this political crisis and instead trying to formulate a response that sustains their agency. In the process they articulated foundations for climate agency, from despair at the difficulties posed, to anger at those who wilfully exercise 'apocalypse blindness', as Beck termed it, to the construction of hopes vested in the capacity of the climate movement and in the assertion of ethical values for the movement. We can suggest that, in the process, climate activists were constructing a new language of climate protest that offers real insights into the potential for such initiatives in the future.

6 Direct Action

The upsurge in grass-roots activism heralded a new momentum in climate politics that could be observed throughout many industrial countries around the world. The activism was born of the frustration with the failure of governments in the emissions-intensive countries to implement any really decisive measures to arrest climate change and the failure to negotiate an international agreement to set in place the required emissions reduction targets. There was a growing appreciation of the impact that this intransigence would have for the global South and that this called for action that engaged social justice concerns. While environmental NGOs had added social justice, and more recently climate justice, ambitions to their climate politics lexicon, grass-roots activism was regarded as a necessary antidote to the ineffectiveness of these organisations' lobbying efforts. A new, more animated climate movement, one that was not as acquiescent to political convention and was prepared to confront the status quo, was considered to be essential if there was going to be any progress on mitigating climate change. Civil disobedience and non-violent direct action were essential components in the repertoire of this grass-roots movement.

The turn in climate politics evident in Australia was particularly significant because it confronted the Conservative Coalition Government which had over a decade aligned with the Bush Administration's opposition to the Kyoto Protocol and opposed any initiatives to cut emissions that could disadvantage energy-intensive industries and the export-oriented resources sector, including coal and natural gas exports. Grass-roots activism flourished in the major capital cities, as well as in Newcastle where the port had developed into the world's largest coal export facility. Following the example of the metamorphosis of climate politics in Britain, the establishment of Climate Camps emerged as the most important development in the middle of the first decade of the new millennium. Climate Camp aimed to mobilise into a broad coalition the disparate array of climate activists and others desperate to see government implement progressive policies. In setting up in the vicinity of emissions-intensive enterprises or coal mines and coal-transport facilities, Climate Camp brought together people from diverse origins and political backgrounds to debate their wide-ranging concerns and the challenge of climate change, with a view to developing a community of solidarity and a praxis to contest the legitimacy of emission-generating enterprises and the poverty of government policy.

Diversity, reflecting much of the theoretical literature on social movements, tends to be a dominant characteristic of climate movements. This is evident in the differences in the origins of the personalities who join forces, and in their motivations and personal political beliefs. Diversity can be a rich ingredient in contributing to the dynamism of the new movement. It can also test the cohesion of the movement, and one of the features of the organising strategies of Climate Camp was the endeavour to engage this diversity in bringing people together to better understand the nature of the challenge to be confronted, the urgency of this challenge, and how to make the most of the potential in fostering a range of actions to contest the prevailing damaging emissions-generating activities, and the ideas and politics that underline these.

The Climate Camp project was a comparatively unique approach in the development of climate politics. Although similar actions involving a period of sustained protest and direct occupation of a site were not unheard of in Australia, especially in the anti-logging campaigns and the anti-uranium mining movement, like its British counterparts Climate Camp was premised on building larger communities of activists and injecting more momentum into climate politics.

Through the concerted endeavour to develop the confidence of individual participants and trust in one another, Climate Camp became a community of activists equipped to launch a number of strategic non-violent direct actions to block emissions-generating activities, and through these actions engage wider support for the cause. It was thus a quite distinctive moment in the development of climate politics, and one that we felt warranted critical scrutiny. While there have been a number of studies of Climate Camp, and most notably of those held in Britain, most of these do not really provide much critical reflection on the nature of the coalescence that was so critical for the Camp and how this shaped the political project. They generally do not explore the nature of activists' participation in Climate Camp and the development of the sense of community and solidarity that this engendered, nor the confidence in direct action as a political strategy that could drive efforts for some decisive action to mitigate the causes of climate change. It was this interest in the exercise of agency and praxis that aroused our intrigue in this political project. Here, in focusing on the stories of the many individuals in Climate Camp, we explore the dynamics in the making and unfolding of the political project.

Climate Camp – igniting a climate movement

Climate Camp was launched as a much-needed panacea for the failure of the environmental NGOs to make any headway in their lobbying efforts with the

Howard Government. As Samuel, a staffer with one environmental NGO, reflected:

> ... being an activist on climate change issues for quite a while and recognising for a significant proportion of that time that, um, the advocacy about climate change ... need[s] to step up a level because [of] the urgency of the situation, and the science of climate change is demanding a really strong and maybe even radical response ... the community needs to step up their action to make it clear to community leaders, business leaders and all levels of government that the action that they want to see is really strong.
>
> (Samuel, 2008a)

The urgency for meaningful action on climate change called for a new politics. A not uncommon refrain was that, 'it's an emergency, we have to do something about it now ... we have to sort this out now' (Beatrice, 2009). Fermenting a climate movement was seen as essential if the political landscape was to be transformed. Speaking at the Switch Off Hazelwood Climate Camp, Ben maintained that:

> ... I see it as part of building a movement. And I think to get real solutions we are going to have to build a movement of millions of people.
>
> (Ben, 2009b)

Alison was equally emphatic about the need to build this movement and Climate Camp was held up as a crucial vehicle in this project:

> ... we need a really strong people's movement that is making demands of decision makers ... It's gonna take everything that everyone, we need everyone working on climate change ... We need to be the biggest social movement that the world has ever seen ... I think Climate Camp is one of the first real big examples of that people's movement in action in, um, Australia. I think it has been in the UK, um, and in the US last year ... And so if you want any political response that is anywhere ... then we need to provide political cover – the strong demand from the citizenship of Australia – to say that nothing less than real action on climate change, nothing less than deep cuts to emissions. I think that Climate Camp is the perfect example to be doing that.
>
> (Alison, 2008b)

While there was unanimity on the need to forge a movement that could drive the demand for urgent action on climate change, the immediate challenge was that of establishing a forum that could accommodate the different motivations and ambitions of the climate change activists, while retaining the grassroots emphasis of the movement.

Building a climate politics community

Diversity was a defining feature of this new politics. The movement brought-together people with quite different experiences of involvement in political activity and campaigning. It engaged seasoned environmental campaigners, many of whom had been involved in campaigns against uranium mining or forest blockades. They were joined by 'tree-changers', people who were mapping lifestyles that minimised their ecological footprint. The resurgent climate politics attracted people who had never really been actively involved in a political movement before, such as Cathy, a mother of three young children and a CAG member, who went to Climate Camp in Newcastle. University students, many of whom were involved in campus-based environmental collectives and ASEN, and the students and others who were members of some of the small socialist groups or of anarchist groupings, were active contributors to building this new politics. Staff from some of the ENGOs also contributed to the making of this movement, as did members of trade unions and faith-based groups.

The diverse origins of those who joined Climate Camp were also reflected in the political philosophies or persuasions of individuals. According to an organiser of one of the Camps:

> we've got people, you know, who come from a Marxist political tradition, then there's anarchist political traditions, um greenies, hippies, ferals, you know, whatever, that whole mob all here together. And then just a lot of people who don't come from any political tradition and who are just citizens concerned about climate change. And there's been a bit of you know background work to try to smooth those differences and help them work together.
>
> (Alistair, 2008b)

This diversity was regarded as one of the great strengths of the emerging movement, evidence that the movement was open to newcomers and welcomed the exploration of new ideas:

> in terms of how I think about social change and policy issues and environmental issues I very much take the diversity approach that, you know, you need all sorts of people with different theories of change and different ways of working and different tactics and strategies working on the same kind of issues to achieve a really broad shift … That's not to say I don't come across tension in other people going 'You should be doing more of this, and less of that.' I mean I don't get that a lot … And so, I see tension, but it's not something that affects me personally.
>
> (Samuel, 2008b)

The tension that Samuel considered to be one of the corollaries of the diverse participants in Climate Camp did not, as he observed, necessarily detract from the effort to project a united front. Indeed, one of the organisational ambitions of Climate Camp was the way it sought to accommodate difference.

> ... even though at Climate Camp for example everyone had different ideas about how best to achieve change and what society they would like to live in. But they were all working towards it in their own way, and prepared to talk about it and come together to do this one big action together. And that's pretty amazing for me just that people can cooperate like that.
>
> (Harriet, 2008b)

Establishing a forum that could draw on different perspectives was regarded by some as one of the great strengths of Climate Camp as a movement. Different understandings of the nature of the challenges to be confronted could be discussed, and the various ways of responding to these challenges debated. While the site where the respective Camps were set up anticipated a particular campaign action that would likely be pursued, the diverse nature of participants opened up the possibility for a range of actions to be considered, and this was facilitated by the ways in which Climate Camp was organised.

The Climate Camp organisation

Following the British Climate Camp model, the Climate Camps established in Australia were organised around a multilayered structure. Within the campsite, a sense of community was based on setting up groups around *barrios* or neighbourhoods, which generally grouped activists according to their geographic origin, although particular communities were established in recognition of particular social characteristics or preferences such as queer members. The neighbourhood provided a space for participants to develop trust in their fellow members and to establish a space that maximised the opportunity for members to voice their opinions and ambitions and to debate issues and action.

As one of the organisers of one of the Camps explained, establishing communities in this manner would help individuals and groups bond with one another and thus establish solidarity among participants. Newcomers would find it easier to join with others, and the sense of solidarity could also provide a springboard for the continuing development and strengthening of the climate movement:

> ... the camping area is divided up into neighbourhoods. So basically we divided up the paddock into areas roughly similar to a map of Australia where people from Tasmania were camped over in this corner, and people next to them were the people from, you know, Victoria, and then the people from South Australia and so on. Um, the idea behind that was people who came to the camp from Victoria that may not have known the

other people from Victoria and if they were camping near each other it might give them an opportunity to get to know each other more and help build communities of action that can go home together from the camp and organise in their State and their own regions.

(Alistair, 2008b)

The effort to construct an inclusive environment was bolstered by setting up communal kitchens to cater for participants, and the principles of sustainability and minimising the Camp's carbon footprint were adopted. Such thinking reflected the determined effort to formulate and put into practice a climate sensibility. Included among many of those who expressed such sentiments were individuals and friends who adopted their established practices of minimising their ecological and carbon footprints. Climate Camp provided a vehicle for exploring these practices on a larger scale. Solar panels provided much of the Camp's energy requirements, and pit and compost toilets were set up.

Another crucial facet in developing a sense of community at Climate Camp was the organisation of workshops to canvass a broad range of issues. There were educative workshops that concentrated on debates around the science of climate change or the different climate change policies that were being introduced by governments. Some were conducted to introduce people who were just beginning to reflect on the issues, others to debate anticipated or alternative policy focuses. The workshops also provided an important space to consider possible campaign actions, underscoring the fostering of a political community.

... the workshops creates that nice, um, easier to enter environment ... to be able to allow people to learn more about climate change ... And to explore ideas about why they would want to take action, what kind of form that action might take, and sort of share and learn in that setting.

(Rosalind, 2008a)

The neighbourhoods were also critical for ensuring that the grass-roots character of the movement was the fulcrum around which the Camp was organised. They provided a reasonably intimate space for participants to develop and share their ideas as well as differences, and to discuss their involvement in Climate Camp. As Alison (2008a) described, this promoted trust and encouraged 'people to be self-determining. And that was really exciting.' The neighbourhoods also provided the arena in which action teams, or 'affinity' groups, could be formed. Affinity groups formed a crucial node for developing the multi-headed strategies for breaching the fence line of the export terminal, and supporting individuals to take part in civil disobedience. Within the neighbourhoods, affinity groups were formed with the intention of planning each group's role in direct action.

... we've worked with this idea called action teams, or convergences and social movements. It's termed affinity groups where people have formed into teams that have similar ideas about direct action and social change and they've organised together to do a particular thing on a day. So, for example, there was a group called Apocalypse Bloc who did an amazing job at the action – they were doing drumming, sort of visual distractions and theatre ... they were very strategic on the day, and they had a really good crew of people, they know what they were gonna do. They had a plan for the day and they did it really well.

(Alistair, 2008b)

The multiple spaces in climate camps enabled debate and openness, the sharing of ideas and differences, to shape an emergent climate action consciousness. This contributed to engendering a sense of purpose which did not presume a singular or homogenous form but provided for and accommodated diversity while acknowledging different capabilities and capacities among activists.

... climate change is such a huge issue, and there's so many ways you can target it ... So, it's kind of hard to rally around particular ways of campaigning ... I think it's always going to be stronger to have autonomous groups campaigning on issues that they care about and are excited about working on ... So I think there's a strength in diversity, and, um, that you can often do more if there are different groups asking for similar things instead of one group which is larger asking for one thing ... we're always trying to encourage people to take the initiative, start their own things, we can provide support, offer skill sharing, but now saying 'Here's a project for you to work on, go do it.'

(Kylie, 2009b)

The settled opinions of the neighbourhoods could be conveyed to the key decision-making forum of the Camp, the 'spokes council'. The convening of spokes councils each night at the Camp was an exercise in direct democracy, reflecting democratic principles within activist traditions dating back to peace and environmental protest camps in Australia in the 1970s (Margo, 2008a). Spokes councils provided a forum for discussing and cohering the Camp activities, from food, energy and waste tasks to the protests planned for the weekend. The model was enacted through groups positioning themselves in concentric circles. Discussion was convened by two facilitators. The innermost circle was constituted of one representative from each neighbourhood and/or 'action team', and behind them, these individuals were usually flanked by other groups' members, ready for quick caucusing. All camp participants and others were welcome to attend the councils, although it was the neighbourhood spokespeople who were given the floor to represent a given position on the issue of the moment on behalf of their neighbourhoods. Transparency in decision-making was a crucial feature of Camps.

Differences were openly debated and resolved as the council strove to ensure that decisions were arrived at by consensus, and this was one of the strengths of Climate Camp that endeared participants to the movement. For Rosalind, the Camp could accommodate an array of actions and retain the integrity of affinity groups:

> I see spokes councils as a really great model to use … it's not necessarily a decision-making body and each group is still able to do what they plan on doing, but it's kind of a space to come to some common agreements and dialogue and to kind of share information.
>
> (Rosalind, 2008b)

This is not to say that there were not some heated differences of opinion on, for instance, the causes of climate change and how these might be countered. There was a remarkable degree of amity.

> I think people generally had an idea of a vision at the time that everyone came together that sort of worked to a fair degree. And I think that there was a lot of tolerance shown where a lot of groups that things that were said wouldn't have been able to be tolerated so amicably.
>
> (Robert, 2008b)

Political differences could be accommodated to a degree within this model, according to many of the participants. Even those who seemed set on a more confrontational path

> … were listened to and dealt with by the mass of people there … harmoniously … and peacefully generated. There wasn't abuse, there wasn't immature responses … well developed responses that a society could base a lifestyle on.
>
> (Robert, 2008b)

However, there were some criticisms of this autonomous form of structuring debate and decision-making. The open forums aimed to give all a voice and to frustrate the potential for some political factions to shape council decisions, and this mode of organisation helped to block *entreeism*. Participants from Solidarity questioned the 'anarcho conceptualisation[s that fuelled] a reluctance to actually openly discuss and debate people's ideas around.' (Lillian, 2008b). There was a feeling among the socialist groups there was too much focus on developing direct action plans, and not enough attention being given to addressing bigger-picture political concerns. During the Newcastle Climate Camp, Solidarity sought to open up debate about the use of autonomous self-organised direct-action teams during the rally and planned occupation of the coal export terminal train line. They also argued for the Camp to produce a political statement on topical issues that year: energy privatisation in NSW, and the announcement of the climate policy green paper that same weekend. The green paper was the first detailed description of Labor's CPRS – the national carbon trading scheme (Commonwealth of Australia, 2008). The heated discussions this generated tested the decision-making structures of the Camp.

At the Newcastle Climate Camp there was confusion as to whether the spokes councils were decision-making bodies, or, as described by the organising collective and facilitators, a place where information is shared between autonomous groups, but no binding collective decisions are made. The rationale embedded in this was that the structure for organising instituted by the organising collective, and more broadly their framing of the protest, was not up for revision at that stage. In response to Solidarity's interjections about the final rally and occupation of the coal export terminal, the spokes council was unable to accommodate their calls for a full reappraisal of the Camp's strategy to use direct action and affinity groups for organising. However, a spokes council did agree to endorse a collective statement critiquing energy privatisation and the green paper. Here, the political traditions of autonomism and socialism came into tension with one another.

Personal empowerment as a key to the exercise of collective agency

The openness of the Climate Camp organisation model and the support mechanisms that were in place were regarded by many of the participants as being personally empowering, and this was crucial to igniting the momentum of the climate movement. The multiple layers of the organisation provided the spaces into which individuals could be initiated into communities, be given a voice and be listened to.

> I think collective organising is really empowering because it makes people feel listened to and feel that they can make a difference.
>
> (Harriet, 2008a)

> You get to feel empowered and you get to feel like you're the one making the calls on this.
>
> (Rosalind, 2008b)

Participants universally described how being able to discuss ideas for pursuing actions contributed to them developing the self-confidence and the confidence and trust in others that gave them the courage to take direct action:

> ... it was really exciting that there were these small self-organised teams who made a plan and changed their plan and were able to react to the circumstances. And I think that's [the] kind of strategic and reactive movement that we need.
>
> (Alison, 2008a)

The merit in this form of organising was that it opened up opportunities for individuals to decide on the kinds of participation they felt most comfortable in taking (Sarah, 2008b). There was no pressure or compulsion for individuals to be involved in actions that they felt uneasy about, and ensuring that individuals felt safe and comfortable in participating in actions was also a conscious objective of Climate Camp.

The space provided to encourage and support individual involvement in Climate Camp was not only personally empowering, it was also critical in developing the sense of solidarity that consolidated the collective enterprise. Climate Camp was a

> chance to learn a bit more about how I can be involved and meet like-minded people, and to get a bit of a sense that something is happening, that we can do positive action ... also to have my views nurtured and validated. So being again with a group of like-minded people so we can get an energy going together, build that big community.
>
> (Sarah, 2008a)

> Everybody came together and started, that energy, you know you knew everybody stood around you was on your side. They understood, and that was really empowering and energising.
>
> (Sarah, 2008b)

However, at least one member of one of the socialist groups that had participated in the Newcastle Climate Camp felt that there was too much emphasis on personal empowerment. With regard to direct action, Lillian 'felt like the clapping of people going over the fence and chaining themselves to the train was a bit about this individual heroism, which [she felt was] ... a bit strange about that dynamic'. Lillian argued that activists' references to Rosa Parks and Ghandi in their narration of the Climate Camp strategy tended to abstract these individual personalities from the collective mobilisations that stood behind them (Lillian, 2008b). Rather than affinity groups organising autonomously to breach the train line at different points, Solidarity argued for mass action, in practical terms, with the 1200-strong rally breaching the line together in one place, rather than spread out along the kilometre stretch.

Climate camp: coalescing and collective civil disobedience

Climate Camps were set up in locations to expose, confront and obstruct activities at emissions-intensive enterprises or coal facilities and to challenge the politics that sanctioned the energy-intensive and fossil-fuel based preoccupations. This was perhaps the most distinguishing feature of Climate Camp, setting this political strategy apart from all other campaigns and activities that had contributed to the invigoration of climate politics.

The sites selected were determined for a range of strategic reasons. The factor that was uppermost in the selection process was whether or not there were any plans or indications that a fossil-fuel intensive activity was about to be intensified or expanded, which was an obvious factor in the Newcastle actions and the Helensburgh Camp. The Hazelwood power-plant action had been launched in response to the State Government's decision to extend the life of the plant, in contravention of an earlier decision to close what was the biggest polluting electricity generating power station in Australia.

The principal object of Climate Camp was to pursue actions that directly challenged the legitimacy of activities that fuelled the carbon economy. Some participants, such as Samuel, who worked with an environmental NGO, clearly saw this as the overriding rationale for developing this form of expressing climate politics, although in his instance he saw the shift as supplementing the campaign efforts of ENGOs:

> I think collective action is obviously and has been the key to successful social movements and successful social change ... in relation to Climate Camp, non-violent direct action, civil disobedience is a critical element but it's a critical element among many other elements which are all equally important.
>
> (Samuel, 2008a)

Others looked upon Climate Camp as making a decisive break from the corporatist politics that had characterised the ENGOs' deliberations with Labor governments but which had proved completely moribund and politically emasculating over the course of ten years of conservative government.

The idea of bringing together a community of activists was moved by the conviction that the science of climate change pointed to the imminence of a crisis and the need to act. Robert (2008a) reflected the sentiments of many in articulating his thoughts: 'we are in a period of dangerous climate change already ... we're on the edge of a cliff' and this called for urgent action. In Robert's opinion, governments have a short-term vision, and 'collective action is an incredibly powerful method of changing politicians' views of the impact of global warming, and Climate Camp is part of it.' Reflecting back on her participation in the Newcastle Climate Camp, Beatrice (2009) was even more emphatic: ' ... a lot of people got involved because it's an emergency, we have to do something about it now ... ' And for all Climate Camp participants we interviewed, 'doing something' translated into a call for direct action, for adopting the tactics of civil disobedience and non-violent direct action that give people a voice.

> I think the direct action is essential. I don't think it's going to happen without direct action. You know I think that relying on some of the governmental processes like Copenhagen or even the Federal government setting realistic limits to carbon emissions, is highly problematic. I think

that often those arguments that happen in that sort of political arena around carbon trading, um, it is highly problematic, and that they're going to be pushed because that is what works best for industry.

(Vicky, 2009)

I think the civil disobedience part of it, like Climate Camp, is particularly important. I mean if it's symbolic it points to that just politely protesting is falling on deaf ears ... we need to do things which will make a difference.

(Ben, 2009b)

[D]irect action gives[s] people an avenue to express what they want ... [and this can be] fantastic.

(Cathy, 2008a)

[N]on-violent direct action ... it's a tried and tested ... people actually [signaling] with their feet and with their presence going to a point that is either seen as being part of a problem or directly is part of a problem and showing by numbers, and by what they do that they want to make change.

(Ruth, 2008a)

Direct action as a means of promoting climate politics

There were some differences of opinion within Climate Camp about the main rationale for launching direct actions. Exposing the connection between an emissions-intensive enterprise or coal exports and climate change by occupying a site or locking down on a coal train, was a spectacle that could attract the media and this could provide the prospect of the event being broadcast and thereby engage a wider audience. Some participants adopted a somewhat taciturn approach to adopting actions that played to the media, and there was a suggestion that this was a consideration among organisers:

> You know if you're running a campaign, you do some kind of direct action so that you get media attention in order to do something. In terms of a campaign plan, you think of it as a tactic.
>
> (Alistair, 2008c)

Others advocated a more careful and strategic engagement with how actions should be pursued in order to try to avoid the action being dismissed as the action of troublemakers:

> In terms of media coverage ... sometimes I think it can be why you've gotta be really careful because I think that, ah, sometimes it can work

against the cause, um, in that people can dismiss the action, dismiss the issue by saying that's just a bunch of angry individuals who wanna go and ... So it is really important to make sure that it's peaceful and, um, constructive, really constructive. And you have really intelligent spokespeople and people creating a really intelligent sort of argument for the media ... that's got to be handled really well because you do sometimes get angry people in activism and you can shoot yourself in the foot.

(Cathy, 2008a)

One of the activists who had participated in a number of non-violent direct actions in Newcastle suggested that a more sanguine assessment of media reporting on such the actions was warranted. The media, he argued,

tried wherever possible to exaggerate or make out as though there was some sort of violence. But my point is that every time that action was put in the media there was an ensuing clip about the environment and the problems associated with the environment and about global warming and the potential harm that was being caused. So, to me, there was a massive amount of media all around the country and even globally because of those action ... And whether the actions themselves were positive or negative even in the eyes of the media, the resulting media was putting a message across that climate change is happening and that it is dangerous. And that would not have happened if those actions didn't happen.

(Robert, 2008b)

Angus, too, recognised the fine line that had to be traversed if one of the purposes of direct action was to get a message through the media to the broader community:

I'm not sure. I think the spectacle of being on the news and that kind of thing, doesn't help [engage more people in the movement. ... However, in] some ways you have to have that because otherwise how are most people going to know it ever happened, but I don't think it helps to make people look at it and go 'Oh yeah, that's something that maybe I'll do next time.'

(Angus, 2008b)

For most, negative media did not matter because the environmental movement had exhausted all other efforts through the established political channels in trying to get some action on climate change. Civil disobedience and non-violent direct action seemed the only remaining course of action. Robert, who was an active parishioner in a local church and who would not describe himself as a radical, had prefaced his support for the campaigns waged by Rising Tide, maintaining that:

You know, I think society needs to turn away from the idea that you know, you be an upright little citizen and do as you're told and you know everything will be fine because we've already tried that. You know, the last generation's already tried that, and it's not working. Our world's falling apart. There's got to be a different way to do things.

(Robert, 2008a)

Ruth reinforced these sentiments:

[Direct action] might not be popular all the time. It might not be the best way to do it, but what is the best way? And how do we ever have a voice? If I was sitting here and, as Mrs concerned citizen, the planet's burning, what do I do? I can write letters to my local politician. I might even be able to go and see him. He'd pat me on the head and say 'On your way'. But what do I do to really affect everyone else who lives around me to get them to understand it, to hear the message?

(Ruth, 2008b)

Contesting the power relations of the carbon economy

Climate Camp was organised to concentrate the energies of the climate movement on bringing an end to the ambivalence, if not opposition, of government and corporations to adopting measures that would mitigate climate change.

... something needs to change. Um, governments and corporations are clearly not going to solve the problem for us, so it's up to people to take direct action, to shift the terms of allowable political debate, to put pressure on government and companies to really shift the agenda to try and avert climate change. And so I think that Climate Camp is a really exciting opportunity to get together, to learn, to build their confidence and skills in direct action, and to take direct action against the expansion of the coal industry in Newcastle.

(Alistair, 2008a)

This necessarily meant contesting the power relations that underpinned the carbon economy by directly challenging the expansion of coal mining and coal exports and the right of energy-intensive enterprises to continue to generate emissions.

I think that we often think about civil disobedience as a tactic ... But I think civil disobedience is best thought of, or most powerfully thought of, as a strategy, then the most powerful thing people can do is to engage in civil disobedience and say 'I'm no longer consenting to the government killing our planet and ruining our future.' And it poses a profound challenge to government when it grows. Not just one-off isolated events, but when you have large numbers of people systematically and regularly withdrawing their consent and questioning the authority of the state – it's very powerful.

(Alistair, 2008c)

As well, while considering that the government would play a necessary role in any moves to dismantle the carbon economy, many of those involved in Climate Camp adopted a somewhat circumspect approach to placing too much confidence in government to take the lead in adopting policies to decarbonise the economy. The state and government were not insulated from the power relations that underpinned the carbon economy, and the focus of civil disobedience was as much directed to challenging the role and legitimacy of government policy and the state more generally because the state was an institutional force in the construction of the fossil-fuel intensive industrial complex. Indeed, many activists at Climate Camp drew on a range of radical critiques of the state, and especially anarchist traditions, to argue that the legitimacy and role of the state was as much a target of direct action as the fossil-fuel installations. Some were quite explicit in arguing the need to avoid being caught in a trap that had rendered ineffectual the lobbying efforts, and ultimately the political force, of the environmental NGOs:

> I think sometimes even the environment movement can put too much emphasis on, um, governmental decision-making processes, on Copenhagen, and then when things like that fail, you can feel completely disempowered. And ... so I think actually making sure that there's a focus on 'we can make a difference on the street, we don't necessarily have to feed into government processes to do that. I think that is a really important aspect of it as well.

(Vicky, 2009)

As Fiona explained, the failure of government to act justified non-violent direct action, and a valid legal justification could be made for this. Civil disobedience was a case of legal necessity: 'it's sort of the concept that you had to break the law to stop greater evil taking place' (Vicky, 2009). And while there were those who were not so resolute in questioning the authority of the state, there was a general acknowledgement that non-violent direct action could well necessitate defying the law.

Climate Camp aimed to take control of the political agenda, and challenge the dominant and, hitherto emasculating, form of conducting climate politics by determining the ground on which the campaign would be played out:

> ... in a sense like I feel it's more proactive than following summits around the world ... Like it's kind of a little bit more on our terms. So that's one really exciting reason to come.

(Rosalind, 2008a)

While one of the main aims of Climate Camp was to mobilise participants in a mass action, Climate Camp councils invariably focused on coordinating a mass action to celebrate the culmination of a Camp. But this did not preclude the execution of a raft of smaller non-violent direct actions. Indeed, the grass-roots nature of the climate movement, the organisation of affinity groups or action teams, and the determination of some groups to assert their autonomous identity, injected a degree of anarchy and, for the police deployed to protect sites from being occupied, unpredictability and uncertainty as to how civil disobedience would unfold. On some occasions, a mass action masked other actions by small teams to lock down infrastructure, such as occurred at the Helensburgh Camp in December 2009 where police resources were mobilised to protect the Peabody mine site from being invaded. The concentration of policing on the entrance to the mine allowed another small team to lock down the coal loader at another local mine site. This highlighted the strategic advantage that could be had from organising around autonomous groups. In other instances, a combination of mass action and breakaway teams disrupted police efforts to contain protestors' ability to occupy transport infrastructure. At the 2008 Newcastle Climate Camp a phalanx of direct-action teams over-turned the capacity of the police to restrict the movement of protestors. As Angus indicated, what was seemingly an anarchistic, disorganised protest belied the fact that the chaos was a coordinated action (Angus, 2008b). And the success of the day's direct-action efforts was clear testimony to the self-confidence and trust in one another that made the affinity groups such potent forces.

Nor was the diversity among the participants and the different strengths and capabilities of affinity groups the only factors that shaped how the actions at Climate Camp would unfold. The spaces that were occupied were selected because of their iconic significance within the carbon economy, but, as a number of participants remarked, the sites chose the Camp: 'we're not entirely choosing the site, obviously we're in the largest coal exporting town in the world' claimed Rosalind, referring to the 2008 Newcastle Climate Camp (Rosalind, 2008a). And the actual site and target of protest influenced the character of the respective political projects. Just as the decisions as to where the British Climate Camps would be located were determined strategically, so this was also the case for Climate Camps in Australia.

The particular emissions-intensive or fossil-fuel enterprise that was the object of the campaign and the location of the site shaped the character of the campaign actions. Setting up Climate Camp at different sites confronted different aspects of the carbon economy, and forced different ways of engaging with fossil-fuel based and emissions-intensive processes. How this shaped campaigns and political discourse has been the subject of some debate in Britain, especially with respect to the different ways in which Climate Camp sought to engage the public around its actions in occupying a Heathrow Airport facility, in contrast with the Drax power station action.

The significance of the activity being called into question and the location of that activity was critical in how the campaign developed. An intriguing illustration of this was the 2009 Helensburgh Climate Camp to protest against the Peabody underground coal mine, which had recently had approved plans to extend the reach of the mine. Helensburgh is located about 45 kilometres south of Sydney, surrounded by the Royal National Park and Sydney's main water catchment area. The mine is a source of metallurgical, or coking, coal, which is used in the manufacture of steel. The township of Helensburgh has a population of some 5,000 and because of its location possesses a village-like atmosphere. Camp organisers selected Helensburgh as a site to conduct an action partly because members of the local community had formed a group, Rivers SOS, to draw attention to what they maintained were the deleterious effects of mining on the river systems and aquifers. The decision to set up a Camp at Helensburgh was also motivated by the fact that Peabody was the largest coal-mining company in the world, and a campaign to protest against the company and its planned expansion would highlight the transnational origins of climate change. This was a unique opportunity for fermenting a local campaign to protest against the environmental implications of coal mining, and it had obvious and fundamental global implications.

While the Peabody mine employs comparatively few members of the local community, the company went to some lengths to portray itself as a being an active supporter of community-based ventures, such as sporting facilities, so it was evident from the outset that there would be some opposition among locals to the Climate Camp project (Focus Group Participants, 2009a). Camp organisers were very mindful of this, and invested a lot of effort in working within the local community to debate climate-change concerns. Regular information stalls were set up in the shopping precinct, houses were leafleted, and open public forums held to debate the issues.

Despite all of these efforts, there was a counter-Camp protest involving a large number of the local community, who lined the street with placards as the Climate Campers marched towards the mine entrance. Alistair was not the only Camper to observe that ' ... there was quite a lot of angry people there, quite a lot of frustration that was clearly on display' (Alistair, 2009). The mood was indeed quite testing and there was what might be regarded as aggressive action against the Camp marchers when teenagers began throwing eggs and fruit in the direction of the mine entrance where many Camp participants had sat down in silent protest.

The event threw up some divisions in the movement, some questioning whether there had been enough preparatory work to engage the community, even though there had in fact been a substantial amount of groundwork carried out. Others argued that not enough thought had gone into selecting the site given that the mine produced coking coal for steel making rather than the thermal coal for power stations.

And, yet, there were some positive reflections on the experience among Camp participants. Cathy (2009) described an exchange with one of the residents who took issue with the Camp as being a polite and respectful con-versation. The resident queried 'How am I going to feed my kids if I don't, if I stop mining? Why do I have to bear the brunt of change [were the mine to be closed]?' Cathy responded by telling him that her family had made the decision to live on less, that they had made a choice to reduce their carbon footprint, and that everybody makes those choices. She thought that the exchange had prompted some rethinking: 'then a little while later, you could see something went clunk, and he just sort of said "okay". And he was very respectful and he was a really nice guy.' The Camp did manage to engender some quite constructive dialogue about climate change and the challenges this presented, as discussions with some members of the Helensburgh community revealed after the event (Focus Group Participants, 2009b).

In a further reflection, as one local activist observed, some of the aggression displayed by teenagers towards Campers was not out of the ordinary:

> [T]hose problems that occurred at Climate Camp between local kids and Climate Camp, they're occurring in Helensburgh anyway, and it's pretty well reported about there being a bit of a problem in Helensburgh. And those kids were just really grateful they got some variety in who they could target for a weekend.
>
> (Josh, 2009)

Josh elaborated further:

> The mining company went out of its way to put misinformation around Helensburgh, but a lot of people in Helensburgh either don't care or know that's rubbish, and then there was the element who were quite angry about Climate Camp ... I think there was just a redneck element combined with a mischievous effort from the company on that front.
>
> (Josh, 2009)

One of the Camp participants, who was responsible for setting up the solar panels and who had stayed behind at the Camp when the march was being held, had a quite animated discussion with young teenagers who had ridden into the Camp site on their BMX bikes. He described how bored they said they were. There was very little do to occupy their weekends, and they had just been out to have some fun. Contrary to the negative assessments of many at the Camp, he was quite happy to argue that there were some positives in his exchanges with the local teenagers as they expressed interest in why he had set up the solar panels, and he felt this had put climate change on their agenda and given them something to think about (Angus, 2009).

The six-day Climate Camp in Newcastle had a more tangible outcome. The actions, which ranged from incursions onto the site and lock-ins, culminated in the protest that stopped the transport of coal by rail. The success of this well-orchestrated event could be measured in terms of the reduction in the magnitude of coal exports, down by 18 per cent over the week, which was equivalent to removing every car from the road in Australia for one day. There was a not dissimilar outcome from the Climate Camp gathering which involved hundreds of people assembling on the shores of Lake Liddel, near Newcastle. This Camp, which was organised by Rising Tide and its extended network from 1 to 5 December 2010 to protest against the proposed new Bayswater A power station, concluded with the occupation and blocking of the coal rail infrastructure. Such local actions had quite concrete global implications.

By contrast, the September 2009 'Switch Off Hazelwood' Climate Camp action in East Gippsland in Victoria confronted a large police contingent which prevented protesters from breaching a temporary perimeter fence that circled the power station. The operators of Hazelwood were issued with a 'Community Decommission Order', but the symbolism of this was overshadowed by a police contingent that was well prepared to block all attempts to break through the perimeter fence. The 'Switch Off Hazelwood' Camp highlighted the preparedness of the State Government to pull out all stops to defend the continued generation of electricity from this highly polluting power plant. Legislation passed in 2009 that criminalised non-violent direct action and empowered police to disperse and arrest protestors, the *Electricity Industry Amendment (Critical Infrastructure) Act 2009*, illustrated the measure of what this new climate politics was up against.

Conclusion

A sense of urgency to act in the face of government intransigence and the ever-increasing mining and export of coal was the catalyst that prompted efforts to raise the intensity of the struggle against climate change. The adoption of civil disobedience, of non-violent direct action, was considered crucial to shifting the momentum of climate politics, and Climate Camp became a crucial vehicle for pursuing this goal. Climate Camp provided the forum for drawing together a coalition of people from diverse backgrounds and mobilising activists committed to exploring an antagonistic politics that confronted and challenged the status quo.

This marked a shift in campaigning around climate concerns not simply because it broke with an emphasis on lobbying and one-off displays of popular sentiment characterised by, for example, the annual 'Walk Against Warming' event. Climate Camp provided the space for concentrating collective energies on targeting particular iconic sites, coal-fired power stations and coal facilities over an extended time frame.

This focus on particular sites made more concrete the rationale for campaigning, and the opportunity for action to have a tangible effect by contesting and even trying to block the emission-generating activities or the transport of coal. Climate Camp was personally empowering, and through civil disobedience actions provided a means for individuals to physically express their desire to decarbonise the economy. Even when direct action at a particular site had not successfully slowed down or blocked the emissions-generating enterprise, participants could still contend that there were grounds to regard the action as affirming:

> We didn't necessarily close down Hazelwood, but that doesn't mean we failed. It means that we've done an amazing thing ... that really has to be held on to.
>
> (Vicky, 2009)

After all, the success or otherwise of Climate Camp could not be measured simply in terms of the actions launched at a particular site. In drawing attention to emissions-generating activities, the direct actions projected the concerns about climate change into the public arena:

> ... our movement has been successful in getting climate change on the agenda – and let's remember, you could probably three years ago ... climate change wasn't on the agenda ... So that was an achievement that I think we need to recognise.
>
> (Margo, 2008b)

The campaign strategy had to be seen in terms of the broader struggle:

> ... even with sort of, Hazelwood or Climate Camp, it's like there's been so many actions worldwide leading up to fucking Copenhagen that clearly demonstrate that people are highly concerned about this and its incredibly serious ...
>
> (Vicky, 2010)

And, it would be a mistake to measure the success of Climate Camp in terms of the individual events because Climate Camp was a project organised at different sites within individual countries as well as globally. The camps were generally not envisaged as one-off events, yet as a political project it was not clearly formed.

> ... even sort of without a unifying campaign, or whatever, we have done a lot of stuff that has changed the political landscape in many ways ...
>
> (Cathy, 2009)

Moreover, it was recognised that the individual campaign focuses would not alone be transformative. There was quite obviously considerable resistance to winding back the carbon economy which, after all, is what inspired the movement, and change could not be expected to come immediately. Transforming the entrenched emissions-intensive model would require perseverance and persistence, and the Climate Camp project, if it was going to have any political traction, required sustained mobilisations, if the systemic nature of the challenge was going to be successfully confronted.

> ... I think that, um, you know, ... we aren't going to win the change we need overnight. We have got to be in it for the long haul and people need to come up with whatever strategies work for them to stick with it.
>
> (Alistair, 2009)

However, acknowledging that the new climate politics could, at best, effect only gradual change sat somewhat awkwardly alongside the sense of urgency that had incited the shift in political momentum. There was thus an inherent tension in the Climate Camp project that tested the climate movement's capacity to sustain the involvement of activists. This was especially so when the momentum of the movement depended so much on a campaign focus defined in terms of civil disobedience and non-violent direct action, and which, as occurred in Victoria, simply resulted in the government becoming more resolute in defending the carbon economy by shoring up its powers to limit the exercise of the non-violent direct-action project. One could detect a measure of impatience in Cathy's observation that there was an expectation that something more tangible should have emerged out of the Climate Camp project:

> I think these things take time. I know we don't have a lot of time. Hmmm ...
>
> (Cathy, 2009)

There was next to no critical reflection on how the Climate Camp project would unfold, when so much energy was concentrated on the movement, defined in terms of challenging the right of particular enterprises to maintain their emissions-generating activities through non-violent direct actions. As one participant in Climate Camps perceptively reflected:

> Grass-roots action without someone running a political strategy is generally unsustainable. Generally, everyone turns up, gets pushed around, gets tired and goes home. And if there's no-one pushing that further, and it's a fairly thankless task pushing it further, 'cause you're not going to get everything you want unless you're very, very good, or they're very, very afraid of what the grass-roots people will do, in terms of the political ramifications and the support the grassroots people have.
>
> (Josh, 2009)

The decision by Britain's Camp for Climate Action to disband in 2011 seemed to suggest that as a political project Climate Camp had run its course. In announcing the decision to disband, the Camp website declared that the project had matured and it was time 'to launch new radical experiments to tackle the intertwined ecological, social and economic crises we face' (Van der Zee, 2011). While the declaration put a positive spin on the decision to fold the project, an Australian counterpart was much less sanguine in his assessment:

> I think at the moment what we've got is this real frustration where, there's public awareness and concern over climate change, has really ... increased significantly, and we haven't seen the institutional changes, and the policy changes to reflect that. And I think that it's quite a disempowering moment for the movement ...
>
> (Alistair, 2009)

The critical challenge remained that of building a movement that 'is stronger than the power of vested interests'. As the politics of the campaign around the Hazelwood power station had demonstrated, this necessarily meant confronting the government commitment to the carbon economy, and one of the ambivalences of Climate Camp was the ambivalence around the role of government and the state. Direct actions were intended to challenge government policies that underpinned the expansion of coal mining and energy-intensive enterprises, as well as the legitimacy of the state more generally. And yet there was also a predisposition to regard action as bringing sufficient pressure to bear on governments to effect policy changes.

7   Alternatives and Policies

As the climate movement translates its hopes into agendas for political change it enters a realm of 'practical' politics. Here the magnitude of climate crisis encounters the constraints and limits of the political process. The initial default position, from pragmatic NGOs, has been a call for climate action, by whatever means are available. The call is at once unifying and depoliticizing, in terms of avoiding any question of which approach or mechanism is to be preferred. As a call to action it can have the effect of silencing any dissent as potentially creating disunity. Yet denying the need to make political choices, and to campaign for them, serves the politically powerful. If the single unified demand to the authorities is to 'cut emissions', then any measure to do so will be devised in such a way as to serve powerful interests in society. Unfortunately, this logic was made painfully clear from 2007 as the formal political process produced its own answers to the climate crisis in the form of a 'price on carbon', and thereby drastically undermined public support for meaningful climate action. In the context of policy failure, several of the less pragmatic NGOs began arguing the proposals were 'worse than nothing'. Denial of politics in this respect had proved signally counterproductive.

The 'radical' climate movement that we engage with here displays these depoliticising tendencies, but also seeks to break from them and develop a common strategy. In doing so, it confronts some of the key political problems of climate action, and addresses the question of what kind of mechanisms will achieve it. This chapter discusses alternatives and policies projected by activists through a two-part lens of 'problems' and 'mechanisms'. In terms of problems, activists cite the urgent and abstract nature of climate crisis as defining a particular politics for the climate movement, marking it out as a significant departure from other social movements. The debate about mechanisms, by contrast, tends to reflect longer-running ideological debates between preferred sites for political change.

Disagreements over which social institutions can achieve the required changes pose a broadly community-centred approach, against market-centred and government-centred approaches. Community-centred advocates, what we term 'communitarians', are generally opposed to making claims on government and instead focus on constitutive politics and prefigurative initiatives.

Those who put faith in markets, in alternative consumer sovereignty and the emergence of new modes of economic relations, take a more 'economistic' approach, and tend to posit the need for a groundswell to transform economic relations. Those focused on governments share 'statist' assumptions and view social-movement political activity as pressurizing for changed policies, as an instrument for policy change.

Across these three domains we found a strong tendency to default from communitarianism and economism into a pragmatic form of statism. Where transformation of the community and economy fails to meet the urgent need for emissions reduction there is a slide into accepting government action as better than nothing. The key challenge for the movement, we argue, is then to define a radical programme for government action, capable of healing the metabolic rift, for a post-growth society, beyond capitalism-as-we-know-it.

From urgency to strategy?

Unlike most social movements, people are not directly experiencing the climate problem they are trying to address. Yet at the same time there is an overbearing urgency for action. These two factors together produce a sharp dilemma for activists, as one NGO representative argued:

> I think for me one of the biggest issues is the lag between the, what the science is telling us what people actually experience … by the time we do experience these things as an absolute crisis that is experienced by a critical mass of people, um, well a lot of the science is telling us we've already gone past a lot of these sort of threshold points where various devastating things happen. So I see that as an enormous political challenge.
> (Bradley, 2009)

The combination of minimal experiential immediacy with powerful temporal immediacy militates against the development of longer-term strategic capacity. Here we discuss how climate activists approach these issues, in terms of seeking strategy in the face of urgency, and finding material immediacy in the context of an abstracted climate crisis.

In the first instance the key political barrier to climate action is the power of vested interests. The failure to achieve effective action is read as a failure of the political system: 'You know, we live in a democracy, in theory, so in theory we should be able to just elect people who are going to do the right thing. But that's just not how politics works. And there are so many vested interests, very powerful vested interests of the fossil fuel industry' (Alistair, 2008a). The power of vested interests is, ironically, enabled by the abstracted and systemic challenge posed by climate change. As Josh (2009) argued, climate change is particularly abstracted from day-to-day experience – 'you can't see it in the same way you can see a tree being felled' – but at the same time the science of climate change is all-encompassing and apparently unremitting in its downward slide, creating 'a distinct urge in everybody to want to not believe in it. I'd like to not believe in it.'

As reflected in the earlier discussion in Chapter 5, the urgency of climate change can create political stasis. As NGO representative Tim suggested, climate change seems 'like this insurmountable problem: you get this danger of oscillating between apathy and denial, and being completely paralysed' (Tim, 2009). Apathy, arising from a sense of powerlessness, is the key issue for activists to address. All social movements face this problem, but climate change imposes a premium for disengagement. To counter this, climate pragmatists habitually resort to scientific necessity as a political imperative. In this context, climate science is often deployed as a substitute for political strategy, as delivering a universalising message to galvanize the movement.

The assertion of necessity, though, suppresses internal debates that may, themselves, enable the movement to gain a transformative capacity. Cathy is particularly concerned about dogmatism from 'evangelical' advocates of techno-science. The frustration was palpable, and very damaging to the movement: 'there are people who have a complete technological focus on the solutions who will just argue and argue and argue and just, I think, show an incapacity to see the bigger picture and not realise that they're just burning everybody out with this stuff' (Cathy, 2009). The techno-scientific discourse had defined climate politics as a place apart from politics 'as normal'. As Beatrice put it:

> It feels like this isolated thing that you go and do climate activism, it doesn't feel that related to other activism which is maybe affected by similar things, it doesn't feel that related to people's lives generally. Like it feels like a box that you go and do things in.
>
> (Beatrice, 2009)

Positioning climate action as a requirement of the science is commonplace. Clearly this reflects a desire to rise above more mundane political concerns, but in doing so climate activists cancel out political content. As Harriet argued:

> I think a lot of people are so freaked out about climate change, that they don't want to have to deal with ... making really drastic changes to our social structure because they think it will put people off and will divide us, we don't have time to be divided, and we don't have time to not encourage more and more people to join this movement. And I can totally sympathise with that, but I do think we are [at] risk of having a slightly meaningless movement ... it seems like we shy away from a lot of the important discussion.
>
> (Harriet, 2009)

Several interviewees linked self-censorship to the rhetoric of urgency, reflecting on how debilitating this can be for movement development. Lillian, for instance, argued there was a 'major confusion' among activists over 'who's responsible, and what a solution looks like, or what sort of solutions look like,' and at the same time, she felt there was 'a reluctance in the movement to actually openly discuss and debate people's ideas' (Lillian, 2009). Nevertheless, after two years of mobilisation, she found

> some people are coming to a point where they do want to have the discussion about what kind of movement, what kind of politics, what kind of campaign, and I think that's taken a couple of years but I think that's a good place, it's a positive place.

Yet, some argued against the idea that a unified strategy was possible, or even desirable. Here we find a strong pluralist undercurrent in the movement. Alison (2009), for instance, argued for dialogue, for debate across the alternative approaches, stressing 'there are lots of people trying to figure out how do we negotiate those worldviews and those different theories of change, and work together as a movement'. The objective, for her, was not to arrive at a common strategy, but to achieve mutual understanding. Along with many other interviewees, she emphasised political diversity and the different roles played by different players in the movement, from community education to direct action, arguing there 'is no one right way' (Alison, 2009).

This assertion of diversity against a single strategy is commonplace. The sheer scale of the task – of reducing greenhouse gas emissions to acceptable levels – drives a perspective that calls for comprehensive action at multiple levels and in multiple ways. From the perspective of diversity, all climate action geared to reducing emissions is by definition desirable. As Samuel argued, climate crisis

> requires recognition and willingness to address the problem right across the global community and down to an individual and right up to an institutional level whether that be governments or corporations.
>
> (Samuel, 2008b)

This suggests a demand for individual and household commitments as well as government and international policy change. The nature of that change is not a concern, provided it delivers emission reductions. Those arguing for diversity see it as a political unifier. Samuel favours a

> diversity of techniques that will allow us to reach the broadest audience possible, which is what we need to achieve what we want to achieve with climate change.
>
> (Samuel, 2008a)

Deliberate eclecticism may be designed to sidestep political disagreements and enable mobilisation, but in doing so it is deliberately apolitical and can ignore the power structures that render some solutions viable and others unimaginable. Those from a socialist perspective most often argued the need for a shared political agenda, stressing that any shared strategy would require some shared analysis of power structures, and sources of agency. As Ben argued, at the most basic level 'you have to have some idea of how you're going to bring about change to want' (Ben, 2009b). Lillian agreed, arguing against the notion that it was sufficient for the movement to say 'if you're against climate change come and take non-violent direct action' (Lillian, 2008b).

To a large degree, the absence of a political agenda for transformation was tactical, reflecting a desire to avoid political dispute, but it also reflected the weakness of political critique in the movement, and the absence of consensus amongst climate activists around a positive alternative agenda. At its worst, embracing diversity had become code for not challenging neo-liberal climate policy. Lillian (2009) argued, 'there is a real confusion about what needs to be done within the movement.' Some favoured pricing reform such as through carbon taxes or carbon trading, others were focused on technical solutions such as renewable energy, some were saying the community was the solution, and were actively anti-state. Lillian expresses personal surprise at support for carbon trading which is, for her, quite clearly a 'neo-liberal attack'; the capitulation to neo-liberal reform by the movement is seen as an indication of 'how far the right has won', demonstrating the need 'to start rebuilding in the politics of the environment movement' (Lillian, 2009). However, it would be an exaggeration to say an appreciation for the need to move beyond neo-liberal prescriptions did not exist. For instance, Margo reflected on the challenge of sustaining popular movement for climate action after the first flurry of movement activity, and in the context of the financial crisis.

> Now the challenge is how you keep that impact going. Because people have so many pressures in their life like now with the economic debacle, but I'm hoping that we can use this economic crisis to highlight if we're going to solve the economic crisis we can't go back to the old neo-liberal ways. This is the opportunity to meet the challenge of climate change, meet the challenge of peak oil, and meet the challenge of reorganising society. I'm hoping there are people who can bring that message forward.
>
> (Margo, 2008 #600)

The drama of reaching a weak international agreement in the UNFCCC Copenhagen Accord December 2009 had accentuated the depoliticizing tendency as it had mobilised people but negated strategy. Alistair (2009) argued that from 2006 'there was this real awakening to the urgency of climate change ... [that] scared the living daylights out of people': people began believing that if Copenhagen failed in 2009 'then we're all toast'. The campaign redubbing the Copenhagen Summit as 'Hopenhagen' could not have been more apposite. In the rising upsurge, Alistair recalls, we tried to change the world in a year ... [and] ignored our experience as organisers and suspended disbelief and just tried to achieve what we knew was utterly impossible. You know, you need to be ambitious with campaigning, I'm not saying you shouldn't be really ambitious, but you kind of need to have some sense of reality as well ... it was really feeling that if we don't turn the world upside down by December, then, we might as well give up.

(Alistair, 2009)

The loss of political bearings was understandable, but counter productive: the movement needed long-term strategy and perspective to sustain involvement and to make solid gains. Urgency had to be managed politically, or it could morph into a blind, ill-considered panic, and become destructive.

In this conundrum the key question for activists (as posed by the interviewer in one of the interviews) is how to strategise for the long haul while mobilizing people around the necessity for urgency. Campaigning for an agreement at international summits was counterproductive. As Vicky argued, the focus on Copenhagen was simply unstrategic, a case of 'working towards something that actively disempowers you' (Vicky, 2010).

The insistence of urgency was not simply disempowering, it was also alienating. Several interviewees argued it had generated a kind of arrogance and disregard for others. Susie (2009a) said that some had an 'attitude of "we know what's best for you" kind of thing ... It just still felt kind of awkward.' Reflecting in late 2009 after a period of moving away from climate activism, Beatrice (2009) felt the urgency for action created 'a kind of callousness to how we do things'. Invoking an emergency produced a kind of activist elitism, 'a kind of attitude of knowing what's best and telling people what's best and not having enough time to listen to people properly'. Exacerbating this, the movement had attracted relatively privileged people, comfortable with expert-based knowledge centred on abstract targets and statistics. The result, when faced with people directly employed in the coal industry, was telling: 'There was a lot of talking down to people, not really listening ... being very dismissive, not being very prepared to think about what people were saying.' The insight, that climate activists were, when pushed, not necessarily as progressive as they considered themselves to be, is incisive and highly self-critical. Beatrice ends with the devastating statement that people were simply 'childish and not compassionate,' that 'there was something selfish about what we were doing' (Beatrice, 2009).

The hierarchy was internal as well as external. Community-based CAGs were often assumed to be more conservative, what one interviewee described (with intended but revealing irony) as the 'tennis club committees for either climate emergency, or tennis club committees for climate totalitarianism, or tennis club committees for the global revolution' (William, 2009). CAG members were assumed to be foot soldiers; as confirmed by William, there had been a conscious 'process of politicising CAGs to get them to feel comfortable with direct action' (ibid.). Others argued that extending participation through the CAGs would take the movement beyond 'a traditional grass-roots activist space' to engage 'the more conservative areas of the climate movement' (Samuel, 2008b). In this formulation a value hierarchy is drawn between established climate activists as 'the grass roots', and the community-based action groups as conservative allies. For some, avoiding debate about strategy compounded the disrespect, both of 'allies' and the wider public: NGO representative Ashley (2009) reported a generally held 'assumption, which is wrong, that people say "oh we need everyone to be involved, so we won't say anything that might offend people."'

From abstract to concrete action?

The abstract logic of climate change also imposes another burden on climate activists, that of sufficiently animating the issue amongst people who generally cannot experience it. Several interviewees stressed the success of the movement in putting climate change on the political agenda, but argued that this begged the question of how to act on that agenda. Margo, for instance, stressed the central agenda-setting role of the movement:

> [I]f we had not have had the actions against the coal industry, the walk against warming, people running the stalls, the petitions, all that sort of thing, the Government and the Coalition could ignore climate change … it's on the public agenda because there has been so much public outcry about it.
>
> (Margo, 2009)

In terms of shaping the response, though, the movement had been found wanting. Several activists acknowledge the difficulty of not making specific demands. Rosalind stressed the need for coordination to achieve transition, but also the lack of required political knowledge, 'To be honest I really don't know how we're going to do it, I would really like to have the blueprint [laughs] on the way forward and how we coordinate that' (Rosalind, 2008c).

There was a strong consensus amongst interviewees that the climate movement had to focus on the extraction and burning of fossil fuels, rather than on the abstract concept of carbon pollution and carbon policy. Margo's comments are representative of this broad position:

> Our federal and our State governments have such a head-in-the-sand approach to the coal industry, it really is business as usual, there's so many new coal mines opening up, particularly in the Hunter, and that's just exporting tonnes and tonnes of climate change basically. Every tonne of coal that goes overseas is going to come back and impact on us as well as the rest of the world.
>
> (Margo, 2009)

Several interviewees argued that the key contribution of the climate movement was to focus attention onto the material causes of climate change, and
in particular the coal industry, as against abstracted policy proposals. Margo,
for instance, made a very strong argument for forcing a focus on coal:

> You can't be serious about climate change in this country if you're not
> coming up with a plan about ending coal mining and having no new coal
> mines, to be moving away from coal-fired power plants, that really has to
> be the direction we need to go in.
>
> (Margo, 2008a)

Margo observed that through protest actions the movement had played a role
in contributing to the public awareness of climate change, and in turn eliciting
a governmental response, but the ongoing challenge was to extend the political focus to the coal industry (Margo, 2008b). Samuel (2008b) agreed,
describing the future of coal as 'the critical battleground in Australia': the
climate movement needed to focus on this objective, stating clearly that the
coal industry had to be superseded, and so 'completely turn around this thing
about being able to bring the coal industry with us as we deal with climate
change.' Reflecting on these issues in the wake of the failed international and
national policy process, Alistair argued that a shift to refocus on coal was
in the offing, the movement would soon 'move on from contesting the CPRS
to things like stopping new coal plants being built and you know really
practical things like that.' This would be a positive step, away from 'this eso-
teric area of economic instruments and complex policies,' and instead to focus
on actual sites of emissions (Alistair, 2009). Rather than debating the
merits of taxes and emissions trading, the movement would be forcing public
debate on substantive outcomes, such as

> are we building a wind turbine or are we building a coal plant? Are we
> building a solar thermal power station or are we starting a new coal
> mine? Just, you know, into the real world, which I think will be a good
> thing.
>
> (Alistair, 2009)

More broadly, direct climate action is itself seen as translating climate concerns into material contexts. Reflecting this, there is sustained reflection on
the implications of mobilisations, a learning through doing. Alistair, for
instance, stated that the first Australian climate camp was not a game changer,
yet started a process of political education:

> It wasn't a mind bomb. It wasn't something like planes flying into the
> Twin Towers and suddenly everyone around the world wakes up and it's a
> different world. And the terms of public debate around a whole range of
> issues are just shifted. Climate Camp wasn't a mind bomb like that. But it

was part of a process I think of telling the story that people, individual people have got responsibility and power to change the world.

(Alistair, 2008c)

Another interviewee reflected on the political leverage the first Climate Camp gained in being timed accidentally with developments in the Federal politics of climate policy, along with some media capacity to exploit this. The camp, he argued, raised a question about coal that had been absent from the debate, contrasting a 'kind of technical, complicated fix to climate change' with coal production as 'the source of the problem', dramatically highlighted by a

whole bunch of people, a very large number of people out there in the community who realise that this problem is so urgent and this is the root of it, that they're prepared to be arrested, protest, create social disruption.

(Samuel, 2008b)

Concrete actions had allowed for reflection, and activists drew some significant conclusions comparing the politics of the Newcastle Climate Camp and the later Helensburgh event. One issue was the relationship between conservation issues and climate change, which were assumed by many to be complimentary in the Helensburgh case but proved to be in tension, with conservationists arguing for mitigating measures to protect water catchments, while climate activists demanded the closure of the mine in its entirety. As one activist stated: 'I felt like we were pulling in a couple of different directions.' There were parallel tensions over the question of whether mining for metallurgical coal in the Illawarra was the best target given the claim that 'such coal is needed to fire the blast furnaces that produce high-tensile steel needed for … renewable energy.' As one interviewee put it, Helensburgh was 'murky' compared with other targets that more clearly posed the question of coal-fired power. Targeting metallurgical coal posed difficult questions, 'I mean anyone knows if you're going to create the public transport … as well as windmills, turbines, you need steel to make it' (Lillian, 2009). There were further concerns as to whether the Illawarra was politically prepared for a Climate Camp. Unlike in Newcastle there had been no sustained climate activism targeting Illawarra coal (Margo, 2009).

In the context of failing climate policy the movement was seeking to overcome policy inertia by targeting weak links in the coal industry that could relatively easily be delegitimised to undermine reliance on fossil fuels. Clearly the responsibility was a heavy one, and the focus for intense reflection when actions are found to be less than effective.

These political difficulties reflect a wider weakness of shared political analysis. Common agreement on the need to close down coal mines and coal-fired power stations could substitute for a more rigorous political vision. In the process, again, it becomes easy to abstract the immediate demand for no new coal mines, for instance, from the context that is driving the coal boom. Coal mining is a clearly not an end in itself, but a symptom of much wider structural logic. The movement needed a political strategy to address this structural logic, otherwise it is condemned to firefighting and palliative band-aids. Even if the movement is successful at the sectoral level, the underlying problem can be displaced elsewhere, for instance from thermal coal into coal seam gas, or 'natural' gas, or nuclear energy. As the movement subsequent to 2010 has focused more directly on halting fossil fuel extraction and burning it has certainly found new allies and new political traction. Such initiatives, though, are in danger of fetishising fossil fuels as the cause and solution to climate change when the crises are in fact much wider and engage much broader questions of structural transformation.

An example of this problem was the patent horror amongst climate activists when they realised their activism was legitimising the 'dash for gas', including coal seam gas, as Australia's fossil fuel of choice. The blunt demand for 'climate action now', without a strategy of how to achieve it, helped produce a carbon pricing mechanism whose principal purpose and effect was to boost gas. The resulting 'gas rush', as the Australian Broadcasting Corporation put it, is now exposed as emitting considerably more greenhouse gasses than is routinely claimed, and as having serious impacts on water supplies (ABC, 2011). As one climate activist said in an online forum, 'my god what have we done?'

Mechanisms for climate action

There is considerable disagreement amongst climate activists about the required mechanisms to address climate change. These disagreements reflect different assessments of the effectiveness of the various mechanisms, and also different political preferences. Indeed, the debate over the three main mechanisms analysed here – communities, economies and states – reflects wider ideological debates. The focus on communities is strongly influenced by the autonomist political tradition, which has traditionally embraced a model of society free from economic and political power, and expressed in freely determined community relations. This tradition is overlaid with a less radical ecological communitarianism that privileges civil society and embraces autonomous and participatory community-level action to achieve sustainable outcomes. These two tendencies feed into the broad 'communitarian' mechanism, as discussed here. The contending argument that economic forces, properly directed, can carry the required climate transition is a weaker tendency, but no less significant given its dominant status in wider climate policy debates. Activist arguments for consumer sovereignty on climate, for instance, seek to strategically engage with the pervasive neo-liberal underpinnings of official climate policy.

By the same token, critical positions taken by activists on the question of economic measures, for instance to achieve a 'just transition', reveal a strong liberal reformist tendency where communities are supported by government.

Finally, those emphasising the need for state action on climate draw on social democratic and socialist traditions in arguing for state intervention to, respectively, reform markets or ultimately overcome them. From the statist perspective, the community- and economy-focused measures are by definition inadequate: rather than relying on indirect mechanisms, statists argue that action on climate change requires state intervention to directly reduce greenhouse gas emissions.

The debate between these three main mechanisms reflects the extent to which climate activists are embedded in wider debates about social change. Clearly activists come into the movement with pre-existing assumptions, and these are reflected in the political preferences discussed here. Whether activists are engaged on climate action because it is simply the latest means to challenge the status quo, or whether they are engaged solely as climate activists, they still bring their political assumptions to the process of mobilisation. What is perhaps not surprising is the extent to which these political assumptions fall into pre-existing categories. Yet in many respects, as discussed here, activists are required to reconfigure existing political traditions for the climate age. As argued in the Conclusions, this suggests that a more thorough rethink of political categories becomes necessary with the transformation in political agency entailed by anthropogenic climate change.

Climate communitarianism

The ethical political imperatives of climate change can produce a form of expressive communitarianism that is by definition non-strategic, or even anti-strategic. As the primary purpose is to express a set of values, rather than to achieve a policy goal, for instance to reduce emissions, political action becomes self-affirming (and potentially narcissistic). Vicky argued that rather than evaluate political actions in terms of their external impact, for instance concluding that 'we didn't do it this time, we have to try harder next time', actions should be assessed in terms of how they felt for the participants, that 'we did this amazing thing! that's really great' (Vicky, 2009). Climate action from this perspective can become an end in itself, as elaborated:

> 'it's about working out an attitude to bring to doing activism that means I survive in that non-broken-hearted way. ... turning up at the gates and going "No!" is an amazing thing. And that really has to be held onto.' Yet still, the experience is demoralising, you 'get yourself arrested and put your body on the line and maybe it'll change something and each time I do it, it doesn't change anything.'
>
> (Vicky, 2010)

The approach reflects the ethical foundations of climate activism, as arising from the process of collective action itself. Amongst the interviewees activism is often understood to be double-sided, directed 'outwards' to the authorities but also 'inwards' to the construction of political community. Rhianna (2009) argued 'activism for me is not just about asking for change, but it's also about … making a community that you want to live in, that is collaborative and that can support each other in doing what makes us happy and sustains us.' The priority is to explain the political priorities of the activist community, not to strategically calibrate political demands to fit the main frame. As Susie asked: 'Why are we asking the government to change their ETS when we, yeah, when we have our own different idea of social change?' (Susie, 2009a).

Consistent with the communitarian foundation for agency, several interviewees aspire to creating decentralised and locally embedded renewable energy systems that can support re-engagement with locality and community. From this perspective, climate action is primarily prefigurative of a broader shift. Alison, for instance, outlined

> a vision for a world … where communities predominantly have local-sourced energy and food, where there's local governance systems, where, you know, people take enjoyment out of each other's company and, you know, working together and there are less cars and more public transport, there are kids playing in the street.
>
> (Alison, 2008a)

A community-based society, supported by decentralised renewable energy cooperatives, would, she argued, support a 'much lower carbon lifestyle'. An ecocentric life is intrinsically self-fulfilling and fulsome:

> you have less food miles, less consumption generally because people enjoy life and get fulfilment through gardening rather than shopping for example.
>
> (Alison, 2008a)

For some, community-level action was necessary, but not sufficient. Alison favoured 'creating community in renewable energy cooperatives … transitioning our communities, not just our households, but our whole suburbs and towns to being energy autonomous, powered by renewable energy with community control' (Alison, 2008b). In her 'theory of change' this delinking is to proceed hand in hand with direct action to stop coal 'in its tracks' and

> public pressure on decision-makers to, to make sure that they commit to doing what is scientifically necessary to stop climate change, not what is politically possible, but what is scientifically necessary.
>
> (Alison, 2008b)

From this perspective, direct action can become a substitute for formal politics, a way of exiting the dominant frame, as the voice of the community that has the capacity to withdraw consent for the fossil fuel economy. As Angus (2008a) argued,

> people will realise that they need to somehow stop the burning of coal and then realise that they need to make that happen because it's not going to happen for them, I think that's the most important thing.

The turn to community is partly out of frustration with the state, but also reflects anticipation that climate change will endanger households in new ways, requiring community-wide adaptation and self-protection. There is a degree of community survivalism at play, for instance in this statement from Harriet:

> I've been thinking about that more on a community level and start getting people to think more in terms of community and their neighbours and local food and consuming less resources because at some point all those resources aren't even going to be available to us.
>
> (Harriet, 2008c)

More broadly, as Lillian noted, some of the more anarchist-inspired activists committed to community-based solutions will refuse to make demands on the government as this 'is understood as reinforcing the government's power' (Lillian, 2009). For her, 'there are massive problems with that argument'. In some instances of debate in the movement she argued that advocates of the 'self-sufficiency' position silenced dissent, labelling state-focused strategy as by definition politically conservative.

Lacking a political analysis of the state, utopian communitarian aspirations can quickly default into an acceptance of what may be deemed more realistic. William (2009) would prefer a movement 'that can actually through its own power change society', but argued climate activists must engage the state, mainly due to the urgent need to address climate change and partly because an anti-state position can cultivate a self-marginalisation. For him, the prospect of 'climate chaos' meant the immediate priority was for a 'movement to put pressure on the state to manage capital in a sense, in the short term' arguing this was a necessary but transitional reform, leading to and making possible more thoroughgoing transformation (William, 2009). Beatrice was also pragmatic:

> I think ideally, I do like the idea of a more decentralised community approach to like, generating power and, yeah, separate communities that can find ways to do that, but it's a big change to how things are. ... I think trying to stop relying on coal is a big thing that is maybe simpler and easier to ask for than to change the structure of society [laughs].
>
> (Beatrice, 2009)

Kylie favours delinked sustainable towns, but pragmatically

> the fact is we've got to work with what we've got ... I think we need to do it, in I guess the easiest way possible ... it would just be way too much effort and we wouldn't get it done in time if we went on another path.
>
> (Kylie, 2009a)

Consequently, communitarians resist reliance on government action but default to pragmatism when pushed by the urgency of climate action. At this point, communitarianism diverts attention from key power sources in society, notably from corporates and the state, and becomes counterproductive.

Climate economism

In contrast with those who take a communitarian position, several interviews stress economic mechanisms as central to achieving emissions reductions. Here greenhouse gas emissions are to be reduced through price incentives built on enlightened self-interest. From this perspective the key vehicle for climate action is economic preference, not community autonomy or government policy. The prevailing bipartisan political consensus at the time of the interviews was the need for 'market-friendly' climate policy, which would create new incentives for decarbonisation. The political debate turned on the extent to which incentives should be price-based, with permits to pollute bought and sold on a carbon market, or tax-based, through a fixed levy on carbon. Most activists rejected this agenda, although a significant number argued that creating economic incentives could be an important means of reducing emissions.

A few interviewees were happy to endorse carbon trading. One stated that carbon trading could be 'an effective part of the solution'. For this interviewee, the key problem was not carbon trading but the government's continued commitment 'to keeping the coal industry alive' (Samuel, 2008b). The policy mechanism was not so much the issue as the objective to phase out coal, allowing him to be agnostic on the question of which policy may or may not achieve this goal. Many argued that a low-emissions economy offered many economic opportunities, and that these could be exploited if the economic settings were changed. Margo (2009), for instance, stresses 'we really are missing out on huge export opportunities because of the failure of government to back renewable technology and energy-efficiency technology.'

Several interviewees argued that decarbonisation would be difficult, if not impossible, to achieve under the existing growth model. Economic growth on the current model would always produce more emissions; the key was to rethink growth positively, to create a new definition of well-being. For several interviewees this would require a new approach to consumption and lifestyle. Angus (2008b), for instance, argued that 'people need to be able to accept that they need to consume less,', but this had to happen in a positive way: 'I think the main problem is that people imagine that being environmentally friendly is something that has to be a burden.' Some argue that what is required is a lifestyle change, and that this will induce broader structural changes. Alison (2009) stressed the demonstration effects of delinking, to 'build up the alternatives so that they [fossil fuels] slowly become irrelevant.' Robert (2008b) argued, 'I don't think the masses are going to say "Yes it's time to do the right thing." But I think there will be a growing number of people who choose to live that way. And I think eventually they will be the pioneers of a new life and consumption. As Robert stated,

> happiness has got nothing to do with, you know, the corporate line of buying this and buying that. It's got nothing to do with it. We need a simpler lifestyle and, um, it can come from just growing your own food and you know, recycling and doing things that, that, um, people enjoy.

This idea that community change can force corporate change is a strong theme. Sarah made a powerful argument for the demonstration effect of individual actions and for the logic of consumer sovereignty, in terms of the impact of delinking on the corporate sector, stating,

> I'm a bit of a believer that you start in your own backyard. You live how you would like everybody else to live, and I hope that if more people do that then things will have to change. And hopefully it will be a domino effect. Soon everyone will be turning to the sun and the energy companies will have to think again. ... if enough people do it, and if you spread the word about it.
>
> (Sarah, 2008a)

While some embrace consumer pressures to drive climate action, many were sceptical of price incentives, arguing that economic forces are agnostic and will backfire. Angus, for instance, argued that the increased cost of oil, rather than driving renewables, creates demand for other fossil fuels: 'you just turn the coal into petrol' (Angus, 2008b). Assumptions that the exhaustion of fossil fuels will drive renewables are clearly mistaken. 'You can't mine stuff forever by definition, but you can definitely do it long enough to kill the planet' (Angus, 2008b). From this perspective there are real political choices to be made, that cannot be displaced into the market.

In this context, pricing carbon can become counterproductive. For Cathy (2009), carbon trading was undermining prospects for climate action. People could not understand it, and it created an 'enormous black hole where people can bury ... massive handouts and so on to big polluters.' She favoured a carbon tax as it would be more transparent, describing carbon trading as a 'diabolical instrument of deceit'. Alistair stressed that within the entire NGO sector perhaps five to ten people could explain carbon trading: 'even now, after the thing's been debated for nearly two years, most people, even the polls are saying, they don't have a clue what it is, or how it works, or whether it's good or bad' (Alistair, 2009). Carbon trading had created a 'terrain in terms of campaigning and policy that I think really suits vested interests'. Instead, Alistair argued for a 'rules-based' approach:

> if we think that climate change is a major problem, which it clearly is, we need to be serious about the solution rather than leaving it up to the invisible hand of the market to try and fix for us ... When we wanted to introduce seat belts, we didn't set up a market in seatbelt wearing credits that you could exchange with your neighbours, we just said by law you have to wear seat belts, and that's how you do it.
>
> (Alistair, 2009)

Despite the obvious shortcomings of market-based mechanisms, the movement had (so far) failed to develop a critique of neo-liberalism, and thus of emissions trading. Much of the environment movement believed that markets, in principle, could deliver environmental outcomes. While the climate movement had opposed carbon pricing when it surfaced in 2007, this was not an in-principle rejection, but more tactical, concerned with the detail of implementation rather than the mechanism as such. Some groups had pushed for a clearer rejection of carbon trading, but in general the climate movement had avoided a more serious critique, suggesting, at least on this issue, as Alistair (2009) put it, that it was 'not a politically radical movement at all'. In part this was an issue of political maturity and, Alistair predicted, would change as carbon trading is shown to fail and coal mining expands.

The issue of green jobs was seen as central for mobilisation on a positive agenda, but was also an issue which forces debate about how the alternatives would be achieved. Ben emphasises the neo-liberal context for any claim that transition will create green jobs. Carbon-intensive jobs are in place now, unlike green jobs, which are often assumed to emerge automatically from the process of repricing fossil fuels, and the resulting 'adjustment'. Even if green jobs were to emerge, there was no guarantee the jobs would be located in regions that were de-industrialised by the transition, nor that they would be offered to people leaving the fossil fuel industries. Ben recounted his experience with workers in the mining sector, who were happy with the concept of sustainable jobs but highly cynical about a transition, following decades of failed regeneration projects, and given that the unions were generally defensive and on the 'back foot' politically (Ben, 2009a). In this context it was unsurprising that workers were sceptical of climate policy, or even downright hostile. The alternative 'green future', he argued, needed to be made 'real' through government-led industry policy, not through market forces.

More broadly, as Ben argued, relying on price incentives would shift the burden onto those least able to pay. The climate movement had to adopt positive programs that would not simply punish workers and consumers. There were direct implications for mobilisation – and this echoes related concerns about elitism: 'I don't think you can build a movement telling people they're going to pay more for electricity. I just don't think that's possible' (Ben, 2009a). Lillian agreed, arguing that without a clear political programme on how to achieve emissions reductions, climate action translates into an 'attack on workers ... and the poor' while 'giving out free permits to business' (Lillian, 2008b). Climate economism thereby becomes profoundly counterproductive as it entrenches economic privilege and ultimately erodes public support for climate policy.

Climate statism

While some interviewees sought to embrace community action and economic forces or consumer sovereignty, most looked to the government as the chief vehicle for climate action. Rosalind (2008c) argued that governments needed to lead, to be 'at the forefront of the kinds of changes that we need domestically and encouraging other governments to do the same thing'. For Kylie, the government could act: 'I think it needs to be the government coming down and saying "you have to cut emissions" and providing the infrastructure to do that ... We need tough action that you know will have a certain outcome' (Kylie, 2009a). For Margo, the issue would not even require legislation in the first instance:

> Clearly what's needed here is a greater degree of government intervention, and a lot of it isn't rocket science ... stop the subsidies to the coal industry, shift those subsidies over to renewable and energy efficiency. You would make such a huge difference. Put more money into public transport, so much of our greenhouse gas emissions would then be cut.
>
> (Margo, 2009)

There was a common view that while the government has the capacity, it lacks the political will. Several interviewees argued the government had failed to address the issue and would only do so in the face of mass direct action. As Bernard (2009) said, 'The 85 per cent of people who want something done about climate change have been dudded. What do they do?' Alistair argued that mobilisation is needed to 'force governments all over the world, because we aren't going to get it through some kind of enlightened benevolence, because there's too much at stake in terms of self-interest and vested interest' (Alistair, 2009).

Amongst many of the activists there was strong scepticism of climate lobbying by the 'mainstream' environmental movement. Vicky (2009) argued 'the environment movement can put too much emphasis on governmental decision-making processes ... and then when things like that fail, you can feel completely disempowered.' The favoured alternative was to make a direct difference 'on the street'. From this perspective, direct action is an instrument to force government action, as Josh claimed, to take a campaign from the 'battle phase' into a 'tough political skills and science phase' (Josh, 2009). He argued that direct action can be very effective in influencing the formal political process, stressing 'what amazing things you can do with a generally small amount of people ... [when politicians] realise their vote might be compromised.' This may take time, but required strategy that could look beyond what seem like immediate losses:

> So you shouldn't always consider everything a loss immediately, because changes do happen as a result of anything you do, even if you can't see it at the time.
>
> (Josh, 2009)

Particularly important at an early stage was the capacity to polarise the debate. In this context, direct action had a particular purpose. As Josh argued,

> it's capable of shaking things up when things need to be shaken up to move the political possibilities; it can just as likely set them back as well as bring them forward, but, when risks need to be taken, it's a really good option.

While arguing for government action, several interviewees claimed that the Government had manipulated and distorted movement goals. The Government agenda for carbon pricing had especially sidetracked the movement; in rejecting the carbon trading scheme the movement had posed a real challenge to the Government. But the Government had responded by simply co-opting some of the more pragmatic environmental NGOs, such as the ACF, the WWF and the Climate Institute, leading them to believe they had achieved improved targets. For Alistair (2009), these groups were manipulated into believing 'they were more influential than they actually were', adding 'which is often a problem when you rely, when you're close to power, people often confuse access with influence.' More seriously, the Government had as a result constructed a political agenda centred on the economic cost of action rather than the benefits. Alistair stressed the impact, that when 'you're competing in terms of someone else's frame, it's very difficult to make progress'. Alison (2009) had self-consciously worked to 'change the terms of the debate to stop talking about carbon pollution and start talking about a post-carbon society, or a country powered by renewable energy'. For her this approach would accentuate the positive and demonstrate practical examples to build consensus, rather than entering highly divisive debates about carbon pricing. This was critical since, she pointed out, 'doom and gloom' on renewables was in the interests of the polluters

More positively, political leadership by the government was seen as central by several interviewees. For many there is a strong faith in a reclaimed government. As Ruth argued, 'we need a government that's prepared to have a backbone and to make those tough changes, so that our grandchildren will have a future' (Ruth, 2008a). Climate policy suggested a failure of government leadership, or rather a crisis of confidence on the part of the government. Here there is often a strong belief that the general public would support phasing out fossil fuels as the necessary response to climate change, and interviewees point to the lobbying effort required by mining companies and the government to resist this common-sense approach. Gary, for instance, stated that the public were looking for positive leadership; they understand the issue of climate change and would support a government willing to act seriously on it. He argued the government is

> not leading by example, and we should be. People appreciate that, they understand when they see people leading by example. That there is an issue there that's worthwhile. And they'll come on board. They will, they will. They're looking for it. That's why they'll come on board.
>
> (Gary, 2008a)

Cathy (2008b) agreed, and insisted the movement should approach the political sphere in the expectation of a positive response, rather than antagonistically 'raging against the machine' from a position of assumed marginality. This positive framing, she argued, should build on the broad community consensus that climate change must be addressed,

> Because the beauty of the whole climate change issue is that the answers are all there, and fundamentally it's not questioning most people's values, because most people when it comes down to it want a healthier planet.
>
> (Cathy, 2008b)

Ruth agrees that government leadership is fundamental, arguing:

> The government really do not appreciate the fact that the people will go with them if they have strong leadership. They seem to think that ... people are greedy and stupid. And yes, maybe some are. But I think the vast majority would, can see the need for dramatic change and would take the lead of government if they were strong enough to make it.
>
> (Ruth, 2008a)

To build that support, Lillian (2008b) argued, the movement should advocate for public provision, for public transport, and publicly funded green jobs. A green job agenda that could build mass support meant 'putting up a demand ... for the government to directly invest in alternative renewable energy'. Addressing this class dimension to climate politics would help the climate movement gain a mass base, otherwise 'it's never going to go forward'.

These advocates of state action were sceptical of current government policies but also condemned anti-statism. Lillian (2008b) found people at climate camp 'very reluctant to say anything about the state', citing the idea that 'we can't ask anything of the state, we should be able to do it ourselves' as a major problem. She explained this in terms of immersion in neo-liberalism, where 'people are starting to think that, you know, we can't have any expectation on government to provide'. Closing down an industry could only be achieved by creating new forms of work and this would not come from any 'invisible hand'. For most interviewees, this issue of transitional justice was important, but only some had understood it in terms of broader questions of climate justice. Gary, for instance, argued that 'Just as we've got people in the Pacific Islands who have got nowhere to go, we've got people in Bangladesh who've got nowhere to go, and we've got workers here in Australia who need to be shepherded out of the industry and make sure that they don't go on the scrapheap by unscrupulous, rapacious resources companies' (Gary, 2008b). Above all, the movement had to learn 'we can't be glib with people's lives' (Alistair, 2009).

Conclusion

In this chapter we find climate activists struggling with the political challenge of translating climate crisis into climate politics. The urgency for climate action can undermine efforts at movement building, as disagreements over strategy are deferred in favour of a lowest common denominator of metapolitical climate imperatives. The idea of 'climate emergency' might help put climate on the political agenda, and one can say it had been successful in this regard, from at least the early 1990s, but it is less helpful in ensuring the emergence of a sustained climate movement. The climate movement is clearly at an impasse, needing to develop a politics beyond the 'metapolitical'. Some pointers as to the parameters for achieving this are revealed in this chapter. Specifically, we can observe an important double shift, from urgency to strategy and from abstraction to materiality. These prepare the groundwork for a more substantive shift from climate-action to climate-justice agendas (Pearse, 2010b). The interviews discussed here suggest a shift along a trajectory from community-centred and economy-centred approaches to a focus on developing specific programmes of government-led intervention to supersede fossil-fuel dependency.

Drawing from the critiques discussed here, it is clear that positive climate justice programmes, at minimum, cannot hope to rely on community action or markets to achieve emissions reductions. Neither should they be aimed at displacing the costs of structural change onto those with less capacity either to adapt to climate impacts or to pay for emissions reductions. Such programmes must produce a dramatic change in the nature of economic growth, to ecological accumulation and a model of regrowth resting on ecological sufficiency, not ecological efficiency. As defined by many of the activists interviewed for this project, the required policy shift must take a decentralised approach that strengthens autonomy and capacity to transform social relations in an eco-centric direction. Both decarbonisation and ecological regrowth require localisation strategies, and eco-sufficiency in this respect rests upon the primacy of local relations. From this perspective, policy can be explicitly geared to delinking from financial priorities in order to enable relinking or reconnection with ecologies. Within these parameters we can define an emergent paradigm for transitions that can tactically encompass a provisional or transitional program. The key consideration here is to 'start stopping', that is to create means for people to achieve limited objectives as part of an overarching vision.

These elements of a 'realistic' paradigm shift at best only hint as what such a frame might encompass, but at least establish the necessity for a focus on the practical politics of translating metapolitical conditions into a process of realising climate agency. Perhaps such a frame should begin with the normative stance, the ethical foundations of climate action being one of justice. The stance is not simply in relation to an abstracted notion of the ecosystem but also very immediately to all we hold dear. In that respect, the normative imperative is not to act now to save ourselves from disaster, but to act now to express our regard for others and for the world as we know it. In a very real sense, when we deny climate change or avoid climate justice we are denying the relationships that make us human, that is, relationships to others and to our environment. From this perspective there is nothing selfless or self-denying in climate justice – in every respect this is self-affirming and self-realising. Seen from this perspective, there is no possible climate-society dichotomy, or at least not from any ethical standpoint. Climate change in this respect forces a bridging of the metabolic rift created by capitalist order, between society and nature. It forces recognition that the ecosystem is inseparable from us, finally requiring recognition of the 'naturalisation of humans and the humanisation of nature'.

Conclusion

Through the first decade of the new millennium, the political purchase of the climate crisis underwent an extraordinary transformation. The weight of scientific evidence was unambiguous in signalling the force of climate change, and this spawned a climate politics that seemed to withstand the efforts of the climate sceptics and the corporate deniers to cloud consideration of the urgency for action. As argued in Chapter 2, established environmental movements, and more particularly ENGOs convinced by the science of climate change, found new purpose and organisational momentum in taking up the cause of climate politics. The challenge, however, was how to translate climate science into climate politics, and this question was largely avoided through the climate pragmatism of asserting metapolitical agendas and seeking to work the traditional corridors of political power. Characterised by claims that we are all in this together and that there is an absolute moral necessity for emergency action, the mainstream approach to climate change produced a form of command politics that proved decidedly unsuccessful.

The failure of this attempted metapolitical challenge could not be more starkly illustrated than by the debacle of the 2009 Copenhagen UNFCCC conference. More than two decades of international negotiations signally failed to produce a practical political response to the metapolitical demand. Likewise at the national level, metapolitics has translated into political programmes that serve the powerful at the expense of the rest. As has become painfully clear, the climate crisis – as with all crises – can be translated into an opportunity for power holders. The spectacle of climate bailouts for high-emitting industries and of financialisation to provide new arbitrage opportunities for the finance sector is plain. Displacement of the costs of climate policy onto consumers in high-emitting countries, onto workers in high-emitting industries, and onto low-income countries, has dramatically undermined public support for climate policy.

Challenging this political narrative, we have been witness to, and participated in, the endeavours to forge a more provocative and radically formed climate politics, one that is premised on constructing a new kind of political agency, one that is capable of translating climate science into climate politics. A critical feature of this radical political turn has meant the abandonment of the metapolitics of climate pragmatism, instead embracing a transformative climate politics with climate justice at its centre. In engaging with this project, we have observed how this has been founded on the moral imperative for action, on a collective urge to mobilise that is grounded in an ethics of climate sensibility formed around concern for the environment *and* humanity. This climate politics has been imbued with the ambition to construct a new language of climate justice, human rights and social justice. It is also a politics that, critically, has sought to progress its claims through direct actions that contest the legitimacy of carbon-producing sites and challenge the authority and the right of capital and the state to impose their destructive will on the environment and humanity. In challenging the hegemony of the carbon-intensive system, this radical climate politics has worked to eschew established power structures and institutional structures.

This, however, has not been an unproblematic road. In exploring this new climate politics, we have sought to uncover the challenges that have confronted the movement, and particularly the dialectical play of hope and despair. The demobilisation precipitated by the pragmatism that engulfed both the Australian Government and the Copenhagen talks highlights the magnitude of the difficulties that have confronted the upsurge in climate action and the capacity to sustain the commitment to direct action.

As has become abundantly clear, the absence of such a movement contributed to the failure of climate policy and the emergence of climate ambivalence and denialism, and the ultimate unravelling of climate as a political issue. Indeed, as the climate debate moves into reverse internationally, we are witness to the remarkable process of demobilisation and deprioritisation. The global 'walk against warming' initiative now barely exists, and climate-action networks, which once gained the ear of governments, are excluded from the policy process of managing 'carbon pollution'. Remarkably, in Australia in March 2013 the Federal Department of Climate Change and Energy Efficiency was, as the Department put it, 'abolished with climate change functions transferred' to the new 'Department of Industry, Innovation, Climate Change, Science, Research and Tertiary Education' (DCCEE, 2013). This reversal was achieved by a Labor administration that one month earlier had been in coalition with the Australian Greens. Australia is not alone in this. The British Treasury successfully thwarted attempts by senior Whitehall economists to set up a review of resource depletion and climate change to address industry and environmentalists' concerns, and the subject of climate change failed to make the G8 agenda (Pickard 2013; Straw, 2013).

How, then, to not succumb to the pessimism of the will, given this? How are we to investigate global warming in a way that engages with both the science of climate change and the social process of acting on it? In debates about climate change there has been a strong tendency to configure climate action as first and foremost grounded in science, rather than in values or political ideologies (e.g. Low, 2010). This rationalist bent runs the risk of missing the generative potential of affect, values, norms and political vision in the process of collective mobilization, and in generating new agendas for climate agency. As with all social movements, the climate movement is constructed by the collective action of its participants, including disputes over shared political priorities (Hosseini, 2006; Maddison & Scalmer, 2006). It emerges from social and ecological relations and from public awareness of these, but the process of realising agency through a social movement is always a process of constructing possibilities. As with all movements, various components of the network are in constant motion, forming variable and revisable coalitions (Juris, 2004). The climate movement is thereby highly contingent as a series of sites of deliberation and knowledge production for mobilisation, directed at transformation. The movement is always, by definition, a social process, not a social 'thing' that is in any sense fixed or predetermined.

We found climate activists self-consciously engaged in this intellectual process of generating new visions and new models for action in the context of climate change. Clearly the movement is in formation, yet in apprehending the profound clash of histories, activists have been exploring and experimenting in ways of moving beyond fatalism, and creating new foundations for mobilisation. Our research shows how activists produced a new language and practice of ethical protest in the face of a profound historical conjuncture, and created political tools to address the crisis. Many of these perspectives were, and are, half-formed, preliminary and contingent, yet they take us considerably further than the official script, and have great generative potential beyond the current malaise.

Whilst addressing a distinctive challenge with its own logic, we find familiar debates and issues surfacing in climate movements. A key issue, as discussed in this book, is the movement's stance in relation to the issue of the state. There have been intense debates between contending positions, for an instrumental policy focus, as against more prefigurative initiatives designed to offer a means to expressing movement values and alternatives. The debate between instrumentalists, who see the movement as a means to an end, and those who see the movement as an end in itself, are rehearsed across many social movements, and have been debated within the academic domain of social movement studies since the 1980s (see Jamison, 2010; McAdam et al., 2001; Snow et al., 2008).

The Climate Camps and the Climate Action Summits provided unique forums for these strategic visions to be explored. These were extraordinary events in so far as they brought and held together individuals and groups from diverse backgrounds and possessed of disparate interests and ambitions. Yet, as some interviewees explained, the opportunity for developing strategic visions and deepening the political project was too frequently circumvented. This was, in part, to be expected. Debates about the 'how' of social movement strategy reflect more fundamental debates about the 'why' of climate change. Reflecting wider society, there is no consensus amongst movement participants as to the causes of climate change. With no consensus on diagnosis there is also much debate about the necessary, desirable or effective cure.

These debates develop over time and may converge in the context of broader revelations in the logic of climate change and climate policy. For instance, there were, and are continuing, clear disagreements over how the problem of consumerism and growth, and also what alternatives may be available in terms of eco-sufficiency, eco-socialism and eco-modernisation (Goodman, 2010).

The difficulty in formulating an agreed vision was also a product of the fluidity of a movement in formation. Movements are in the process of creating connections between human, non-human and financial resources in order to build power. They are brought together through various means, including protest events, decision-making processes, e-lists and social media, party political or organisation membership, friendships, shared experiences, ideological alliances and antagonisms. Climate activism is constituted as a mix of fluid project-based groups and established groups in the form of collectives, NGOs and political parties.

But, there were organisational challenges that were never resolved, let alone openly debated. Organisers of Climate Camps and Climate Summits were motivated by the desire to avoid rifts within the movement. The fear of *entryism* was an ever-present concern amongst some organisers. The focus on creating a direct action event, while exposing the material foundations of climate change, tended to mean that the movement's political horizons were not as extended as they might have been. And then there were the obvious organisational challenges in trying to sustain the relatively pluralist and inclusive form of the movement, as has been acknowledged by those involved in Britain's Climate Camp (CfCA, 2011).

In telling this story of the peak and trough of activist mobilisations between 2007 and 2010, we do not wish to belittle the significance of the upsurge in climate politics. The upsurge was the product of an extraordinary lift in the political salience of climate change and of a movement that was formed in terms of its materiality. Climate activism in its many forms, which have included Climate Camps, large mobilisations outside UNFCCC negotiations, alternative 'people's' summits and festivals, as well as coordinated rallies such as Walk Against Warming, World Environment day, and 350.org protests, heralded a dramatic shift in climate politics. And each of these sites of movement activity has been an intervention into the political and material production of nature.

The significance of the climate action upsurge lies in the way climate movements have directly contested the domination of nature that has produced climate change, and hence are focused on halting the burning of fossil fuels, for instance. The movements aspire to society-nature relations that are free from domination, although, as we have observed, they disagree on how this may be achieved. Their interventions, in the localities where they are based, reflect the particular ways in which local nature has been produced by the carbon economy. When climate activists in Australia target sites of emissions, they assert a 'withdrawal of consent' (Alistair, 2008c) that rejects the ways in which nature is dominated by coal mining and burning, and instead seek to re-embed society in ecological relations. The contest performs a 'double movement', for, and then against, the commodification of fossil fuels (Polanyi, 2001[1944]). In the process, the movement literally produces new and alternative ecological imaginaries, and constructs new society-nature relations (Goldman & Schurman, 2000: 571).

Our contention is that the story of this period of climate activism holds many lessons for future mobilisations. Coming to grips with the Anthropocene is at once an affective, cognitive and political task. Climate-activist subjectivities are forged in the dynamics of a profound change that societies are still struggling to understand, articulate and act upon. The process of apprehending climate change and finding ways to talk about its political implications is immediately public, but is also intensely personal. Social movements are located at this nexus between the everyday practices of life, the personal-political, and the public-political realms of civil society organisations, corporates, media and the state (Routledge, 1996: 511). Accordingly, an understanding of climate activism requires combined engagement with the public antagonisms of social movements and the personal and affective dimensions of climate action (Connor, 2012).

Indeed, the brief encounters that have sought to expose the contradictions of the human-nature dialectic which have defined the Anthropocene, and the hope that these have engendered, have not been abandoned. Rather, the energies of the movements are being resuscitated and redirected towards confronting emerging challenges, to contest the carbon age and its injustices. In Australia, governments supporting the exploration and extraction of coal seam gas have spawned an unparalleled plethora of campaigns to block the ambitions of energy companies to transform the landscape. A coalition of interests that is both unique and historic in its reach has waged determined civil disobedience campaigns and questioned the legitimacy of government to issue energy companies with permits to test for coal seam gas. The 'Lock the Gate' movement has united farmers and others living in rural areas with city dwellers across the Eastern seaboard of Australia in a concerted endeavour 'to protect the environment, cultural and agricultural resources from inappropriate mining and to educate and empower all Australians to demand sustainable solutions to food and energy production.' (LtGA, 2013). And the success of this campaign, in getting governments to adopt measures that restrict exploration rights on environmental grounds, has not been limited to energy companies' search for gas; the exploration of coal is now subject to these regulations. Moreover, the force of the movement is bolstered by its connections to similar struggles being waged throughout much of the global North, and especially in North America and Europe. Many of these struggles are drawing on the lessons of the upsurge in climate activism, as is evident in the 'Camp Frack' initiative in the UK, and have social-justice concerns as integral elements of the climate action campaign (Vidal, 2011; Environment Blog 2012).

In the face of accelerating climate change, we draw on our analysis of the upsurge in climate politics to anticipate a renewed momentum in climate politics. Current mobilisations build on the advances of the period of climate action upsurge, and hold out the promise of taking them still further. In celebrating this moment in climate politics, this book has sought to reveal the many positive developments, as well as some of the challenges the climate movement will have to confront if the renewal is to have the purchase that will be so crucial to forging a climate sensibility that embraces both climate and social justice.

References

ABC, (2011) *Gas rush*, Four Corners, Matthew Carney, 21 February.

ABRCC, (2006) *The Business Case for Early Action*, Australian Business Roundtable on Climate Change, ACF, Westpac, Visy, Swiss Re, Origin Energy, IAG, BP Australasia.

Adam, D. & Jowitt, J., (2008) 'People power vital to climate deal: Miliband calls for global movement to pressure governments into action', *The Guardian*, 8 December.

Alison, (2008a) Interview, 3 October, Sydney, with Rebecca Pearse.

——, (2008b) Interview, 8 July, Students of Sustainability, Newcastle, with Rebecca Pearse.

——, (2009) Interview, 13 December, Sydney, with Rebecca Pearse.

Alistair, (2008a) Interview, 7 July, Newcastle, with Rebecca Pearse.

——, (2008b) Interview, 14 July, Newcastle, with Rebecca Pearse.

——, (2008c) Interview, 17 October, Sydney, with Rebecca Pearse.

——, (2009) Interview, 24 November, Coogee, with Rebecca Pearse.

Angus, (2008a) Interview, 7 July, Students of Sustainability, Newcastle, with Rebecca Pearse.

——, (2008b) Interview, 20 October, Sydney, with Rebecca Pearse.

——, (2009) Interview, 2 December, Marrickville, with Rebecca Pearse.

Arrighi, G., Hopkins, T. & Wallerstein, I., (1989) *Anti-Systemic Movements*, London: Verso.

Ashley, (2009) Focus group – NGO and union campaigners, 13 October, Sydney, with Stuart Rosewarne and Rebecca Pearse.

Asia Pacific Research Network, (2007) Peoples' Protocol on ClimateChange, *People and Planet over Profits: Conference on People's Sovereignty on Natural Resources*, 23-25 October, Inna Bali, Denpasar Bali.

Bank, W., (2012) *Turn Down the Heat: Why a 4°c World Must Be Avoided*, Washington DC: World Bank.

Beatrice, (2008) Interview, 30 September, Sydney, with Rebecca Pearse.

——, (2009) Interview, 25 November, Sydney, with Rebecca Pearse.

Beck, U., (1992) *Risk Society: Towards a New Modernity*, London: Sage.

Ben, (2009a) Interview, 1 December, Sydney, with Rebecca Pearse.

——, (2009b) Interview, 12 September, Switch Off Hazelwood, Morwell, with Rebecca Pearse.

Bernard, (2009) Interview, 9 October, Climate Camp, Helensburgh, with Rebecca Pearse.

Bond, P., (2012) *Politics of Climate Justice: Paralysis Above, Movement Below*, Scottsville: University of Kwazulu-Natal Press.

Bourdieu, P. & Wacquant, L.J.D., (1992) *An Invitation to Reflexive Sociology*, Chicago: University of Chicago Press.

Bradley, (2009) Focus group – NGO and union campaigners, 13 October, Sydney, with Stuart Rosewarne and Rebecca Pearse.

BREE, (2012a) Australian Bulk Commodity Exports and Infrastructure – Outlook to 2025 Canberra: Bureau of Resources and Energy Economics.

——, (2012b) *Resources and Energy Quarterly: December 2012*, Canberra: Bureau of Resources and Energy Economics.

Bruno, K., Karliner, J. & Brotsky, C., (1999) *Greenhouse Gangsters vs. Climate Justice*, San Francisco: Transnational Resource & Action Center, Corpwatch.

Bulkeley, H., (2000) 'The formation of Australian climate change policy, 1985–1995', in A. Gillespie & W.C.G. Burns, (eds) *Climate Change in the South Pacific: Impacts and Responses in Australia, New Zealand, and Small Island States*, Dordrecht: Kluwer Academic Publishers.

Bullard, N. & Müller, T., (2012) 'Beyond the 'Green Economy': System change, not climate change?', *Development*, 55(1): 54–62.

Bullard, R., (1983) 'Solid waste sites and the black Houston community', *Sociological Inquiry*, 53(2–3): 273–288.

——, (1999a) 'Dismantling environmental racism in the USA', *Local Environment*, 4(1): 5–19.

——, (1999b) 'Environmental justice challenges at home and abroad', in N. Low, (ed.) *Global Ethics and Environment*, London: Routledge.

Burgmann, V., (2003) *Power, Profit and Protest: Australian Social Movements and Globalisation*, Crows Nest: Allen and Unwin.

Burgmann, V. & Baer, H.A., (2012) *Climate Politics and the Climate Movement in Australia*, Melbourne: Melbourne University Press.

Carbon Trade Watch et al., (2004) Climate justice now! The Durban declaration on carbon trading, *Durban Climate Justice Summit*, 10 October, Durban.

Castells, M., (2004) The Power of Identity: The Information Age: Economy, *Society and Culture, 2nd edn*, Oxford: Blackwell.

Cathy, (2008a) Interview, 11 July, Climate Camp, Newcastle, with Rebecca Pearse.

——, (2008b) Interview, 13 October, Rozelle, with Rebecca Pearse.

——, (2009) Interview, 18 November, Sydney, with Rebecca Pearse.

Catney, P. & Doyle, T., (2011) 'The welfare of now and the green, (post) politics of the future', *Critical Social Policy*, 31(2): 174–193.

CfCA, (2011) *Metamorphosis: A statement from the Camp for Climate Action*, viewed 3 February 2012 <http://climatecamp.org.uk/2011-statement>.

CfCA Nottingham, (2009) 'Minutes of 'Where Next?': A day of discussion at the Climate Camp', paper presented to the *Ratcliffe-on-Soar Climate Camp* – "The Great Climate Swoop", Nottingham, 1 September.

Chakrabarty, D., (2009) 'The climate of history: Four theses', *Critical Inquiry*, 35(Winter): 197–222.

——, (2012) 'Postcolonial studies and the challenge of climate change', *New Literary History*, 43(1): 1–18.

Chatterton, P., Featherstone, D. & Routledge, P., (2012) 'Articulating climate justice in Copenhagen: Antagonism, the commons, and solidarity', *Antipode*.

Chavis, B., (1987) *Toxic Wastes and Race in the United States: A National Report on the Racial and Socio-Economic Characteristics of Communities with Hazardous Waste Sites*, New York: Commission for Racial Justice, United Church of Christ.

Christoff, P., (2005) 'Policy autism or double-edged dismissiveness? Australia's climate policy under the Howard government', *Global Change, Peace & Security*, 17(1): 29–44.

CJN!, (2007) Climate Justice Now! Principles, Denpasar, Climate Justice Now!

Claire, (2008a) Interview, 6 July, Friends of the Earth national meeting, Barrington Tops, with Rebecca Pearse.

——, (2008b) Interview, 9 October, By phone, with Rebecca Pearse.

Climate Action Groups, (2009) Joint Open Letter by 66 Climate Action Groups: RE proposed changes to Australia's targets and CPRS, 5 May, to Prime Minister Kevin Rudd, Parliament House, Canberra ACT 2601.

Climate Action Summit, (2009) *Our 2009 Campaign objectives*, Climate Action Summit 2009, viewed 20 November 2010 <http://climatesummit.org.au/campaign-strategy-development-stream-outcomes>.

Commonwealth of Australia, (2008) *Carbon Pollution Reduction Scheme: Green Paper*, Canberra Department of Climate Change.

——, (2011) *Strong Growth, Low Pollution: Modelling a Carbon Price*, Update, September, Canberra: Treasury.

Connor, J., (2010) Carbon markets and regulation for renewables, panel, *Key Forces for Climate Action*, 5 March, University of Sydney.

Connor, L., Freeman, S. & Higginbotham, N., (2009) 'Not just a coalmine: Shifting grounds of community opposition to coal mining in Southeastern Australia', *Ethnos*, 74(4): 490–513.

Connor, L.H., (2012) 'Experimental publics: Activist culture and political intelligibility of climate change action in the Hunter Valley, Southeast Australia', *Oceania*, 82(3): 228–249.

CorpWatch India, (2002) Delhi Climate Justice Declaration, *New Delhi Climate Justice Summit*, 26-28 October, New Delhi.

CorpWatch US et al., (2002) Bali Principles of Climate Justice, 28 August, Johannesburg.

Courtice, B., (2010) 'Natural gas and the climate movement', *Green Left Weekly*, 840.

Crikey, (2012) 'Rich Crusaders', *The Power Index, Crikey*, 7 March.

Crutzen, P.J. & Stoermer, E., (2000) 'The anthropocene', *Global Change Newsletter*, 41(1):17–18.

Davis, M., (2010) 'Who will build the ark?', *New Left Review*, 61: 29–46.

DCCEE, (2012) Australian National Greenhouse Accounts: Quarterly Update of Australia's National Greenhouse Gas Inventory, June, Canberra: Department of Climate Change and Energy Efficiency.

——, (2013) *New portfolio arrangements*, Department of Climate Change and Energy Efficiency, viewed 25 April 2013 <http://www.climatechange.gov.au/>.

Della Porta, D., (2007) *The Global Justice Movement: Cross-National And Transnational Perspectives*, London: Pluto Press.

Dobson, A., (2006) 'Ecological citizenship: A defence', *Environmental Politics*, 15(3): 447–451.

Doherty, B., (2006) 'Friends of the Earth International: Negotiating a transnational identity', *Environmental politics*, 15(5): 860–880.

Doyle, T., (2000) *Green Power: The Environment Movement in Australia*, Sydney: UNSW Press.

——, (2005) *Environmental Movements in Minority and Majority Worlds: A Global Perspective*, Piscataway: Rutgers University Press.

——, (2010) 'Surviving the Gang Bang Theory of Nature: The environment movement during the Howard years', *Social Movement Studies*, 9(2): 155–169.

DRET, (2012) *Energy White Paper: Australia's Energy Transformation*, Canberra: Department of Water Energy and Tourism.

Economou, N., (1999) 'Backwards into the future: National policy making, devolution and the rise and fall of Australian environmental policy', in K.J. Walker & K. Crowley, (eds) *Australian Environmental Policy 2. Studies in Decline and Devolution*, Sydney: University of New South Wales.

Elias, N., (1956) 'Problems of involvement and detachment', *The British Journal of Sociology*, 7(3): 226–252.

——, (2007) *Involvement and Detachment*, S. Quilley, Dublin, University College Dublin Press.

Engels, F., (1953[1876]) *The Part Played by Labour in the Transition from Ape to Man*, Moscow: Progress Publishers.

Environment Blog, (2012) 'Is climate protest making a return to the UK?' *The Guardian* April 27, http://www.guardian.co.uk/environment/2012/apr/27climate-protest-return-uk, (Accessed 12 January 2013).

EV, (2010) *Fast-tracking Victoria's Clean Energy Future to Replace Hazelwood Power Station*, Melbourne: Green Energy Markets for Environment Victoria.

Evans, G., (2010) 'A rising tide: Linking local and global climate justice', *Journal of Australian Political Economy*, 66: 199–221.

Faehrmann, C. et al., (2009) *Joint Statement: Green groups unite against CPRS, Nature Conservation Council of NSW, Friends of the Earth Australia, Greenpeace Australia, Conservation Council South Australia, Environment Tasmania, GetUp!, Queensland Conservation Council*, The Wilderness Society.

Farro, A.L., (2004) 'Actors, conflicts and the globalization movement', *Current Sociology*, 52(4): 633-647.

Featherstone, D., (2005) 'Towards the relational construction of militant particularisms: Or why the geographies of past struggles matter for resistance to neoliberal globalisation', *Antipode*, 37(2): 250–271.

Flannery, T., (2006a) 'Let's talk about nuclear power and other energy sources', *The Age*, 30 May.

——, (2006b) *The Weather Makers: The History and Future of Climate Change*, Melbourne: Text Publishing.

Flannery, T. & Rowley, N., (2009) 'Comment: Carbon omissions', *The Monthly*, May.

FoEB, (2008) *Community Dialogues on Coal: A Listening Tour of Queenslands Coal Affected Communities*, Brisbane: Six Degrees, Friends of the Earth Brisbane.

Foster, J., Clark, B. & York, R., (2010) *The Ecological Rift: Capitalism's War on the Earth*, New York: Monthly Review Press.

Foster, J.B., (2002) *Ecology Against Capitalism*, New York: Monthly Review Press.

Fraser, N., (1995) 'From redistribution to recognition? Dilemmas of justice in a "post-socialist" age', *New Left Review*, 212(July-August): 68–93.

Freese, B., (2006) *Coal: A Human History*, London: Arrow books.

Freire, P., (1970) 'Cultural action and conscientization', *Harvard Educational Review*, 40(3): 452-477.

——, (1995[1970]) *Pedagogy of the Oppressed*, trans. M.B. Ramos, New York: Continuum.

Gary & George, (2008a) Interview, 5 July, Muswellbrook, with Rebecca Pearse.

——, (2008b) Interview, 11 October, Muswellbrook, with Rebecca Pearse.

Gelbspan, R., (1998) *The Heat Is on: The Climate Crisis, the Cover-Up, the Prescription*, New York: Perseus Books Group.

——, (2005) *Boiling Point: How Politicians, Big Oil and Coal, Journalists and Activists are Fueling the Climate Crisis – And What We Can Do to Avert Disaster*, New York: Basic Books.

Giddens, A., (2009) *The Politics of Climate Change*, Cambridge: Polity Press.

Gilbertson, T. & Reyes, O., (2009) *Carbon Trading: How It Works and Why It Fails*, vol. 7, Uppsala: Dag Hammarskjöld Foundation

Goldman, M. & Schurman, R.A., (2000) 'Closing the "great divide": New social theory on society and nature', *Annual Review of Sociology*, 26: 563–584.

Goodman, J., (2009) 'From global justice to climate justice? Justice ecologism in an era of global warming', *New Political Science*, 31(4): 499–514.

——, (2010) 'Responding to climate crisis: Modernisation, limits, socialism', *Journal of Australian Political Economy*, (66): 144–165.

Goodman, J. & Rosewarne, S., (2010a) 'Climate policy: From carbon tax to direct action?', *Chain Reaction*, November.

——, (2010b) 'Special issue: Climate challenge', *Journal of Australian Political Economy*, 66: 17–50.

Green, J., (2010) 'How climate change came to tax us all', *ABC News*, 3 February.

Hansen, J., (2009) *Storms of My Grandchildren: The Truth About the Coming Climate Catastrophe and Our Last Chance to Save Humanity*, New York: Bloomsbury Press.

Harriet, (2008a) Interview, 8 July, Newcastle, with Rebecca Pearse.

——, (2008b) Interview, 14 July, Newcastle, with Rebecca Pearse.

——, (2008c) Interview, 20 October, Newcastle, with Rebecca Pearse.

——, (2009) Interview, 17 December, Newcastle, with Rebecca Pearse.

Harvey, D., (1996) *Justice, Nature and the Geography of Difference*, Cambridge: Blackwell.

Hayward, T., (2006) 'Ecological citizenship: Justice, rights and the virtue of resourcefulness', *Environmental Politics*, 15(03): 435–446.

Hosseini, S.A.H., (2006) 'Beyond practical dilemmas and conceptual reductions: The emergence of an 'accommodative consciousness' in the alternative globalization movement', *Portal: Journal of Multidisciplinary International Studies*, 3(1): 1–27.

Hulme, M., (2010) 'Mapping climate change knowledge: An editorial essay', *Wiley Interdisciplinary Reviews: Climate Change*, 1(1): 1–8.

Hutton, D. & Connors, L., (1999) *A History of the Australian Environmental Movement*, Cambridge: Cambridge University Press.

IEA, (2012) *World Energy Outlook*, Paris: International Energy Agency.

IPCC, (2007) *Fourth Assessment Report: Mitigation Working Group*, Cambridge: Cambridge University Press.

Jackson, T., (2009) *Prosperity Without Growth: The Transition to a Sustainable Economy*, London, UK Sustainable Development Commission.

Jamison, A., (2010) 'Climate change knowledge and social movement theory', *Wiley Interdisciplinary Reviews: Climate Change*, 1(6): 811–823.

Jasanoff, S., (2010) 'A new climate for society', *Theory, Culture & Society*, 27(2–3): 233–253.

Jasper, J., (2008) *The Art of Moral Protest: Culture, Biography, and Creativity in Social Movements*, Chicago: University of Chicago Press.

Jimmy, (2009) Interview, 13 September, Switch Off Hazelwood, Morwell, with Rebecca Pearse.

——, (2010) Interview, 19 January, Melbourne, with Rebecca Pearse.

Johnston, J. & Goodman, J., (2006) 'Hope and activism in the ivory tower: Freiean lessons for critical globalisation research', *Globalizations*, 3(1): 9–30.

Josh, (2009) Interview, 9 December, Sydney, with Rebecca Pearse.

Juris, J., (2004) 'Networked social movements: Global movements for global justice', in M. Castells, (ed.) *The Network Society: A Cross-Cultural Perspective*, Cheltenham: Edward Elgar.

Juris, J.S., (2008) *Networking Futures: The Movements Against Corporate Globalization*, Durham: Duke University Press.

Kylie, (2009a) Interview, 5 January, Wollongong, with Rebecca Pearse.

——, (2009b) Interview, 10 October, Climate Camp, Helensburgh, with Rebecca Pearse.

Leggett, J., (ed.), (1990) *Global Warming: The Greenpeace Report*, Oxford: Oxford University Press.

Lillian, (2008a) Interview, 11 July, Climate Camp, Newcastle, with Rebecca Pearse.

——, (2008b) Interview, 21 October, Sydney, with Rebecca Pearse.

——, (2009) Interview, 17 November, Sydney, with Rebecca Pearse.

Linacre, N., Kossoy, A. & Ambrosi, P., (2011) *State and Trends of the Carbon Market 2011*, Washington DC: World Bank.

Lohmann, L., (2006) 'A Critical Conversation on Climate Change, Privatisation and Power', *Development Dialogue*, 68(September).

Lovelock, J., (2004) 'Lovelock: 'Only nuclear power can now halt global warming'', *The Independent*.

Low, N., (2010) 'Power of persuasian creates critical mass for climate action', *The Age*, 6 September.

Low, N. & Gleeson, B., (2002) 'Situating justice in the environment: The case of BHP at the OK TEDI copper mine', *Antipode*, 30(3): 201–226.

Lowe, I., (2005) *A Big Fix: Radical Solutions for Australia's Environmental Crisis*, Melbourne: Black Inc.

LtGA, (2013) *Mission, principles, aims*, Lock the Gate Alliance, viewed 26 April 2013 <http://www.lockthegate.org.au/missions_principles_aims>.

Luke, T.W., (2005) 'Environmentalism as globalization from above and below: Can world watchers truly represent the earth?', in P. Hayden & C. El-Ojeili, (eds) *Confronting Globalization: Humanity, Justice, and the Renewal of Politics*, London: Palgrave Macmillan.

——, (2008) 'The politics of true convenience or inconvenient truth: Struggles over how to sustain capitalism, democracy, and ecology in the 21st century', *Environment and Planning A*, 40(8): 1811–1824.

Luxemburg, R., (1916) The Junius Pamphlet: The Crisis of German Social Democracy Berlin: Politische Schriften.

Lynas, M., (2007) Six Degrees: *Our Future on a Hotter Planet*, London: Fourth Estate.

Lynch, M., (2000) 'Against reflexivity as an academic virtue and source of privileged knowledge', *Theory, Culture & Society*, 17(3): 26–54.

Maddison, S. & Scalmer, S., (2006) *Activist Wisdom: Practical Knowledge and Creative Tension in Social Movements*, Sydney: UNSW Press.

Margo, (2008a) Interview, 11 July, Climate Camp, Newcastle, with Rebecca Pearse.

——, (2008b) Interview, 16 October, Sydney, with Rebecca Pearse.

——, (2009) Interview, 16 November, Sydney, with Rebecca Pearse.

Marx, K., (1964) *The Economic and Philosophic Manuscripts of 1844*, New York: International Publishers.

McAdam, D., Tarrow, S. & Tilly, C., (2001) *Dynamics of Contention*, New York: Cambridge University Press.

McGregor, I., (2009) 'Policy Coalitions in the Global Greenhouse: Contestation and Collaboration in Global Climate Change Public Policy', Doctoral Thesis, University of Technology Sydney, Sydney.

Melucci, A., (1996) *The Playing Self: Person and Meaning in the Planetary Society*, Cambridge: Cambridge University Press.

Milman, O., (2012) 'Australian 'mega mine' plan threatens global emissions target', *The Guardian*, 18 September.

Milne, C., (2009) *Why the Greens could not support the CPRS*, Canberra: Australian Greens.

Monbiot, G., (2006) *Heat: How to Stop the Planet Burning*, London: Penguin.

——, (2011) 'Greens must not prioritise renewables over climate change', *The Guardian*, 8 August.

Müller, T., (2012) 'The people's climate summit in Cochabamba: A tragedy in three acts', *Ephemera: Theory & Politics in Organization*, 12: 70.

Newell, P. & Paterson, M., (2010) *Climate Capitalism: Global Warming and the Transformation of the Global Economy*, Cambridge: Cambridge University Press.

Norgaard, K.M., (2006) '"People want to protect themselves a little bit": Emotions, denial, and social movement nonparticipation', *Sociological Inquiry*, 76(3): 372–396.

O'Brien, K., (2008) 'Rudd in the hot seat', *The 730 Report*, 11 December.

O'Connor, J., (1998) *Natural Causes: Essays in Ecological Marxism*, New York: The Guilford Press.

Participants, (2009a) Focus group - Helensburgh residents, 05 October, Helensburgh, with Stuart Rosewarne and Rebecca Pearse.

——, (2009b) Focus group – Helensburgh residents, 13 October, Helensburgh, with Stuart Rosewarne and Rebecca Pearse.

Paterson, M., (1996) *Global Warming and Global Politics*, London: Routledge.

Pearse, G., (2010a) 'Australia's precious place in the coal industry's world', paper presented to the *Climate Camp 2010*, Lake Liddell Recreation Area, NSW, 3 December.

——, (2011) 'The climate movement: Australia's patrons of climate change activism', *The Monthly*, September.

Pearse, R., (2010b) 'Making a market? Contestation and climate change', *Journal of Australian Political Economy*, 66: 166–198.

——, (2013) 'Back to the land? Legitimation, carbon offsets and Australia's emissions trading scheme', *Global Change, Peace & Security*, 25(1): 43–60.

Pearse, R. & Creenaune, H., (2011) 'Contesting the climate: Movement, politics, justice', *Chain Reaction*, 111(March).

Pickard, J., (2013) 'Treasury kills green study' *The Australian Financial Review* 5 March: 20.

Pittock, A.B., (2006) *Climate Change Turning Up the Heat*, Melbourne: CSIRO and Earthscan.

Polanyi, K., (2001[1944]) *The Great Transformation: The Political and Economic Origins of Our Time, 2nd edn*, Beacon Press: Boston.

PWC, (2012) *Too Late for Two Degrees: Low Carbon Economy Index 2012*, London: Price Waterhouse Coopers.

PWCCC, (2010) People's agreement, World People's Conference on Climate Change and the Rights of Mother Earth, *Cochabamba*, (22 April).

Redclift, M. & Sage, C., (1998) 'Global environmental change and global inequality', *International Sociology*, 13(4): 499–516.

Reitan, R. & Gibson, S., (2012) 'Climate change or social change? Environmental and Leftist praxis and participatory action research', *Globalizations*, 9(3): 395–410.

Rhianna, (2009) Interview, 10 October, Climate Camp, Helensburgh, with Rebecca Pearse.

——, (2010) Interview, 19 November, Sydney, with Rebecca Pearse.

Riach, K., (2009) 'Exploring participant-centred reflexivity in the research interview', *Sociology*, 43(2): 356–370.

Rising Tide International Network, (2011) *The Rising Tide Coalition for Climate Justice Political Statement*, Rising Tide UK, October, viewed 1 January 2013 <http://risingtide.org.uk/about/political>.

Roberts, G., (2009) 'Why green leaders backed the carbon plan', *The Australian*, 9 May.

Roberts, J.T. & Parks, B.C., (2007) *Climate of Injustice: Global Inequality, North-South Politics, and Climate Policy*, Cambridge, Massachusetts: MIT Press.

Rootes, C., (2008) 'The first climate change election? The Australian general election of 24 November 2007', *Environmental Politics*, 17(3): 473–480.

——, (2011) 'New issues, new forms of action? Climate change and environmental activism in Britain', in J. van Deth & W. Maloney, (eds) *New Participatory Dimensions in Civil Society: Professionalization and Individualized Collective Action*, London: Routledge.

Rosalind, (2008a) Interview, 8 July, Students of Sustainability, Newcastle, with Rebecca Pearse.

——, (2008b) Interview, 13 July, Newcastle, with Rebecca Pearse.

——, (2008c) Interview, 14 October, Sydney, with Rebecca Pearse.

Rose, A., (2007) 'Gray v Minister for Planning: The Rising Tide, of climate change litigation in Australia', *Sydney Law Review*, 29: 725–734.

Rosewarne, S., (1992) 'The green accord in Australia', *Capitalism Nature Socialism*, 3(1): 11–17.

——, (2003) 'The Kyoto Protocol and the Australian state's commitment to capital accumulation', *Capitalism Nature Socialism*, 14(1): 1–36.

——, (2007) 'Global warming and discourses of uncertainty: Buying time, buying business and engendering risk', in G. Birch, (ed.) *Water Wind Art and Debate: How Environmental Concerns Impact on Disciplinary Research*, Sydney: University of Sydney Press.

——, (2010) 'Meeting the challenge of climate change: The poverty of the dominant economic narrative and market solutions are subterfuge', *Journal of Australian Political Economy*, 66: 17–50.

Routledge, P., (1996) 'Critical geopolitics and terrains of resistance', *Political Geography*, 15(6): 509–531.

——, (2011) 'Translocal climate justice solidarities', in J.S. Dryzek, K.M. Norgaard & D. Schlosberg, (eds) *The Oxford Handbook of Climate Change and Society*, Oxford: Oxford University Press.

Ruth & Robert, (2008a) Interview, 7 July, Maitland, with Rebecca Pearse.

——, (2008b) Interview, 22 October, Maitland, with Rebecca Pearse.

Samuel, (2008a) Interview, 3 July, Sydney, with Rebecca Pearse.

——, (2008b) Interview, 3 October, Sydney, with Rebecca Pearse.

Santow, S., (2013) 'Ok Tedi', *ABC Radio National*, 21 January.

Sarah, (2008a) Interview, 8 July, Newcastle, with Rebecca Pearse.

——, (2008b) Interview, 23 October, Newcastle, with Rebecca Pearse.

Saunders, C., (2012) 'Reformism and radicalism in the Climate Camp in Britain: Benign coexistence, tensions and prospects for bridging', *Environmental Politics*, 21(5): 829–846.

Schlembach, R., (2011) 'How do radical climate movements negotiate their environmental and their social agendas? A study of debates within the Camp for Climate Action (UK)', *Critical Social Policy*, 31(2): 194.

Shalhorn, S. et al., (2008) An open letter to Kevin Rudd: We need a strong target to cut greenhouse emissions, 3 December, Parliament House, Canberra ACT 2601, 55 NGOs and community groups.

Simonis, U.E., (2009) 'The IPCC and climate politics: Small potatoes', *The Environmentalist*, 29(3): 330–332.

Six Degrees, (undated) *About Six Degrees*, viewed 15 January 2013 <http://sixdegrees. org.au/content/about-six-degrees>.

SMH, (2008) 'Range of groups form climate coalition', *Sydney Morning Herald*, 6 July.

Smith, N., (1984) *Uneven Development: Nature, Capital and the Production of Space*, Oxford: Blackwell.

Snow, D.A., Soule, S.A. & Kriesi, H., (2008) 'Mapping the terrain', in D.A. Snow, S.A. Soule & H. Kriesi, (eds) *The Blackwell Companion to Social Movements*, Malden MA: Blackwell.

Spash, C., (2010) 'The brave new world of carbon trading', *New Political Economy*, 15(2): 169–195.

Spratt, D. & Lawson, D., (2008) Government carbon pollution target announcement Monday, 12 December, Melbourne, Climate Action Centre.

Spratt, D. & Sutton, P., (2008) *Climate Code Red: The Case for Emergency Action*, Brunswick: Scribe.

Steier, F.E., (1991) *Research and Reflexivity*, London: Sage.

Stern, N., (2007) *The Economics of Climate Change: The Stern Review*, Cambridge: Cambridge University Press.

Straw, W., (2013) 'Failure to put climate on G8 agenda will cast a shadow on "greenest government"', *The Guardian*, 10 April.

Stryker, S., (2000) 'Identity competition: Key to differential social moevment participation?', in S. Stryker, T.J. Owens & R.W. White, (eds) *Self, Identity and Social Movements*, Minneapolis: University of Minneapolis Press.

Susie, (2009a) Interview, 2 December, Sydney, with Rebecca Pearse.

——, (2009b) Interview, 11 October, Climate Camp, Helensburgh, with Rebecca Pearse.

Swyngedouw, E., (2010) 'Apocalypse forever? Post-political populism and the specture of climate change', *Theory, Culture and Society*, 27(2-3): 213–232.

Tarrow, S., (1998) Power in Movement: Social Movements and Contentious Politics, Cambridge: Cambridge University Press.

Taylor, L., (2010) 'Greens offer interim carbon deal', *The Australian*, 6 February.

Tim, (2009) Focus group - NGO and union campaigners, 13 October, Sydney, with Stuart Rosewarne and Rebecca Pearse.

Touraine, A., (1995) *Critique of Modernity*, Cambridge: Blackwell.

Trembath, B., (2007) 'Environmentalists furious at Anvil Hill coal mine approval', *ABC Radio National*, 7 June.

UNFCCC, (1992) The United Nations Framework Convention on Climate Change, The United Nations Framework Convention on Climate Change, Opened for signature 4 June, FCCC/INFORMAL/84, (entered into force 21 March).

——, (2011) *Trends in aggregate greenhouse gas emissions, 1990–2010*, United Nations Framework Convention on Climate Change, viewed 1 February 2013 <http://unfccc.int/files/inc/graphics/image/jpeg/ghg_total_incl_2012t.jpg>.

Urry, J., (2011) *Climate Change and Society*, Cambridge: Polity Press.

Van der Zee, B., (2011) 'Climate Camp disbanded', *The Guardian*, 2 March.

Vicky, (2009) Interview, 12 September, Switch Off Hazelwood, Hazelwood, Victoria, with Rebecca Pearse.

——, (2010) Interview, 19 January, Melbourne, with Rebecca Pearse.

Vidal, J., (2011) 'Activists organise "Camp Frack" in protest of shale gas drilling in UK', *The Guardian*, 22 July.

Wallerstein, I., (2002) 'New revolts against the system', *New Left Review*, 18: 29–39.

WCED, (1987) *Our Common Future*, World Commission on Environment and Development, Oxford: Oxford University Press.

WEF, (2012) *Global Risks Report*, Geneva: World Economic Forum.

William, (2009) Interview, 9 October, Climate Camp, Helensburgh, with Rebecca Pearse.

Wright, M. & Hearps, P., (2010) *Australian Sustainable Energy: Zero Carbon Australia Stationary Energy Plan*, Melbourne: The University of Melbourne Energy Research Institute and Beyond Zero Emissions.

Index

For Product Safety Concerns and Information please contact our
EU representative GPSR@taylorandfrancis.com Taylor & Francis
Verlag GmbH, Kaufingerstraße 24, 80331 München, Germany